NO WAY
HOME

The terrifying story of life in a children's home...
and a little girl's struggle to survive

SUE MARTIN

Vermilion
LONDON

11

Published in 2007 by Vermilion, an imprint of Ebury Publishing

A Random House Group Company

Copyright © Sue Martin 2007

The Random House Group Limited Reg. No. 954009

Addresses for companies within the Random House Group can be
found at www.randomhouse.co.uk

A CIP catalogue record for this book is available from the British Library

The Random House Group Limited supports The Forest Stewardship
Council® (FSC®), the leading international forest-certification organisation.
Our books carrying the FSC label are printed on FSC®-certified paper.
FSC is the only forest-certification scheme supported by the leading
environmental organisations, including Greenpeace. Our
paper procurement policy can be found at
www.randomhouse.co.uk/environment

MIX
Paper from
responsible sources
FSC® C016897

To buy books by your favourite authors and register for offers visit
www.randomhouse.co.uk

ISBN 9780091917371

Printed and bound in Great Britain by Clays Ltd, St Ives plc

For my daughter Chrissie and granddaughter Robyn

Preface

I wish to make it absolutely clear to readers that this is a story of what I suffered in what was then called 'Dr Barnardo's Homes' from 1944–1957. The perpetrators of the horrors I write about must be long dead and, with them, the sort of behaviour I experienced. That said, even though there were appalling Homes, there were also wonderful places run by caring, lovely people, dedicated to the welfare of the children in their charge. It was my misfortune to spend most of my time in the former and all too little time in the latter; just long enough to discover the positive experience that I was to miss out on.

Barnardo's, as it is now called, closed the last of its Homes over twenty years ago. I am glad to say that Barnardo's is, today, a very different organisation from the one I experienced all that time ago.

Prologue

My very first memory is of me, a tiny girl, standing between the knees of a man. He was wearing thick dark trousers, which felt rough against my skin; so it wasn't an entirely comfortable place to be, but I do remember feeling blissfully safe and secure. We were in a kitchen; there was a black range, a door so laden with coats on hooks that they seemed to defy gravity, and in front of me was a window. In the middle of the room a woman worked at a table; my fascination centred on the drawer she occasionally opened. The open and shut movement changed the underside of the table completely, showing bits not previously visible.

Throughout a frequently sad childhood, I comforted myself with this treasured picture, yet for years I reflected on the reality of the scene. Was I really standing by my dad before he died? Was the woman my mother, who abandoned five of us to our fate in care – so shamelessly soon after the early death of our father? Was it an enduring memory of a warm, happy family life or the dream of an imaginative little girl who wished so much that it was real? Placed in Dr Barnardo's Homes at two and a half years old, without even the comfort of a doll or teddy bear at bedtime, this picture had been mine to hold on to.

When I left the Homes in 1957, fourteen years later, I described this memory to my maternal grandmother; I even drew a sketch for her. She said that it was indeed my father. In her estimation, I must have been between 18 months and two years old, and everything I told her about this scene was exactly right. The range was lit only during the winter months; by the following summer my dad had died and we left that house. However sad the circumstances it was a thrill to know my memory had been a reality.

Our personality is largely formed in infancy and a little beyond, by the extremes we see and hear; the gloriously happy and the heartbreakingly sad. We remain unaffected by the mundane and the mediocre – the everyday experiences. War-torn countries and disaster areas produce traumatised children because of these extremes; horrific events mean they cannot properly develop or control their emotions. With insufficient kindness to create a balance, these children struggle and flounder, their personal horrors lasting a lifetime.

My time in Barnardo's was deeply traumatic, most especially in my formative years. Lesbian paedophilia is rarely discussed; however, my personal experience of shocking assaults carried out by certain of the all-female care staff, accounts for its existence. Aside from this horrific exploitation of power, too many of the staff frequently resorted to wanton bullying and gratuitous punishment in their desire for controlled discipline. Although impossible to ignore, I tried hard to develop a strong mind and body to cope with this misery. I decided when very young to make it a battle; my survival instinct took over, the staff became my enemies; I would not allow myself to be beaten down. Once they realised that I would not play by their rules, they sank to even greater depths of degradation and humiliation. Sometimes this proved to be a challenge almost beyond my own endurance; so I struggled harder and tried to remain undaunted. Determined to beat them, and, when older, driven by the utter misery of some of the other children treated similarly, I used my natural physical and mental strength to my advantage; the rest was sheer guile. Although my childhood journey was fraught with fear and pain, I faced it with fortitude and hope. That hope and the strong determination never to give in – that was the success of my childhood. *No Way Home* is my account of that journey.

~ 1 ~

It has been many years since I left Dr Barnardo's Homes, but the first memories have not been dimmed. I was almost three years old and had just been placed in a cot; it must have been bedtime. Barnardo's seemed to have children leave and arrive in new Homes in the evening time. Perhaps I had travelled throughout the day and now awaited the next unknown in this completely strange environment.

My father had died at only 32 years old, of tuberculosis. This was my first night in the Homes away from my young widowed mother, and my five brothers and sisters.

Feeling tiny in this massive high-ceilinged room, I looked around. To my left was a large window; by sitting up at full stretch I could see outside. The sky was still a rich deep blue with soft fluffy clouds barely moving across my line of vision; silhouetted against this backdrop I could *just* see the tops of the tall trees. Turning away and feeling completely bewildered about where I was, I looked into the room; there were many more cots like mine lined up along the walls with other children lying in them.

In the far right corner were three or four women wearing identical green dresses with white aprons and caps. They were deep in conversation and did not seem to be aware of me sitting up. I stared at them hard, hoping one would look towards me, but no one did. For some reason I was too scared to call out and disturb them.

Behind me in the other corner was a huge door which was closed, and that really worried me. I wanted very much for it to be open.

The unfamiliar surroundings and aloofness of the chattering women was becoming too much to bear; I was feeling isolated, alone and completely insignificant, and suddenly rather afraid. Sitting up hugging my knees, I turned again to the window and saw the open space; oh, I desperately wanted to be out there! The more I gazed at those treetops the stronger my longing became.

I felt an overwhelming sadness, but with nobody there to take away the loneliness, I laid my head down to rest on top of my knees and I began to cry, at first almost silently, but then, as real misery overtook me, with big sad gulping sobs. The crying seemed somehow comforting and was helping, so I continued.

I had not heard a sound, but suddenly and forcefully my hair was grabbed from behind and my head was jerked back; it was one of the women from the corner. Her red face was ugly with anger and literally just inches from mine; her equally ugly distorted mouth began shouting at me. The smell of hot breath and the feeling of her spittle on my skin was really scaring me.

With this unexpected and dreadful change in the woman, my crying reached a loud crescendo; she lifted me roughly from my cot and thrust me just as roughly beneath her arm. Wide-eyed in fear, I remember the green and white linoleum of the floor flashing below me as she marched me head down through the nursery. Put upright, I saw a hand remove the heavy metal lid from the dirty-linen bin; I was dropped unceremoniously on to the pile of urine-wet sheets within, and deep below. The woman's head appeared above me; she shouted loudly again, then all was black as she slammed down the lid.

I was terrified. My ears were ringing from the banging of the lid and my cheeks were on fire with burning from the tears. It was becoming more and more difficult to breathe with my sobbing and the ammonia stench from the sheets. Filled with a terrifying apprehension I waited for something else to happen . . . something even worse? The blackness within and the outside silence were frightening and the continuing apprehension was exhausting me. Eventually, I must have quietened down to their satisfaction – I may even have dropped off to sleep. I don't remember being returned to my cot, or how long I remained in that stinking disgusting place, but in my state of fear and desperate sadness it seemed for ever

My cruel initiation was over.

Children learn very quickly to avoid further pain and suffering; in my case 'don't ever cry again' was the first lesson I learnt in the Homes. I would learn many more in the years to come.

*

The next thing Barnardo's did was take away my name, literally overnight. I was called Pauline but there were already two other kids with the same name, so they made me use my middle name, Susan.

Ordered regimentation is the only way to maintain discipline in any large institution, be it the Forces, Hospital or School, and that was how life was in Dr Barnardo's Homes, but they went much further with a desire for *total* control of the children in their care. In their bland Victorian 'seen and not heard' world, we were all just 'the kids'; there was no encouragement toward individuality, we were just lumped together as nobodies. Anyone, adults and children alike, who did not live in the Homes, was simply known as 'Outsiders'. The un-named carers we referred to as 'Staff', as in the army when the senior officers are called 'Sarge' or 'Sir'. (The alarm warning, 'Staff's coming!', was a term often heard to alert others to a possible threatening encounter.) This anonymity ensured their desired uniformity; that was how it was – a clinical, distant, institutional way of life.

With no outward signs of warmth or affection and little or no provision made towards our personal development, our lives were a rather empty, lonely affair.

Daily life was order in the extreme; everything was done by the Rule Book. . . and the clock. The routine was the same in all of the many Homes throughout the country; everyone up by 6.30am, washed, dressed and downstairs so that breakfast could be served by 7.20a.m. After breakfast, a meagre meal of porridge, bread and butter and a cup of tea, we all had certain jobs to do. The intensity and importance of these tasks varied. As we got older, they increased *and* had to be carried out before we left for school. Once free of the cot I clearly remember making my own bed when I was small enough to reach the level of the bedstead, and could see right under the mattress!

The first chores for toddlers were to clean under the dining tables and dust the chair legs, the sort of thing we could manage with ease at the tiny height we were. We also dusted the ornate carved banisters; anything less than perfection after inspection meant we had to start from the top and do them all over again. That was very boring and interfered with our play time! And at the other end of this scale, as older children, *all* the cleaning of the Home, including a very thorough weekly spring clean, was our responsibility; this too had always to be done to absolute perfection, or else.

Meal times were *strictly* to time; we were summoned to table by a bell or gong. What we ate and drank, the enforced rest after lunch, permission to go out to play, what clothes could be worn – all these were orders, never a choice. At the end of the day bed time was the final ruling, strictly adhered to without compromise; the youngest were upstairs at 6.00pm; the latest – up to and including those aged sixteen years old – was 7.30pm.

There were very strict rules about where we could go within the building and the gardens. Every one of these conditions and orders was obeyed religiously; the fear of inevitable punishment was simply too great to do otherwise.

Every day continued in exactly the same grindingly oppressive routine, smoothly, with no breaks to upset proceedings – or the staff. Because of this, my personal institutionalisation was swift and simple, until Michael came along.

I had not been in this awful place for very long but his arrival changed everything. It was as if the sun shone again for me; he brought me genuine joy. His new illuminating presence gave me a sense of reality, warm friendship and *fun*.

Michael and I very quickly became best friends. With the regime, the numerous petty rules, the constant fear of being shut up again in a bin, I had in the short space of time before Michael's arrival been totally withdrawn from the throng of kids. Staff always appeared to be shouting and cross; I was too absorbed in trying to work out why rather than suffer any more of their dreadful punishment.

Michael was a mixed-race boy with beautiful coffee-coloured skin and a mop of black, curly hair. It was soft to the touch yet it looked so wiry. His eyes were jet black and sparkled when he smiled, and disappeared completely when he screwed up his face to laugh, which he did frequently. His teeth seemed whiter than anybody else's and his long eyelashes looked like baby spiders that lay on his chubby cheeks.

We were the same age and size and just clicked from the start. When he arrived, we were both about three years old; we could make each other laugh with ease and I suddenly had an opportunity to play in relaxed freedom. I remember no other kid at the time at all; they were unimportant, I had Michael.

Each day we met on the dormitory landing; went downstairs holding hands, into the dining room, and sat next to each other at the table. Talking during a meal was strictly forbidden; instead, we would often just look at each other and grin in a comforting, reassuring way. As soon as the meal was over, we carried out our chores of clearing the table and sweeping any crumbs from the floor as quickly as we could. After a staff inspection we were gone into the playground, into a world of absolute bliss that was all our own. We did everything together.

We even shared the routine of the 'Potty Line' in the early days!

In many ways, the Barnardo regime was unbelievably Victorian, demonstrated by their obsession with bowels! Daily after breakfast, potties were placed on the floor of the nursery, in a long line down the middle. We had to face opposite ways alternately in the row; I never understood that, and never found out why. We were expected to 'go', and if this had not occurred in the given time there was a smack awaiting. Very harsh, but illustrated perfectly their desire for total control over us tots.

'Babies' Castle' was the name of the Home, a splendid building with grounds and gardens surrounding the vast ivy-clad walls. It was a mansion in the real sense of the word; small castellated turrets on the roof, great sash windows and an impressive heavy solid oak door allowing access to the equally beautiful interior. Huge entrance gates safely secured us but the areas into which we were allowed were *very* limited indeed; quite simply the dormitory in which we slept and the room where we ate and played, these were our boundaries.

At the back of the Home was a playground; an enclosed area reached from the dining-cum-playroom through French windows. With plenty to do, we had our happiest times out there. It was our only chance of the freedom to do what we wanted and let off steam; we all loved it. It had a sandpit, proper swings and an enormous weathered log that became for us a pretend boat – or train – or even a rickety bridge. Michael fell off this one day and I was fascinated to see that the skin of his graze showed as pink as my skin underneath; I imagine by the time we finished examining and analysing this discovery it probably didn't hurt any more!

Goodness knows what kids chatter about all day but we never stopped. The earlier days I spent in an almost mute nervousness were gone; now I was really at ease and found my voice. Michael's favourite expression was 'Cor!' – used when quietly intrigued or in excited expectancy, it was always said with enormous enthusiasm in his husky voice. The first time I heard it was outside, in the small shrub area beyond the playground.

We had found a hefty-sized stone and between us managed to flip it over. We sat down on our haunches to inspect this discovery. . . it was alive and crawling with all sorts of very red thin worms, those leather jackets that curl in a ball, and so on. It was utterly disgusting, and as I let out a very girly-type 'Urgh', he simultaneously said with loud excitement, 'Cor!' He pushed and poked at the various wildlife lurking in the wet slimy mud while repeating this expletive with varying degrees of interest and enthusiasm. It was only because I loved to be with him so much that I put up with this revolting sight!

I have referred to the strict, extremely harsh discipline surrounding all our day, but meal times were especially Victorian: absolute silence was the basic rule. Additionally, if tea was slurped or cutlery accidentally dropped, that was it: end of meal. Regardless of age, we were forced to leave the table and endure the misery of no (or not enough) food – with further punishment of cleaning or similar, designed to interfere with precious play time.

Beyond all the petty instances that occurred, one frightening breakfast time stands alone.

Some months after I had first met Michael a new girl had arrived, about four years old like us; however, we had already nearly eighteen months' experience of the rules . . . *and* the irrational behaviour of the staff. Placed opposite the two of us, our jaws dropped at the same time as we heard her say very loudly, 'I don't like porridge.'

We shared a look of sheer horror, and then quickly returned an exaggerated gaze to our own dishes. Firstly I was extremely puzzled: what did she mean, she didn't *like* it? I most certainly didn't *like* the staff, I didn't *like* being kept inside when it rained, I didn't *like* being shouted at and smacked, but this was just food! As far as I was concerned you just sat at the table, shovelled the food down, drank your tea and left the table. I really had no idea what this girl meant.

Suddenly everything changed up a level.

Staff had been trying to cajole and encourage her but had clearly had enough; the ensuing bedlam made us again glance up. To our amazement, she and her colleague had this new kid in a headlock; they were trying to force the food into her squirming mouth, but were being unbelievably and cruelly forceful. Thrashing her head from side to side in an attempt to escape, we could hear the spoon clashing against her teeth; she was making horrible gurgling sounds in her attempt not to swallow. They held her mouth closed in a vice-like grip; she was choking and this made her cough, and the porridge all sprayed out of her nose: it went everywhere! It looked revolting to us and was clearly very painful for her, as she seemed to be gasping for breath.

At this, completely out of patience, Staff threw the spoon clattering on to the table. This poor girl's bright red face was covered in sweat; her hair was sticking to her forehead and her eyes were staring out in sheer terror. Now shaking and out of control she put back her head and, still gurgling on the porridge, tried to scream as Staff tightly grabbed one of her arms and hauled her upwards and out of her chair. Still held aloft by one arm, thrust forward at Staff's waist level, she was removed from the room like a puppy that had pee'd on the carpet. *Her* cruel initiation was over.

Some of the younger ones began to cry; Michael and I turned slowly and just looked at one another in fear of what they were doing to her now. He barely opened his lips but breathed out almost silently, 'Cor!' That made me laugh a little bit inside, and took a lot of the angst out of the situation. The remaining staff did not notice, so we didn't get into trouble.

We were frequently told to 'pipe down', even when drawing and doing jigsaw puzzles together on the wet days when we were not allowed out to play. In fact, as long as we were doing things together, it didn't really matter what we did.

Most afternoons the staff took us out for a long walk; Michael and I remained as ever stuck like glue. To keep us together we walked in a long 'crocodile'; we loved this time of being away from the awful restrictions of the Home and the warm comfort and sheer pleasure of holding hands, laughing and chattering all the way. Michael and I shared a mutual deep feeling and under-standing of one another; we cried a little, laughed a lot, our life was a blissful state of childish happiness. We spent hours in almost complete oblivion of our austere surrounding and life-style; he was the first and only person I greeted in the morning and the only one to whom I wished goodnight.

We spent a year or so in this magical happy state – same routine from day to day, week to week – until one morning I went on to the landing in the normal way; Michael wasn't there!

This had never happened before: I lingered until barked at to go downstairs but he wasn't there either. I could feel an awful state of breathless panic; strictly against the rules and the risk of punishment, I darted back upstairs. Still no Michael – he was nowhere to be seen. I was now really scared and anxious and went to the dining room as the bell rang. His chair was empty, it looked dreadful.

I approached a member of staff and nervously asked where he was; with a harsh voice and an even sterner look, she shouted,

'Take your place at the table *immediately*. If you must know he has gone away and you won't see *him* again.'

I stood there, stunned.

My mind went funny. I wanted to get out of there, and ran to the open French windows. 'You come back here and sit down *now*,' she shouted, but I wasn't listening. I ran across the playground to the 'pavilion', an open-fronted construction with a bench seat, rather like a bus shelter. I clambered up on to the seat, and with head down, my hands by my sides, I banged my back against the wall, rhythmically and constantly and comfortingly. Staff came out once, but she went back in without saying a word.

I felt desperate. I had been there for some time, hurting more and more inside and fighting hard against the tears trying to come. I just kept thinking, Is he all right? What will I do? Where has he gone? What did she mean . . . *never see him again*? It was impossible for my young mind to take that in. A terrifying thought occurred to me in addition. He had been there at bedtime – *where was he now*?

Slowly my mind adjusted and I felt an incredible change in my understanding and awareness of myself *and* the situation I was in. A mist of some sort had filled my head at the shock of how, and what, she had said, so callously and with sadistic pleasure. Now that mist was slowly clearing; as it did I realised there had always been another mist, but that too was clearing. I stopped banging and looked across the playground to the French windows, I studied what I now saw with new clear vision.

The other kids were all there as before, just the same, but they were how I used to be – compliant zombies – but not any more. The staff too were the same, but now I felt a deep and growing hatred for them. They had taken Michael away. I was desperately fighting back the need to cry with this dreadful loss, but I knew that was what Staff expected – instead of releasing tears, I became angry.

I had grown up there and then and made two resolutions.

Never make another friend.

Never do anything you are told.

I maintained them both whenever possible; my battle had begun, I was four years old.

*

After Michael left, I didn't play as much; I would sit in the warm sunshine in the pavilion just swinging my legs for ages. I preferred being on my own. I loved to watch people, and try to work out what made them say and do the things they did.

In the playground, although allowed to play freely and do the things kids enjoy, I felt forever on my guard, always wary, always observing. There was a new feeling of vulnerability without the support of Michael; I believe this was the reason Barnardo's separated brothers and sisters: as a single unit they could manage their total control so much more easily.

I was always using my newly discovered mind, becoming daily more 'aware' of its capacity. I loved to think things about staff, like 'haven't you got a big nose', and relished the fact they had no idea of what I was thinking. I really enjoyed the *silence* of thought.

The way they told me about Michael leaving had been harsh and had a dreadful effect on my emotions. Was it simply in itself, or because it was a reminder and repeat of another recent rejection by my family? Surely, that was the pain; maybe Michael had taken the place of a brother for me. I only knew there was an enormous emptiness again in my life, and the anxiety and longing for him continued for a very long time.

The promise not to have another best friend was an easy resolution to uphold. I soon realised I couldn't relate to the other kids much anyway; this was where I felt the worst of the emptiness – they were there, that was all. Sometimes I found them to be unbelievably stupid in their ignorance or rejection of the strict rules. Michael and I had soon realised that many of these were in place not only for the necessary smooth running of the Home but also for us to learn a little about self-discipline. Most important of all though was to avoid the punishment involved in failing to carry them out; there were subtleties and craft in being a thorn in the side of the staff, but not many of the other kids seemed bothered to work this out.

I constantly watched the staff. These women, all single, were supposed to be caring, but I soon realised that most of them didn't care. From watching them, something became very clear to me; when they shouted, they did one of two things. From their eyes, and facial expressions, I could see genuine anger, which was scary stuff, like with me in my cot and the new kid and the breakfast. However, there was a second expression. Sometimes in the playground, one of the bigger kids (there was always *one* bully) would snatch a ball from you, or trip you up on purpose, then sneer as you fell. The staff could also have this look on their faces, one of sneering triumph, like when I was told about Michael – the one that portrayed the bully. It was a shock to learn that grown-ups could be bullies, too.

I thought of it as a war; I had learnt which the real enemy among the staff were, those I hated the most. I had already learnt to frustrate and annoy the staff to win my little battles. I quickly realised there were limits to my bad behaviour though; I never *ever* said 'no'.

This tiny word was complete aggravation to the staff and I could not believe the regularity with which some of the other kids used it. The staff's reaction was immediate, harsh and predictable, so why did some kids continue to say it? This same group missed the meal bell and could be in trouble all day; perhaps their minds were devoid of calculation with everything around them so ordered. I never really worked them out. The word 'no' simply upset the ordered regime and staff hated that.

They were in authority – and saying 'no' simply allowed these women to vent their frustration, with a 'cross' attack, or a 'bullying' attack. In practical terms, there was not much difference really, they both hurt.

To get the better of them I decided subtlety was the best approach – get them mad with frustration, then back off before going too far. It took split-second timing, and didn't always work out, but more little skirmishes were won than lost.

Walking away when requested to return indoors worked a treat. 'Come on, Susan – in you come,' moved on to, 'Susan, you heard, *in.*' Then, 'Now, Susan – come in *now.*' Eventually it reached its full crescendo, '*Susan Davis, get in here now!*' I would then turn around, with a 'what *me?*' expression of mild surprise on my face. The timing had to be spot-on to get them hopping mad but not come after you, or the inevitable smack would follow a very unceremonious hauling across the playground; I hated being smacked but they loved it and were always so vicious.

You couldn't perform this routine every time – that was the key; if you did, they would just haul you straight in and smack you anyway. Doing it to a different staff member each time was also essential; their personal anger levels varied amazingly, and I soon learnt how far you could go with each of them. With some guile and even more luck, the outcome was always the same; they got mad because their petty system was interrupted, and that was my intention.

For instance, nobody could take as long to do up coat buttons and shoes as I occasionally chose to do. Everyone else ready for the walk, there would be much tutting and calls to 'come *on*' until just the right tone had been reached, then magic! I was ready.

I mixed this with being so dextrous another day that I was the first one ready. Out through the open front door, on to the drive, before they could say 'Jack Robinson'. Nobody was allowed to leave the building on their own, so I was followed by staff who had to catch me and bring me back. The other kids, eager to see what would happen, rushed their own proceedings, but it would dissolve into a non-crisis, as we met on the doorstep.

Dawdling along behind always made them angry, but being in a public place there was no punishment because they wouldn't let down their public face under any circumstance. I would sometimes run on ahead, which had them screaming like banshees for me to stop.

There was an old granite horse trough a couple of hundred yards down the pavement from the Home. One day I rushed on ahead, and because there was no one in close pursuit I jumped up on to the plinth. The green stuff on the surface was algae, *and* I soon found out was very, very slippery – I fell in.

I was absolutely amazed, it happened so quickly! The staff caught up, and heaved me out by the back of my collar. I had not gone right under, but I was drenched. Staff wasn't all that dry either by the time she got me back on to the pavement, and was she livid! Half the kids viewed this in silent disbelief; the others were laughing their heads off. Michael would most definitely have laughed, but I wouldn't have been so naughty if he had still been there.

My coat was blue, thick wool, and by now, the water was draining off at such a rate I was creating my very own puddle – and I was freezing. The algae was stuck to the fibres and hung in fronds, and I didn't smell all that healthy.

I can safely say I messed up that particular walk, and had accidentally managed to reach a level of madness by the staff that had never before been witnessed. Once we got back, for punishment I had to have a cold bath; was sent to bed straight after tea and missed a playtime, but I didn't get a smack so I considered that a small price to pay.

There was one situation when it never paid to be deaf, dawdling, or under any other circumstances late, and that was for a meal. For punishment they sent you away to do extra work, or straight to bed, depending on the time of day; to skip any food was a very bad idea altogether. I was never exactly hungry after a meal, but never full either; no food at all was purgatory. When the bell went I was there, but I was constantly amazed at the stupidity of some of the other kids who failed to grasp this simple – but cruel – fact. It happened all the time.

From the outset there was little pleasure in my life at 'Babies' Castle', and once I had lost Michael I withdrew; I became more inward-looking in order to survive an existence that was already proving to be quite an ordeal. My naughty behaviour was intentional, it enabled me to win my little battles against the staff and their cruel attitude and unnecessary punishments. They never attempted to show warmth or give comfort; perhaps if they had, we would have all responded very differently. I most certainly would. To have experienced my first night there, so cruelly treated when I was clearly *desperate* for someone to cuddle and make things right, no wonder I made them my enemy and continued my battles. The worst thing of all was when they told me – so heartlessly – that my best friend had gone and I would never see him again. I felt immediately they had set themselves against me, so I would, and did, fight them. It seems fair enough to me now, and certainly did then. If they had told me why or where he had gone, my war would have been less, and so would the accompanying hatred that drove me.

I stuck to the rules rather than face their anger and punishment; however, I was not prepared to be a zombie or a wimp just to fit into their scheme of things. Plenty of the kids were already beaten – or certainly seemed to be – but I had discovered how to use my mind and I loved the privacy and power it gave me. There were any number of ways they could and did control my life, but there were things they wouldn't know or couldn't control; I was determined to keep it that way.

I was nearly five years old when I was sent to the next Home, St Christopher's in Tunbridge Wells.

~ 2 ~

I thought Babies' Castle was big, but St Christopher's was a huge place on the outskirts of Royal Tunbridge Wells. With a main hall, an assortment of cottages, a laundry of commercial proportions and a medical hall known as 'Liberty', my new home was set in the most beautiful wooded surroundings. Once a magnificent old house, the building was now in its old age, and occupied by a horde of screaming children!

The sheer open space and places to play after the confines of Babies' Castle were staggering to begin with; we could, and did, roam the grounds at will and in complete safety. I expect there were 'out of bounds' areas but I do not remember them. The freedom I had so relished in the previous Home's playground, I now enjoyed on an enormous scale by comparison. The familiar routine and ordered regimentation existed indoors but even there the atmosphere was much more friendly and relaxed. From my first day I played with, and actually enjoyed, the company of my new peers. The awful withdrawn and guarded feelings after Michael left had now gone; I became a free-spirited, happy child again.

I lived with about a dozen other girls and boys of varying ages in one of the cottages within the grounds; there were other cottages of a similar size accommodating the rest of the kids. Huge buildings housed the trainee nannies. After their training, many went to work for important people all over the world as well as for the Homes. They shared their accommodation with the staff required for caring for us kids and for the running of the enormous laundry. St Christopher's was virtually a small hamlet in its own right and was largely self-sufficient.

I rarely went into 'The Hall', the main building of this rambling nine-acre estate, but it was an awesome place to behold. Through the enormous front door, you entered a porch, which itself was the size of a small room. The second door then led into the main area with a floor covered in huge square black and white tiles. It was church-like with high ceilings and a stairway at the very end with decorative wrought-iron banisters – very grand. Down to the right was Matron's Office; there were many other rooms, the contents of which remained a mystery. Upstairs was called Nursery Landing for obvious reasons as that was where the babies lived, but I only went up there once. The staff there wore the same uniform I was already used to seeing at Babies' Castle: green nurses' dress and starched white caps that stuck up at the front.

The grounds consisted of lawns, flower borders, vegetable plots and woodland all lovingly cared for by a small army of gardeners. The head person was called Mr Chessen; he always had a smile for us kids and the time for a warm friendly greeting and chat. I loved to help him and one day managed to push his giant wheelbarrow to the grass tip. As a reward, he pushed us all back – four of us fitted inside! Then there was Mr Meadows, the handyman who did the repairs to our own 'street lights' system that illuminated the many paths and drives and was also called upon to solve any problems in our cottages. I liked him because he smiled a lot and would always let me hold his tools when he came to our cottage.

Within the grounds, and fenced for safety on all sides, was a wood-framed small nursery school. This was to be my first learning experience. Here, for only a couple of hours in the morning, we painted and drew pictures. Music was provided from a wind-up gramophone which used to 'skip' a bit when we bounced too close; we danced and played organised games together which helped us to develop team skills and to understand direction and order. It was brilliant; we all loved it.

The well-learnt work ethic continued as ever and the various items of apparatus and equipment were our responsibility; everything had to be cleaned and packed away neatly into its rightful place. It was a darned sight more fun than polishing banister rails and was a great lesson for our future life.

We ate our lunch there and the preparation for this meal was our first attempt at helping to prepare our meals. As we had a hot dinner with the older kids who went to the outside school, the lunch food was cold. Staff always managed to make this fun and exciting; she would cover the table with a wax cloth and butter the bread for us. We took our turn in applying the filling for a sandwich each, with more mess than filling, and the shouting and laughter was luxury to me after my miserable existence in my first home. After we were fed and cleaned up, next on the agenda was 'rest', where we would lie under a blanket on a foldaway camp bed, and I would frequently doze off to sleep. After our nap we then returned to our own cottages for the remainder of the day.

The nursery was a fun place and very relaxed. Unlike outside school, there was no long walk involved, and all the others attending were the staff and kids I shared my life with anyway. It taught me how to 'learn to learn' rather than great achievement, which was a fine way to start an education

The tiny Miss Mitchell was the matron and head of the Home; it was she who oversaw this whole operation. At last, I had found a human being – she, and all her staff it appeared, actually *liked* children *and* she was fun. Now here was a first in my short experience of adults. I could not imagine any of her staff being allowed to treat her charges in the manner I had already experienced and observed; she would not have tolerated that.

I did once have to spend quite a bit of time with Miss Mitchell in her magnificent office. We did not see much of her in the normal run of things but I had to make a daily visit to have gravel rash removed from my legs.

I was a tomboy and was always getting into scrapes. I was by nature a strong child and, largely because of the atmosphere in Babies' Castle, I'd become very competitive and virtually fearless. I've forgotten what caused the injury – but that's not what was important. What is imprinted on my mind was the care and kindness Miss Mitchell took over my knee. If she had told me off for whatever caused the injury, it must have been so mild as to not have even registered.

The operation was quite a painful procedure, requiring lots of gentle scrubbing to remove the skin that covered the gravel, and then she gently took out the pieces embedded below. All the time she let me watch; quite a story to tell the others! She explained what she was doing and when it would hurt; she was so gentle I would have got more gravel rash just to go back!

The office itself was a grand room, reflecting clearly the days when this was a house of some status. High ceilings, wood-panelled walls with enormous lead-glass windows that looked out across the gardens – quite an atmosphere in which to have something as mundane as gravel dug from my legs! To fill in some of the considerable length of time required for this delicate task, she taught me the capitals of the world. On her side table, she had a great globe brown with age that had its own stand and rotated at the slightest touch. As I sat with my legs up she would point out the different continents, then each country and its capital city. Because I loved the sound of the word, my favourite was Reykjavík; it has always been my dream to go there.

Another fascination was her office 'seal'; she explained that this was used in addition to her signature at the end of an important letter. She demonstrated how to melt the sealing wax and once it cooled a little, would press the seal into it: very posh! There was no doubt in my mind: the whole world should be made up of Miss Mitchells, starting with all the staff of Barnardo's.

The end of the long summer holidays heralded my move away from the nursery and on to an outside infants' school; it was exciting being able to join in the preparations after previously just watching the others. Ordinarily I would have to get myself washed and dressed – but my first day found me being helped considerably more. My hair was thoroughly brushed and my teeth-cleaning supervised; clearly only perfection would be acceptable. We did not wear an official school uniform but had a jumper and skirt that was only used on school days and woe betide you if it was not changed out of the very minute you arrived back! Even in this considerably happier environment, time-keeping and ordered regimentation, the usual Barnardo's rules, reigned supreme.

The walk to school was quite a surprise on that first day as it was over a mile towards Tunbridge Wells and was paved all the way. Because the Home largely ran itself, I hadn't seen much of the 'outside world'. I had been on the very short walk to Dunorlan Park, a beautiful place with a vast lake opposite St Christopher's, but this was a real trek and I was fascinated. The few houses we passed were enormous and were screened from the road (and nosy children) by high hedges and huge double gates. We marched along as was usual in a 'crocodile', holding another kid's hand, and Staff conducted neatness and good behaviour from the rear of the group. Any adult we met along the way knew where we came from, and warm noisy greetings would be exchanged.

The school building was an old grey stone affair with a friendly welcoming air. 'St James's Infants' was carved proudly into the arch above the main entrance. My first impression was how small everywhere appeared; the playground looked overflowing with all the pupils playing before the bell announced the start of the lessons. The rooms were small and housed our individual desks, and the tiny chairs were similar to those we used in nursery.

The desks had a scroll of fancy wrought iron supporting the wooden, lidded top. On the right hand side of the desk was a china ink well; writing correctly was considered extremely important then. One day I dipped my pen into the ink in a way that created a bubble, I stood up to blow it away. Well, I had never heard of a vortex; the next thing I knew a big splash of wet ink had covered my face, and the whole class burst out laughing – including the teacher! Lucky for me it had missed any clothing but it took ages for the blue stain to disappear. I didn't get into trouble from the Home because although it was a bit daft it was clearly an accident.

All the teachers were very kind but this was proper schooling and I knew I had to be very attentive. Learning not to chatter and to watch the blackboard was hard, but being chosen to clean it off was the reward and a great honour at the end of the day. I enjoyed my classes and especially liked drawing. Staff would be waiting to supervise the return and I loved the walk back holding my latest 'masterpiece' for Miss to see.

The 'Royal' part in the name of Tunbridge Wells came from the Royal visits to the world-famous seventeenth-century 'Pantiles' where many of the upper-class gentry visited to drink the healing waters. St Christopher's was a flagship of the many Barnardo's Homes, and Miss Mitchell was sufficiently a Lady to mix in noble company; an announcement was made of a Royal Visit. This caused great excitement throughout the whole place. I am afraid I do not remember who this dignitary was, it may have been the King, who was the Patron, or at the very least Princess Elizabeth.

Miss Mitchell called me to her office to tell me that I was to be the one to present the bouquet; I greeted this news with a genuine mixture of being thrilled to bits and terrified! She said I would have to practise very hard and learn from her how to do everything perfectly *and* I would be allowed to dress up in some special clothes. This was a brilliant bit of news and suddenly my worries were ebbing away. Everything we wore was donated to the Homes by charitable well wishers and usually rather 'ordinary'; there was a 'dressing-up' box at school but I knew my clothes were not going to be like that.

A buzz surrounded St Christopher's and preparations for the visit were keeping everyone busy. We kids were given the task of cleaning the brass plates and handles on every door, not just in our cottages as usual but through the Hall and other staff areas; hundreds of them and all polished to perfection as they ever were! Mr Meadows made sure all the windows were gleaming; Mr Chessen saw to the paths being weeded and he cut and shaved all the lawns to bowling-green standards. But throughout all of this bedlam I was only interested in my beautiful clothes.

I first tried them on in Miss Mitchell's office and she seemed to be as pleased and excited as me. Luckily they were a perfect fit. There was a gleaming white broderie anglaise dress with little puff sleeves and a belt; short white ankle socks and black patent leather shoes with a button: all *brand new*. Having lived in hand-me-downs for as long as I could remember, it was as if I had died and gone to heaven! I felt like a princess when Matron allowed me to show some of the other staff; their comments and compliments were thrilling. Miss Mitchell spent *ages* teaching me how to curtsy with a little nod of my head, and to smile! I was so intent on getting it right without toppling over, I kept forgetting, but practice made perfect and everything at last was ready. I could hardly wait for the day!

The last special thing she did was cut my hair and find me a pretty ribbon; my hair was jet black so she chose pink. It was wonderful being a little girl if only for a day; I felt so pretty and proud.

Then disaster struck: I caught chickenpox. I could not believe it and no one else could either.

Instead of being a bouquet carrier, I was promptly dispatched to Liberty, the clinic and isolation unit within the grounds. Tuberculosis was still prevalent during the forties and any contagious disease needed to be contained to stop an epidemic throughout the whole place.

I was quarantined and taken to a bedroom right at the end of a long corridor, a lovely bright room but the window sadly did not give me a view of any of the proceedings. The day arrived and I missed the whole thing. I imagine Miss Mitchell must have looked lovely.

That winter the great cold and snows came to Kent. It was 1947 and I had turned six in July. Once the thaw came and the snows went, so did I.

Away from dear Miss Mitchell, St Christopher's and happiness. I was on my way to Hell.

3

I first saw 'High Broom' in Crowborough through grey murky drizzle but even that could not spoil the splendour of yet another magnificent building: red brick, mullion windows, high chimneys and a tower at the very top. Across the front of the house and over to the right were lawns and a games field, surrounded by high trees and shrubs. The three playrooms and the main office looked across this front lawn; immediately above were the many dormitories. The long drive swept up and around to the left to the huge heavy front door; I entered through here into the main hall.

Grand appearances can be *so* deceiving; as soon as I was inside my old guarded feelings returned. The dark threatening atmosphere instantly wrapped itself around me in a stifling, suffocating way. The difference between this hall and St Christopher's was unbelievable; I immediately sensed that there would be not a lot of joy or happiness within *these* walls.

Two matrons met me; one was retiring shortly, and the other was to take over the running of the Home. The current matron, Miss Wallis-Myers, was a lady of the same school as Miss Mitchell but altogether much more old-fashioned in her ways; at least a hundred years behind the times. She was extremely tall and very well spoken. She wore tweedy, rather county clothes, with thick lisle stockings and brown leather brogues; she could have been born to that house and never shamed any of her ancestors! Although I would never know her well at all, she seemed kind. She had a red setter dog; the sight of them strolling down the drive together, with feet splayed at identical angles, was hilarious.

I was then introduced to the woman who would eventually take over the Home: Miss Boagey.

I am certain I could be forgiven for making an amusing comment about a woman with such a name in charge of a children's home; believe me when I say it is impossible for me to bring myself to do so. She was the most dreadful person one could ever wish to meet and the contrast between her and the current matron was tangible and horrifying. To say that when I first met her I felt fear, real genuine fear, would be no exaggeration; I also knew she was aware I felt that. It was obvious from those mean eyes that looked right through me; she was an iceberg compared with the matron's vague attempts at warmth. Collaring one of the passing kids she instructed abruptly, 'Take her to A'; that was to be my playroom.

The lot in there were friendly and smiled a greeting but I felt lousy after the Boagey 'welcome' so I didn't go immediately to join them but stood at the door to take in my surroundings. The atmosphere of misery extended from the Hall; the air of threat just seemed to prevail throughout, even extending to the playroom: 'dark and bleak' were my first impressions. There were two huge windows across the wall in front of me, but the light from these was reduced by the heavy dark wood floor and panelling around all the walls. What did look interesting were the 'stepped' window seats, without cushions but could be a comfortable place to sit and read.

As in the previous homes, the playrooms doubled as dining areas and two long tables all but filled the far end of the room. Most of the kids were at these tables playing and I responded to them by shyly smiling back and sitting down when asked to join them. We chatted quietly about which Homes we had come from and how long some of the others had been at Crowborough, until Staff told us to stop whispering. We would have also been in trouble for raising our voices so you could never win! Leaving the group I walked across the room and from the edge of the window seats I looked across the garden. I could see the tops of tall trees silhouetted against the early evening sky and my mind shot back to my first night in a similar place. I did not feel the same lonely desperation or isolation but my first meeting with Boagey made it seem as though a very long time had passed since. All the strategies I had developed in my first home to keep me safe in my body and my mind had rescued me, but my God, I instantly knew I was going to need all the strength I could muster here.

Boagey's desire to crush by bullying was evident from first sight of her but I knew that my experience of battling with the staff at Babies' Castle would help me deal with *this* hateful situation. It was obvious already I was facing the same mean behaviour.

Boagey was a tall slab of a woman – flabby and grossly overweight. Her bejowled face would take on ugly expressions even when she was not cross. She wore heavy glasses and her undergarments creaked as she breathed (very embarrassing in a quiet church). She was the Head – the dominant one; even the staff were scared of her, so we had no chance. Her rules were cast in stone offering no leeway whatsoever; she derived great pleasure from punishing us when they were broken, and often when they were not.

In the Roald Dahl book *Matilda*, there is a character named 'Trunchbull': Boagey was her to the letter, a bullying domineering lump. The comedy was there too, but that was from us laughing behind her back at her frequent crass stupidity. She could act too, switching with ease to a sugary sweet persona for visitors, especially if they were likely to leave a donation in the 'Cottage Homes' Barnardo's charity box that sat on the hall windowsill.

In addition she possessed her own personal power; appropriately strong for her size she could, in boxing parlance, 'punch her weight'. I once skidded across the wooden hall floor, when all she had done was smack me across the back of my head. My instant revulsion, and eventual hatred, of Boagey were justified: time would prove me right. And I was not by any means alone in my hatred of this woman; it was universal. The other kids, the staff, even the blooming gardener!

I will honestly admit I was scared stiff of Boagey, and the atmosphere in the Home as a whole. High Broom wasn't as big as St Christopher's but it was an altogether darker, almost sinister place. This was nothing to do with the décor, it was simply the dreadful atmosphere of the matron's creation. I could see the battle before me like a mountain, and the only equipment I had was my mind, a rapidly developing natural strength. I was determined to survive better than some of the kids I had already seen pass through the doors. Far too frequently, kids who were left-handed, or suffered with a stammer – even one little soul with a strawberry birthmark – were taunted and utterly crushed by the bullying treatment from some of the staff. These poor devils lacked the strength needed to fight back. Their sadness was dreadful to see but as I had all my strength I frequently repeated to myself, 'Don't be a wimp, you can beat them.'

I knew the early days of being an aggravation after Michael had given me courage I may not have otherwise had. I knew too that the mean spitefulness I had already experienced at Babies' Castle was also here, but I felt I had the situation pretty well understood. I could see and feel the difficulties, and knew I would very soon find methods of coping and dealing with them. I guessed I had plenty of time; there were kids in here of fifteen, I was still only six.

Already familiar with the Barnardo's ritualistic routine of time and rules I settled in quickly. I hated the place but then we all did so we just got on with it. The awesome threat I felt from Boagey was lessened somewhat because she mostly stayed in her office. Although this was off the main hall, if we were very quiet we could shoot past without attracting her attention. 'Let sleeping dogs lie,' we would whisper.

There were sixty of us and we all had different lengths of time within the institution; my own amounted to close on three and a half years, while some had only just come in, poor beggars. The arrival of some and the departure of others occurred at an alarming and sometimes very confusing pace.

About six months after arriving at Crowborough I had, with a couple of the others, a six-week 'break' at another Home near Canterbury; an odd sort of holiday but we enjoyed it. To be away from Boagey was the best thing but six weeks wasn't long enough unfortunately, and the return was hateful. This procedure was repeated for most of us; we enjoyed it at the time but in reality it meant a sense of stability and order was permanently denied.

While I was at Barnardo's they had some pretty strange ideas about bringing up kids; I believe the system was to make us unsettled *by arrangement*. It was planned *and* it made money for Barnardo's. It was most definitely bewildering; one girl had moved seven times in five years for no apparent reason, until one of the older kids explained what she had heard.

She said that for every child in each Home, the local council would have to pay a charge to Barnardo's as a 'placement fee' because they were saving the councils the cost of looking after us in their own establishments. For instance, moving me through Babies' Castle and St Christopher's to High Broom constituted three placements. And also, my trip from Crowborough to Canterbury was deemed a placement; my return to Crowborough was another and this immediately changed my number of placements from three to five. I heard this same explanation when I was much older, from a teacher in secondary school; I have always felt it to be the only logical conclusion to what appeared complete madness otherwise. An even greater sadness attached to these placements was only discovered by some folk many years after leaving the Homes. Their Personal Files became available to them with the Freedom of Information Act and that is when they found that back in those days Barnardo's had justified uprooting them by describing them variously as bullies, slow learners, disruptive, liars, thieves and so on. For many of them this was the final 'kick in the teeth' from the so-called 'caring establishment' who felt fully justified in this unsettling treatment: a prison sentence just for being born.

4

A few months after I arrived at High Broom there were a few harrowing incidents which took place that I remember clearly, not just because of the pain, but also because they caused me to seriously doubt that I was as strong in mind or body as I had thought.

My emotional self was already dead. I had made my decision and would not – could not – cry. Not to become emotionally involved was not difficult in my environment; instead, I put any anger and pain into my physical and mental self. I had quickly realised that if I were lacking strength in this new hostile environment, then I would have to do something about it. I knew I had the capacity to do so; well actually, I hoped I had.

Miss Warren was not the head of any playroom, she just interfered everywhere. Once I heard her described as Deputy Matron, but I never learnt whether that was her correct title or not. Nobody liked her mainly because she was a replica of Boagey; just as ugly and similar in size – perhaps a bit younger – and she was *mean*: a vicious bully. Unfortunately for us, unlike Boagey, she didn't have an office in which she could work and keep out of our areas. She was the dreaded inspector who oversaw any work carried out by us as 'Duty Rota'; famous for ordering sixty pairs of shoes to be re-polished because a little spot of dusty mud could be seen *underneath* the instep. She would wander about and suddenly confront you – or creep up unheard from behind. She would not even *try* to hide her pleasure at seeing you staring terrified with surprise at these unexpected encounters, and awaiting the unknown frightening consequence. Sometimes she would just sneer with derision and go away but too frequently she would quite wrongfully accuse us of something that deserved a clip round the ear, or worse. I met her on many occasions going from playroom to toilet – was accused of being where I shouldn't be, then smacked for it. We all hated her.

On this particular occasion, I have no recollection of doing anything wrong, but Miss Warren never needed a reason. I had left my playroom and once in the hall Warren suddenly grabbed me by the arm; saying 'Right, you' she frogmarched me upstairs and hauled me into a small side room I did not know existed; I hadn't been there very long. I knew it was getting close to bed time but I had not heard anyone call me to go, and no one else had made a move. By the way she dragged me up the stairs I knew she was very cross, angry even. I just did not know what I had done, and she obviously was not going to tell me.

Warren spun me round to face her. She was red-faced with a sort of rage; I could not hide my fear. She pulled my arms out in front of me in the strongest of grips, turned them palm up so my shoulders became locked at the joints, and holding me tightly by my elbows, began to shake me. Jerking back and forth, back and forth, with a violence I could never have imagined; only my head was moving and my feet were slipping from under me. I could not keep my mouth closed and was not at all sure I was breathing. Little groaning sounds were coming involuntarily from me, but she just continued. My mind was dead and my body was hurting like mad but even if I had felt like crying, it would have been a physical impossibility.

Suddenly she stopped. She threw me away from her and I slammed into the wall after sliding across the linoleum floor. In a dreadful state of pain and confusion, I stared at her; the hair at her temples was wet with sweat and her face was redder than ever, but she did not seem to be cross any more. Just red. She told me in a breathless, menacing voice to stay there until she came back. I was becoming more worried and frightened wondering what that meant – could it, was it about to get even worse? In a very short space of time I'd had my fair share of 'punishment' from her, but this was different and I waited in absolute dread to hear her footsteps outside the door again.

I lay curled up on the floor for ages, trembling with cold as much as from fear. My arms were very red where she had gripped me so hard, but the worst thing was the pain in my neck and head. When eventually she returned she told me to join the others and get ready for bed . . . *as if nothing had happened.*

When I got to my dormitory I looked at the other children to see if they had missed me or whether they noticed that I looked different because I felt it; neither seemed to be the case. As I had my wash, the marks on my arms were quite visible but Staff didn't make any comment. I *dreaded* that if something like that could happen and no one noticed or cared, what was going to become of me? Why had she done it?

Once changed and into bed, my neck hurt so much I really wanted to cry, but I could not. Even with the chickenpox, I had not experienced such a bad headache – now it was thumping and I could hear my heart beating. The pain in my shoulders and elbows was burning and they felt bruised. Obviously, no one else knew what had happened and in a strange sort of way I was glad they didn't; for some reason I would have felt ashamed had they known.

A repeat of this event took place some time after, but this time it was brought to the attention of other staff. Everything happened almost as before, except I was on the landing having had my wash and heading for the dorm. She dragged me to the same side room; I was immediately terrified because I *knew* what was coming next. I am certain the shaking was even more aggressive and violent; then it happened. My neck flipped back and stayed there. To me it was as though the back of my head was touching my shoulder blades; I am sure it was not, but that was how it felt at the time.

In the moment it happened I think I let out a yell; she suddenly stopped, lowered me very gently to the ground, and left the room. I was immediately freezing cold and shaking; the skin from my chest to my chin felt tight and painful, I could not close my gaping drying mouth, nor could I swallow. The pains were there again in my arms and I was becoming frightened as I did not know where she had gone or how long I would be there. However, I had not lain there as long this time when she came back, with another member of staff.

Warren and the other staff member carefully lifted me off the floor; the new woman held me very firmly to her, with my backwards head completely supported. She carried me to another strange place and sat with me in a chair; at least we were alone because Warren had gone. The Staff said nothing to me and still my head stayed back. I felt freezing cold but the shakes had stopped; I was glad about that as they seemed to make the pain worse. She stroked my forehead and it was calming and relaxing; my fear was passing.

As gently as before, she carried me from the room and took me to my bed; just as gently she laid me down and covered my freezing aching body with the blanket. The others were asleep so goodness knows how long I'd been gone or what the time was. Amazingly, I slept too, and in the morning, although my neck was still extremely painful, my head was back where it should have been. Even more amazingly, no one, including Warren, made even the slightest mention of it!

Years later, I spoke to a nurse who was familiar with the Catholic nuns in Ireland. She knew about 'shaking' and according to her, it was one of the favourites of the female sexual pervert. Firstly, they had power over their victim; but also, unbelievably, the small mouth of a child with chubby cheeks, when shaken, made a similar sound to a stimulated vagina! They would invariably orgasm before they stopped the shaking.

It beggars belief that I still now carry an untreatable double whiplash injury to my neck because some sexual deviant obtained, and kept, a job in a children's home.

I have always said . . . if you like Maths, get a job in a bank.

If you like English . . . become a teacher or journalist.

If you like abusing kids . . . get a job in a children's Home.

I believe those who did not participate personally allowed by their silence and acceptance those who did. With the strict regimentation that tracked our every move each minute of the day and night, no little child could just disappear for some length of time without anyone knowing!

Of course most of them must have known; and that made those that did as bad as one another in my view.

*

I recovered gradually from the shaking incidents by Warren; no word of reference was ever made, she merged into the background more, and slowly I decided she posed no further threat. The physical pain had been miserable for a while but even harder to deal with was the associated worry and utter confusion. I could not work out why she seemed to hate me enough to do it in the first place, or why the other staff had not bothered to address the matter since. With a sense of restored confidence, and deciding I was at least safe from it now. . . I got on with the daily routine and eventually 'forgot' it. One of those times clearly when asking unanswerable questions was proving to be a waste of time.

Upstairs and getting ready for bed one evening I was again walking alone along the landing from bathroom to dormitory.

Two Staff came along and one picked me up in a hug. I was so surprised I laughed as she did, it was such an unusual thing to happen, but at less than seven years old I thought it was fun. She jogged the short distance down the landing and I continued to laugh at the pleasure of being wobbled along in her arms; then the other Staff opened the door of the sluice room. This room was familiar to me, because we used to have to help in there sometimes; it housed all the equipment to rinse through bed-wetters' sheets that would have stunk by the time they got to the laundry.

It was a long, narrow room with a shallow butler's sink, a surface for folding sheets and an enormous mangle. I began to sense a sudden change in the mood: they were still laughing, but it was more of a giggle now; it made me feel anxious. They giggled throughout, and that haunted me for ages after.

There was a little water already in the shallow sink. They removed my nightdress and lowered me into the water where they proceeded to wet me and cover me with soap. I had already had my wash and preparation for bed so I was now feeling frightened and cold. The soap wasn't frothy and smooth like in the bath, it felt sticky and hard. There was not enough water to make it really wet, so it was forming a thick cloying coating on my skin.

I was totally at their mercy. I knew I was justified in being terrified and yet I was too scared to make a sound; I doubt if a sound would have come out anyway. Still they giggled. They lifted me from the water; my eyes were tight shut and I had clamped my jaws together. I was trying not to see what they were doing – *and had a sound escaped me?* I did not dare think about that. The soap and their hands were all over my body – they felt absolutely enormous.

Then the unbelievable happened. Staff forced her finger right up into my bottom. It was painful and the soap was stinging, but as I moved to escape her, she told me in a threatening whisper not to fight. She moved her finger around, and I felt sick. She stopped, but the pain from her leaving my body was almost worse than when she had gone in. I felt I'd be sick at any moment, but the soaping started again. Then, with one holding me firmly – trapping me – the other forced her finger into the front of me. I thought I was going to die!

Still I could make no sound. The pain seared through me. The soap was like thick white paste all over my legs and thighs. I opened my eyes and looked down after she had taken her hand away. My blood was smeared all over the soap and it looked like pink marble. My head and limbs seemed to be disjointed from me. I could not say if I was standing or not, I was conscious only of the pain they were causing deep inside me, and the almost intolerable level of coldness was making me shake uncontrollably. I could still hear their giggling and was terrified that at any moment I would be violently sick.

They seemed to have stopped at last and although I had opened my eyes – I wanted to ask them to let me go – I could not look at them. I felt my degradation and humiliation to be complete, but then they turned me face down to the sink and, incredibly, *fed me through the mangle feet first*. I knew enough about this piece of equipment to realise that the enormous wooden rollers were 'at rest' and therefore could not crush me, but I was once more engulfed by terror. I had gone through as far as my tummy; my own bodyweight forced out my breath as I lay over the rough wooden roller, above me the other roller squashed heavily on to my back. Because they could not use the handle with the mangle in the 'resting' position, one was supporting my arms as the other was pulling me through by my legs. My head was hurting and my thoughts were unfocused and unclear, and I had never felt as freezing cold in my life.

Inexplicably, into my mind came a picture of the dead birds we sometimes found on the drive. Wet and flat on the ground –

with wings spread out – dead head flopped to one side. I felt like a dead bird.

Whether I fainted, or just shut down mentally with the pain and horror, I do not know, but I remember nothing more until later that night. They had obviously returned me to my dormitory because I woke up in my own bed.

No one was allowed out of bed at night without first calling Staff. A painfully desperate need for the toilet made me call her. Once there I had the most dreadful attack of diarrhoea and the wind pains on my inside were terrible, doubling me up; I was shaking again and scared to leave the room. Each time I attempted to stand or even move, the pains would start all over again. Staff said nothing at all but she was kind enough to stay with me. I didn't think the wind would ever go, however, I felt better eventually, but she saw some blood when I wiped myself. She said it was from my bottom and she took me to the bathroom and ran some water in the sink. Oh no . . . not again, was all I could think, and I immediately felt frozen and trembled all over. She quietly tried to reassure me as she very gently lifted me into the sink and told me to wash myself, adding, 'It is private down there.'

This comment crashed with amazing force and woke up my inert mind; I could feel again the dreadful turmoil of confusion. How could one member of staff offer dignity and show such compassion when two others in the same building had abused me so badly? It was beyond my comprehension. I felt bruised and in pain and more tired than I could have ever imagined. I was just happy to return to my bed. Two other occasions that night I had to call her out. In the morning I was in agony. The stinging from the soap was still hurting at the front, indeed I seemed to be hurting all over. The mangle had caused a bruised feeling all down my front, but my arms and legs too were sore, and they felt as heavy as lead. The top roller had hurt my head but now my ears were also burning with bruises and I was freezing cold and could not get warm. Night Staff came back before she went off duty and she said I was to stay in bed and rest. I was in pain, humiliated, and could not see myself recovering.

I was beaten. They had done it and it had taken them such a short time. I may have wanted to but I don't think I had even the energy to cry. I was done for, finished as an individual and well on the way to being a zombie. I stayed in bed all that day, and for much of the time I slept. Staff came in and brought me hot tea but I could not eat, not even bread and butter.

When I woke again my whole body ached from the mangle; little vein marks had come up on my arms and tummy. The bruising to the rest of me seemed to be getting more uncomfortable not less. I felt awful.

I was allowed to go out to the toilet on my own because of the runs during the night. It stung so badly when I spent a penny I did not want to go again. Thankfully, there was no blood anywhere, front or back. While lying awake, the night's events kept playing repeatedly in my head. The aches and pains were most definitely there, so I had not had a nightmare. My mind was clear but jumbled up. Then a horrifying thought occurred. I could not remember who they were, *or even their faces*! I was shattered. There was no apparent reason to me that this should be the case. When first picked up, I had been laughing – *she* had been laughing – and yet I could not remember her. They had become faceless. The giggling and the hands were all I could recall.

As I lay there curled up in a ball, warm now under extra blankets, I realised that to survive this I would have to sort myself out.

The following day must have been a Saturday because all the other kids were in doing their work. I had said to Staff that I still felt ill, and imagine I looked it because there was no objection to my staying in bed under the comforting blankets. I desperately needed that comfort. The dorm was very quiet considering the cleaning was being done in there. I feigned sleep because I wished to speak to no one, and the most unusual sight of someone being allowed to stay in bed made them realise something was wrong, so they kindly left me alone. The polish smelt revolting and I had to go to the bathroom, but there was nothing left in me to bring up. Staff was concerned and asked me if I wanted to go to Liberty. I was horrified. Liberty was on the staff landing and, like at St Christopher's, was the term used to describe the sick bay. The thought of being on my own in a bedroom was too dreadful to contemplate.

They really had got to me physically and I was beginning to wonder what they had done to my mind. I concentrated on that, and as the hours passed and the physical pain diminished, so my thoughts and reason seemed to come back, albeit slowly. I lay there and thought: *Never mind yer body – mind yer mind.* Good, I liked that!

Again I realised that some things are beyond understanding, that to try and find reason was just a waste. What I also now understood was that no matter how guarded, how 'aware' of threat I had become, some things would happen for which there could be no forewarning. In this brainwashed world of demanded obedience and total compliance nothing I could do would help me, and most of the staff could not care less anyway.

During all the hours that I stayed in bed not one member of staff had asked me what was wrong. I considered this to be a deliberate omission – not because they didn't care, *but because they already knew.* No wonder I hated them.

By the Sunday, I was out of bed but did not have to go to church; I must have looked as bad as I felt. However, my thoughts were assembled and clear, and once I had some food in me I was well on the way to being me again. 'Never mind yer body – mind yer mind' became my mantra, but I knew I had to get stronger to get through this miserable existence.

The realisation that there was an undercurrent of malice and cruelty came to me fully one day in the garden. I was still feeling an alien strangeness and although I was slowly healing, the constant anxiety was real. Not wanting to join in games or even chat was unusual for me, but I was kindly left to my own devices because all the kids knew by now that I had 'not been well'.

Sitting on the sloping front lawn gave me an excellent vantage point to observe what was going on around me. There were staff who would join in the fun of playtime always looking as if they were enjoying the games; everybody taking part would be happy and relaxed, as indeed I had once been. Warren was there showing one of the kids how to correctly hold a tennis racquet. I could hear loud laughter when the ball was missed, which happened frequently. The stark contrast of this outwardly normal behaviour, and what she had done to me, I found deeply disturbing. The two who had just abused me so disgustingly were still faceless, but their outward air of normality would have masked completely their cruel behaviour in which they had so clearly revelled. I would have to re-double my efforts to overcome the cruel evil within the Home. I realised that when entering an institution such as this all you had was yourself; to discover they wanted to take that from you as well was awful.

I refused to accept I would turn out the same as so many of the other kids; to me many were like zombies with no thoughts of their own. They did things I could never bring myself to do: carry a bag for Boagey, just because she ordered them to; stand up, just because the staff had said so to 'prove' their authority. And on one occasion, I saw it with my own eyes, a kid got down on her hands and knees and tied Boagey's shoelaces. I would have done it if I could have tied the two shoes together and then watched her fall over as she walked away!

The little ones with the minor physical disabilities were understandably too scared to 'make things worse'. The others who were as fit and strong as me but who did nothing, I could not fathom at all. Very sadly, their fear of the staff and punishment was greater than the desire to help themselves; I did try to persuade and encourage them to change, but without effect.

Not for me though, no way, I had to buck my ideas up. Then a miracle occurred.

5

Uncle Tom and Auntie Dodd came into my life, and everything changed.

Having been summoned to Boagey's office, I went along with the usual trepidation. Now what am I supposed to have done wrong, I asked myself yet again. In genuine surprise I heard her say there were two people who wanted to be a Barnardo Auntie and Uncle, and they had chosen me to take out. Apparently I fitted their desire to have a little girl of about seven years old who would be fit and strong enough to enjoy their rural way of life. To add further to this exciting news I then learned that our outing was to be the next day, a Saturday in the Easter school holidays. I found this all very exciting but I could not grasp the reality of it all. I realised I would also get out of doing cleaning duties, because they were to collect me in the morning and bring me back at night.

The next day arrived and to my amazement, I was to wear my Sunday best clothes; this was serious stuff. I had seen some of the others go out but it left little impression because, well, if it was not you there was not much point in thinking about it really. Now my thoughts were racing and I was getting very excited with the idea. Some of it was to be going out with real outsiders, but it was also the knowledge that I was getting out of the Home for a whole day!

I was suitably scrubbed and polished, and cleaned up quite well really; I liked my Sunday clothes, especially my coat, and felt good inside. I was told to sit in the hall when ready and eventually I heard the scrunch of tyres on the drive. I stood up without having to be told, and waited with butterflies in my tummy doing gymnastics. Boagey answered the knock on the door and greeted them with her 'visitors' voice' – this duplicity made me sick.

At last I saw them: he was tall, as indeed was she. They both had an upright, patrician bearing and yet kindness exuded from them. With the preliminaries over we went out to their car – and what a car. Uncle Tom – that was what I was to call him – opened the huge back door, I slid in as gracefully as I could. Auntie Dodd sat in the passenger seat beside Uncle Tom; with a sweep round the drive in great style, we were off.

I sat back quietly at first, and studied my surroundings. The inside seemed bigger than it had appeared from outside and the seats were made of red leather that smelt delicious. I stretched as high as I could go but could still barely see out until Uncle Tom asked me if I would like to stand on the hump on the floor that ran between the seats. I didn't have to be asked twice, and I felt my excitement build as we swept through the Kent countryside. I had an arm resting on each seat and as Auntie Dodd was looking ahead, I could study her without her knowing.

She was beautiful with smooth pale skin on her face and long neck. Her hair had a natural wave and you could tell it was soft without even touching it. Her hands were elegant; long nails with shiny but not coloured nail varnish were folded delicately on her lap. I decided she was delicious, absolutely lovely and quite obviously gentle. I very slowly moved my hand forward to rest on her shoulder because, well, I really wanted to. She responded by unfolding her hands and patting me softly on mine. Oh, God, I felt happy.

'Don't I get a hand on my shoulder too?' laughed Uncle Tom, who had seen all this unfold in his rear-view mirror!

We sped along – and beginning to feel more relaxed, I asked him about the car. He explained that the badge in the centre of the enormous steering wheel was a Viking ship, and that all Rovers carried that symbol. The clock on the dial was obvious, but he pointed out all the other instruments to me. I was intrigued to watch the numbers on the dial change as the miles went by.

We didn't seem to have been travelling very long when Uncle Tom announced, 'Soon be there,' and all my attention was back on the road and our surroundings. We had passed the signpost to Pluckley when the road came to a fork; we turned up to the right, which was nothing more than a narrow lane. Slowly we bounced along the unmade road, passing cottages with big front gardens. At the very end of the lane, he eased the car to a halt.

He turned to me, smiling. 'Can you manage to open those great big gates for me?'

I slid out of the car and found the handle on the white five-bar gate, leading to their drive and the cottage. I had to pull very hard to get it open and then strained to push – but once moving it was easy. I stood right back as he swept past and then securely closed the gate behind him. (Once indoors, I had to look up 'initiative' in the dictionary; he said that was what I had shown. I was so proud.) I helped Auntie Dodd carry her bag to the front door; but before we entered the house we stood and looked around, allowing me the chance to take in my new surroundings.

I was in front of the cottage beside a large lawn with a weeping willow tree hanging its branches over a pond; this, I was assured, was full of fish. Beyond the gate was woodland; Uncle Tom said we would explore in there later. To the right was a field and countryside for as far as the eye could see; I was told that somewhere in the field was Uncle Tom's horse. At this point, the front door opened; a round lady stood there and for a moment we just looked at each other.

'Cook – meet Susan,' said Uncle Tom. She hurried out and wrapped lovely large squishy arms around me in a breathtaking cuddle. I was in heaven.

Without warning I began to cry. Unfamiliar with cuddles and warmth, a pain had arrived in my chest; I did not know what to do, I was finding it hard to breathe.

'You aren't used to all these kindnesses, are you, my dear?' said Uncle Tom as he lifted me up in his arms. The relief that he knew how I was feeling was immense and when he tickled me under the arms I was in hoots of laughter, partly with the tickling but largely because of his understanding. He continued to hold me until all the tears were dried and then checked with Cook and Auntie Dodd that there was time to show me around outside before lunch.

At the back door porch were loads of wellies, all made for giants.

'Doddy,' called Uncle Tom, 'which are the smallest here that would fit our guest?'

'Oh dear,' she answered. 'They are all so very big, aren't they?' I was seeing my first disappointment poking its face around the corner, when Auntie Dodd called again from the hall. 'You better have these then,' she said. We all laughed and I was scooped up again in a great big hug. She had arrived with a brand new pair, black and shiny and purchased just for me. *Nothing* could have given me more pleasure at that moment.

Off we trekked; it was not a garden, it was land. We walked down the narrow path and went to the orchard at the furthest point first – with Uncle Tom's loyal English bull terrier following us all the way. Beneath one of the apple trees was a little row of graves, each with the names of the dogs who had preceded our present canine company. Uncle Tom pointed these out to me; he had obviously given much love and attention to these animals so it didn't seem at all unusual or macabre. Under the trees on the other side were some beehives; I was promised some of their honey for tea. To the right of the path was a chicken run full of beautiful big red shiny hens, 'Rhode Island Reds' he called them; and all down the opposite side, fruit bushes and a kitchen garden neatly laid out in row upon row of vegetables.

'Shame you couldn't meet the gardener,' said Uncle Tom, with such affection he could have been referring to a member of his own family.

We had been out exploring for ages but now it was time to go in and wash for lunch. The dining room, with pictures on every wall, was beautiful. I said so, excusing myself if it was rude to comment.

'Not at all,' replied Uncle Tom, with enthusiasm. 'I'll show you round the whole place after lunch, and then we'll go and find the fish in the pond.'

Immediately after the meal, we went into the drawing room. 'Is this where people used to do art?' I asked, knowing already that I would be able to ask any questions without receiving the usual scorn, and that I'd be given a friendly reply.

'What a clever idea,' he said. 'No, it's a shortened version of the old term, "withdrawing room", a place where people, usually the ladies, would withdraw from the dining table to rest after a meal and catch up on the gossip, while the gentlemen would go to the smoking room and, well, smoke.' Auntie Dodd added that as the cottage was so small, Uncle Tom had to use the drawing room for his pipe. Everything was relaxed, I was so *happy*.

Uncle Tom sat in an enormous leather chair with me beside him on a soft pouffe he told me had come from abroad. Auntie brought us a beautiful silver tray about the size of a tea plate, with feet that looked like tiny silver peas. 'Have a piece of marshmallow, Susan, it's delicious and a lovely way to end a nice lunch.' It appeared to be a very different confection from anything I had ever seen before and this was confirmed when I had picked out my piece – white rather than the pink.

I felt a bit hesitant. I didn't normally have many sweets and this looked potentially very difficult to eat, so for a moment I just held it between finger and thumb. 'Oh it's all *squishy*,' I said, as I gently squeezed the little square a few times, and then popped it into my mouth. They laughed as I had pondered over this and because they had told me I would have to eat it 'all in one go' because it would be too messy to nibble. They laughed as well when my cheeks puffed out with this mouthful, 'Just like a little hamster!'

The taste was an *explosion* of sweetness; I had to borrow a handkerchief to put to my mouth, as the delicious softness seemed to embrace my every taste bud.

What a luxurious flavour, what luxurious surroundings with these two wonderful people, and what laughter! It seemed to me to be a moment that illustrated perfectly the entire experience.

I guessed they might like to rest then and coincidentally heard Cook removing things from the dining room. I asked if I was allowed to help. I was assured she would be delighted and I was gone like a shot. I knocked gently on the door and she opened it to me.

'What are you up to then, Miss Susan?' she asked and was pleased when I said I had permission to help her. I did some carrying and was introduced to the workings of the kitchen. It seemed to be enormous compared with the size of the rooms in the rest of the cottage. Cook explained it had been added on at some time to allow for the catering for the many parties that were held there.

I told her I liked parties, 'Especially the jelly!' She laughed and said we were having jelly for tea, as well as honey from the bees on bread she had made that morning.

Through one door was the pantry, full to bursting with rows of jars. 'All my own work,' she said proudly, and indeed it was quite obvious the jars were not bought in a shop. They all had different coloured cotton gingham hats on, to differentiate between jams, marmalade, honey, pickles, and all sorts of other delicious preserves. Through yet another door was a washroom with the biggest, deepest sink I had ever seen. I stood on a box to reach the kitchen sink to wash up, while Cook dried and put away.

Then another surprise and treat; we were going to make buns for tea. Other than making the lunch sandwich at St Christopher's I had never been this close to preparing food, and had never been in a kitchen. I watched in awe as her powerful arms had the mixture done in no time and I helped fill the bun cases. I had a lick of the mixture but was warned in a very jovial fashion, 'Don't you lick the bowl out, that's Uncle Tom's treat!' And it was. He came in as the first batch was coming out of the Aga; with spoon in hand, he cleaned that bowl so thoroughly it hardly needed washing up. The laughter in the room was wonderful; I decided I never *ever* wanted to leave. Don't think about going, I told myself, and carried on enjoying every moment.

Later, true to his word, Uncle Tom showed me round the upstairs. Everywhere just looked like a doll's house, pretty covers on the beds and matching curtains with frills covering the tiny lead-light windows. I went over to peer through and from there I could see the horse.

'Come on, let's go to the paddock and I'll introduce you,' said Uncle Tom enthusiastically. We went back downstairs and I got into my new wellies again. We took some cake, proper pony cake of course, to give him a treat. As we approached, he let out a loud whinny of recognition and greeting.

'He knows you are new and wants to meet you.' Reassured, I ran on; he met us at the gate and I was allowed to climb up to be closer (until I was staring up into a huge black nostril). The way Uncle Tom and the horse seemed to communicate and nuzzled each other was amazing; they were friends, not just horse and rider. We went into the paddock.

'Watch this, Susan.' Uncle Tom playfully smacked him on the shoulder and with another whinny and a deep sweep of his head, almost like a bow, he was off! His hoofs thudded on the ground as he went charging around the hedges; he seemed to be gaining speed all the time and then would slow and shake his head and mane before charging off again. I could feel the power; it was magnificent. Eventually tired out he returned for some cake and more nuzzling, but was now blowing hard with all the effort.

'We'd best get back, Susan, I want you to show me how well you read.'

I had mentioned the books in the drawing room before I went to help Cook. From the shelf, Uncle Tom selected *The Wind in the Willows*. He sat again in his huge leather chair with me contentedly beside him on my pouffe. I'm afraid I then showed off. I loved books and read at every opportunity. I did well too, asking him a few times to help where words were unfamiliar. After his pipe was over and I had read many pages, we put the book down.

'You are a very clever young lady; keep reading and learning and you will be able to do anything when you grow up and leave school.' I puffed up with pride; no one had ever praised me before and Uncle Tom, to my young mind, was a Gentleman with his own horse, so I figured he would know! Auntie Dodd came in and he told her that he thought I was not just clever – I was *very* clever.

'There is nothing to beat a clever mind and a healthy body, and you've got both,' she said. I knew then I would always remember those words; it's what I had thought but here was a grown-up confirming it.

Shortly after, Cook called us to tea. She had put out the honey and new bread as promised and we had the cakes I had helped to make. The tea table was a livelier affair than lunch had been; I talked nineteen to the dozen and I knew exactly why: I could not face the thought of leaving. I had put it to the back of my mind, but no longer able to maintain my stoicism I laid my arm on the table, my head on my arm, and broke my heart. Uncle Tom came around the table and silently lifted me into his arms where he held me tightly, as I nestled sobbing into his shoulder.

Gently patting my back he whispered, 'Susan, shhh, shhh, you will make Auntie Dodd and me cry.' I was horrified at this possibility and tried to stop. Uncle Tom sat back on his chair with me on his lap and handing me an enormous hanky, looked at me with all the wisdom in the world and asked, 'When did you last cry, Susan? Are you allowed to cry in the Home? Do you ever let yourself cry?'

I told him I never did because it made the punishment worse – as they put it, 'now I'll give you something to cry for'. I'd heard it so many times and had seen the resultant smacking, so I did not cry. 'You stay brave, young lady, and fight the buggers!' he said. He roared with laughter, and so did Auntie Dodd, at my reaction to the language! Soon the mood had lifted and we were back in the car and returning through the same Kent countryside. On the way they told me they would come and get me again, very soon, before the end of the school holidays. That would not be the last visit either; they were going to ask me back for weeks in the summer holidays too.

I hated to wave goodbye to them and went into the Hall rather than watch the car go down the drive. It was late, the end of the day, and I went straight upstairs to bed. Not one person asked me if I had enjoyed myself but that was fine by me. Uncle Tom and Auntie Dodd were special inside my head and I was going to be, unnaturally for me, very selfish and share them with no one. Having met them, I felt I now had a protective shield around me.

~ 6 ~

I still find it vaguely amusing to hear 'crime' and 'punishment' linked together. For me, or indeed anyone raised in the Homes, the relationship between the two was unclear at best. If I had done something wrong, then of course I would expect a punishment and would do my best to bear it with dignity; however, for us there were two systems at play.

Firstly, the punishment meted out would seem invariably to far outweigh the misdemeanour. Secondly, there didn't have to be any sort of wrongdoing to raise the anger of some of the staff, especially Boagey. In my young mind it was their device to simply alleviate one frustration or another; yet surely a punishment without justified reason, a punishment that is effectively a beating, surely that could never be considered rightful?

I felt I was growing stronger by the day; having healed from the mangle incident, and through knowing Uncle Tom and Auntie Dodd with their encouragement to 'fight the buggers!' I resolved to deal with the threat of punishment in a way that was as annoying to the staff as it was painful for me, but we were all being treated in this same manner anyway, why make it easy for them?

I had finished my designated chores after tea one day, but because I was delayed and behind the main crowd going into the freedom of the garden I ran through the Hall to catch up with the others. Boagey appeared as if from nowhere, grabbed my arm tightly, and pulled me roughly to a halt. As she shouted at me for breaking the rules (the standard precursor for a walloping), I stood stock still with my head cast down, deep against my chest.

'Look at me when I'm talking to you.' I remained as I was.

'I told you to LOOK at me,' she said in a raised voice while trying to move my head, without success.

'Right, you come with me, young lady,' she said as she marched off towards the office, finding when she had walked those few steps that I had stayed where I was. She returned to me and then pushed me to move. I dropped on to the floor on purpose. Then she tried to get hold of my arms, but they were now underneath me so that was impossible. She screamed at me again but I again stayed where I was.

'You stand up now and look at me or woe betide you,' she said in a now quiet, threatening voice. I obeyed but stared at her so face-on I could see it was disturbing her. 'Right. You get out of my sight this instant and get yourself upstairs – you are going to bed early.' I felt safe as the younger ones were already up there. I turned and walked upstairs in silence, without once taking my staring eyes away from her.

As I lay in bed, listening to the others playing in the garden, I allowed myself a smile. I had dealt an unexpected blow to her 'authority'. I had avoided a smacking and felt a new strength from that success. Frequently thereafter, adopted by me as a way of coping with their constant bullying, Boagey even gave it a name: 'dumb insolence'.

That the bullying was such a normal practice was the frightening thing: we were trapped. All the staff were influenced by Boagey and with her approval were free to act in exactly the same way. And even though not all of them would mete out physical punishment, by their silence they condoned those who did.

All of us kids were in the same boat. There was no adult in whom we could confide about this senseless treatment and why we were hurting as badly as we were. Sometimes it would really get one of us down and we would talk a little amongst ourselves, but we all agreed: who would believe us anyway?

To be brutally honest, it was not a major issue. Because of its frequency, it just took on an air of normality. Those of us who had been at Barnardo's for so long that it was the only place we had ever known would probably never have questioned this behaviour so deeply if it hadn't been for the 'new' kids. It was they who told us the behaviour of the staff was wrong – but there was little we could do about it.

To experience something is one thing, to pluck up the courage to tell about it is another; not being believed would be too much to bear. On once occasion I thought about telling Uncle Tom, as I felt he would have understood. But one massive thing blocked my way: *I did not know what words to use*. The attack with the mangle had traumatised me for a long time, it haunted me and I felt a need to tell of that horror – it seemed the only thing I could do about it. However, at eight years old, I was too young; I simply did not know what to say. We never ever referred to our private parts, we had no names for them, and it was taboo. I tried to think about how I could explain; sometimes I desperately wanted to; but I realised I had no means of communicating at that level, so I left it. After some time had passed, I was very grateful I had not. Suppose my calculations of him were wrong and he had thought me a dirty little girl, and did not want to take me out again.

It was the perfect trap.

Punishment took various forms, and while we all witnessed abuse, we were not particularly interested in what happened to each other; it was rarely a topic of discussion or complaint. We were not victimised as such because we realised that we were each treated, overall, equally badly – so we accepted it as normal. However, there was one big exception: Gennie.

Sadly, she was a 'wet-bed', not a nasty or rude term, a simple matter of fact. I am aware that attitudes and understanding of this condition have improved greatly but that was not the case for her, or we who shared the dorm and had to witness daily the abuse that poor little girl suffered. I have said already the trials and tribulations of others made little impression upon me, but this was too obscene to ignore.

We shared the same dorm, sleeping at right angles to one another – with the bathroom door making the corner. There were 16 of us, four along each wall. There was always a night-duty Staff around because we were not allowed to use the toilet without calling for her and being escorted to it.

Gennie always went off to sleep very quickly; she had the quietest snore ever heard, barely perceptible, but she was a deep sleeper. Given that many infants are unable to last the whole night without going to the toilet, it makes sense to 'lift' the ones that don't wake naturally from their beds and take them to the toilet. Gennie's problem may have been avoided had this been done for her but that would have spoiled the daily fun for the staff and thus every morning was the same.

We were always still asleep when the staff called for us at 6.30 to get up, and they did so from the bathroom door between my bed and Gennie's. They would turn to her and with a flourish would pull back her bedclothes. She immediately curled herself up and whimpered: she was wet again. The staff would register their daily renewed disgust and physically haul her from the bed, swiftly followed by her bedding. The bath was run with *cold* water; then she, the bedding, wet nightdress and all would be thrown in. How she stood it, I don't know; she was a frail-looking kid with no muscle structure and had a permanently mauve hue to her skin. The staff did not actually hit her, they did not need to; her shame and humiliation were enough.

Poor little Gennie, crying quietly throughout and sometimes

peeing again with cold and fear, had to tread the bath contents while I was getting washed and dressed. Then ordered to get her from the bath to the sink, I was under strict instructions to use only cold water and had to supervise her wash. She was the same age as me but she was very thin and always wore the expression of a terrified puppy. Drying one's skin when cold is a familiar feeling to anyone who has swum in the sea, but that poor kid had to do it every day, and she could not rub hard, it was too painful. I used to say nothing to her while we were in the room together – but did try to tell her how sorry I was for her when we were elsewhere; sadly, I don't think it registered. I often wished I had the courage to shout at the staff but I confess I was not that brave, not on someone else's behalf anyway. Regrettably over a period of time I became more used to the situation and her plight lessened for me somewhat, until the school summer holidays when the whole thing went up another stage, with Boagey as the chief tormentor.

Our beds were low and narrow, built in tubular metal head and tail, with a base of steel springs. Occasionally these springs would 'ping' – which drew great laughter, especially after lights-out when we would almost choke on our pillows to stifle sounds that might raise the attention of staff. On top of the springs was the mattress, a maximum of two inches thick and filled with flock; I know that snippet of information because one day my spring had pinged and torn the mattress cover. As if it was my fault this damage had occurred, I unfairly had to do extra work while Miss Rustan, the seamstress, came and repaired it for me.

On top of the mattress was placed an underblanket of thick grey material, a bottom and top sheet, one pillow, one blanket in summer and two in winter, all topped off by a counterpane in blue and white, emblazoned in the central circle with the legend 'Dr Barnardo's Homes'. Gennie had the same, except she also had a thick rubber sheet, covered with a drawsheet of cotton, to protect the mattress from the bed-wetting.

On the summer morning in question, for some unknown reason, Gennie's drawsheet had moved during the night. The wet had run down over the rubber, on to the sheet and inevitably the mattress. Once the staff had got her out and realised what had happened, well, the place erupted. Frozen in shocked silence as the tirade hit Gennie, we watched as they went berserk. They tore her bedding off in the normal manner and then her wet nightdress and smacked her so hard, she screamed.

Held tightly by one arm she was thrashed to the extent she danced her legs in an attempt to get out of the way of the consuming pain and anguish; I too had experienced that and felt the pain for her. When they let go her arm, they had held her so tightly their grip showed up white on her skin. Staff seemed unaware of us other kids just standing there – watching in silent alarm and amazement. It was dreadful; I felt sick for her.

They put everything into the cold bath and then, unbelievably, in went the mattress and Gennie swiftly followed. I was ordered to help and get it all done before either of us was allowed breakfast. We had to go through the usual routine of washing and drying ourselves, then get the mattress out through the window and haul it to the drying meadow. 'And you will not have another one until that one is dry,' they added. Gennie was, by now, almost out of control. The natural colour was restored in her arm, but her bottom and thighs were scarlet from the smacking and stung when she entered the cold water. She continued to cry quietly; I had rarely felt so utterly helpless, though perhaps just being there with her was some consolation.

Boagey appeared. '*What* are you two doing up here when you should be dressed and down for breakfast?' I briefly explained and she simply went to the window to ensure it was fully open to enable us to do what we had been told with the mattress.

'And when it is in place, you come back here and clean up any water on the floor, and if you are too long and breakfast is over, you will have to do without.'

It was grossly unfair to both of us, but – I felt – particularly to me, being an innocent party; ironically, it was good for Gennie. It was clear she felt awful about my involvement; she stopped whimpering and just got on with the job in hand. Gradually the awful gloomy atmosphere was lifting from us; we even managed a quiet giggle while trying to lift the mattress – it may have been the thickness of a biscuit but it weighed a flipping ton! The water trail left behind was amazing but we got it to the sill. Because I was much stronger than Gennie, we decided to lift it about halfway out and she would go downstairs on to the path and get ready to guide it down safely.

I then shoved it out of the window and let it drop. It did occur to me that if she was underneath it would probably squash her flat, but all was well! Under the circumstances, we were not in bad spirits, and together we lifted each other's mood. Once up the steps with a struggle and onto the back drive, the gardener kindly helped us manage it the rest of the way, and he sympathised with Gennie to such an extent that she felt much better. We left the thing leaning drunkenly against the apple tree in the place where the gardener said would get most sun, and as it was a warm day already, we felt all might be well.

It was summer time and we were only wearing knickers, a thin vest and a thin dress made for us by Miss Rustan – but we were soaked to the skin from where the mattress had leant against us. There was nothing we could do except get back upstairs and dry the bathroom. There was water everywhere! We did a thorough job because we wanted no complaints and we badly needed to get our food.

Then all the kids appeared – *breakfast was over*! Gennie looked at me and nearly started crying again, but I suggested we quickly go downstairs to see if Boagey really meant it. Silly, silly me, of course she did!

When she saw us she went into a state of shocked horror at the sight of our wet clothes. 'How did you manage to get so wet?' Even then I wondered just who was supposed to be the intelligent person. This allowed her another angry outburst of rage and the excuse to say we could not have breakfast. '*And* you can get back upstairs, remove your wet clothing, take it to the meadow as well, then come back and spring-clean the bathroom – and work till your clothes are dry.'

We had to strip off everything – another nightdress was found for Gennie, and I put my own back on. We returned to the meadow to hang up the clothes, with just the wet fronts to the sun. Our mood had dropped again – with no help from me. I felt real anger now; this was not in any way my fault. I was just being victimised by a callous woman who loved every minute of it; she was positively gloating. She also knew I would not have my normal show of temper tantrum because I would not do that to Gennie, who was by now calm. We duly dried out every nook and cranny and thoroughly spring-cleaned the bathroom; then before lunch, we were allowed to go and get our dry clothes. I was always pretty swift but I had never seen Gennie move so quickly; we were definitely not missing lunch too. While there, we inspected the mattress. I did not say so to Gennie, but it was not going to dry in a month of Sundays. What will she sleep on? I asked myself, and at bedtime we found out.

It was customary to be undressed and washed or bathed before going to the dorm. When I got there, I could not believe my eyes. They had made her bed up already; her pillow and everything else were as usual, but in place of the mattress was thick brown paper. We all just stared in disbelief. Then Gennie came in; she was choking back the tears . . . but didn't say a word. She was a brave little kid and my heart went out to her – she didn't wet the bed on purpose for goodness' sake.

'Will you lot stop standing around like utter fools and get into bed?' Staff barked. Dutifully we did. Being in such close proximity to Gennie, I watched her gingerly climb up and try to lie down on the paper mattress without disturbing the undersheets that had started all this off. She lay stiffly with her back almost directly on to the bedsprings, her arms down by her sides. 'How on earth can she sleep like that?' I thought. Once we were settled down, Staff went out through the door, without another word.

I could not believe the whole thing; the events of the day ran through my mind – bizarre and surreal. One of the kids whispered, at risk of drawing more wrath, 'You all right, Gennie?' No reply. I realised she was very quietly crying again. 'Gennie, are you okay?' she repeated.

Then the door loudly burst open to reveal Staff. I nearly wet my own bed!

'Get out of bed, all of you, *now*,' she hissed, so we did.

The most ridiculous situation then unfolded before us. Two other staff came in with a new mattress! Gennie and I were ordered to strip off the paper and remake her bed while the others returned to theirs; the fiasco was at an end. I could barely believe that they had put us through all that, making us think that the poor kid was going to have to sleep on paper; then producing a proper bed that had been *planned all along*. It only compounded my belief of their crass, cruel stupidity. Needless to say, wet-bed normality resumed the following day – but fortunately, I have no recollection of ever seeing the wet mattress in the drying meadow again.

Barnardo's relied entirely upon charitable contributions; this included almost everything we wore. We did not have any clothes that were 'ours'; the only brand new items being the dreadful play dresses hand made by the seamstress, Miss Rustan. A truly remarkable woman whom we all found a little bit scary . . . and believed to be at least 100 years old! Not much taller than many of the kids, she had a hunchback and wore large boots, one of which had a higher sole to raise a gammy leg to the level of the other. Her long bony fingers and facial features were pale and wizened – and rimless glasses somehow defied gravity to stay on her tiny nose. She used a thick, heavy wooden walking stick that 'thump-thumped' on the floor as she walked. I have no idea whether she 'lived in' at the Home, because she was never seen outside the workroom – her domain. This room was at the very top of the house and appropriately peaceful; she could barely hear the noises from elsewhere inside the house or from the garden. Lit by windows in the sloping roof, it had down the centre the longest table imaginable; permanently strewn with the tools of her craft . . . and woe betide if you as much as laid a finger on them!

I was frequently given sewing as a punishment, simply because I hated it! Miss Rustan, equally, hated having to share her particular piece of heaven with an idiot like me, idiotic because I didn't like sewing. I was up there one day, to sew some buttons onto a piece of cloth, or something equally ridiculous, while she was making the summer dresses. From an enormous roll of dark blue cotton material, which some other soul on punishment had already helped her prepare, she cut to size rectangular pieces hemmed all round. On an equally enormous sewing machine she simply sewed up the sides leaving space for the arms, across the shoulders leaving space for the head, and finished by stitching elastic in the waist. Miraculous to watch but awful to wear, they came in three sizes, small, medium or large; as indeed did everything we wore. I once asked Miss Rustan, breaking my vow of silence, did she make our knickers and vests as well? She fixed me with a gimlet eye, sighed and did not reply. I never did discover the answer.

The Victorian influence was apparent again as we changed into clean clothes just once per week, on a Sunday. Items were selected from three piles separated according to size: small, medium and large. There always seemed to be enough to go round. However, when one Sunday Pamela, a petite little thing, complained that there were only large knickers left, Miss Warren told her to 'get them on or miss breakfast', an option that would not require much thought! They looked ridiculous, but also hilarious; they didn't fit her anywhere! The material was very thick heavy cotton and navy blue in colour and once Pamela put them on they resembled shorts; the knicker legs, even though elasticated, didn't touch her anywhere, they just hung there. The only way she could get them to stay up was to fold the top over, then tie a knot. The whole arrangement looked extremely uncomfortable, and very precarious.

After breakfast, we dutifully went to church, up the steep hill and a walk of a couple of miles, in a crocodile of two-by-two. I was in the row behind Pamela, and as she walked, she kept on trying to adjust her underwear but without much luck. Eventually she gave up; there appeared a show of navy blue just below the coat hem, she turned around, we exchanged grins and with a final wiggle and a shake, she was free of them. I just stepped over and ignored them until eventually they arrived with Miss Warren bringing up the rear; she held them aloft, enquiring as to their origin. The crocodile halted and Pamela owned up. Because said garment was now wet and dirty, Pamela continued without and was known after that as Nicholas (knickerless) which eventually became just Nic. Moreover, Nic it stayed for as long as I can remember.

I read somewhere about Barnardo's, 'They ruled with the Bible in one hand and a whip in the other.' Boagey's and the staff's greatest display of their overt hypocritical behaviour was possibly nowhere more apparent than at church: their sugary sweetness that they put on for the outside world was sickening. We were dressed in our Sunday best as if nobody ever saw us in the other raggedy clothes we otherwise wore! Their greetings of the vicar and potential benefactors beggared belief in insincerity; we would frequently make vomiting expressions between ourselves – strictly out of sight of course. We none of us liked to be centre stage or 'on show' and we all shared a hatred of one such example. Whenever the parishioners sang 'Onward Christian Soldiers' we were made to march around the pews to demonstrate our youthful commitment to God! I once stayed in my seat, folded my arms defiantly and would not join in; however I missed my roast lunch and decided afterwards my principles weren't *that* strong.

All sorts of things went on out of sight of the supposed authority of the staff: waves to the choirboys, tongues out to grannies . . . Oh! If they had known!

The other thing – which upon reflection is tragically amusing – was the religious verse 'Suffer the little children to come unto me.' We honestly believed that this meant that if you suffered as a child, you were guaranteed a place in Heaven. One of the older kids suggested that with our record The Lord God would lay on transport!

A Sunday incident, well remembered, began at breakfast. I must mention at this point that the Home had been acquired from three spinster sisters who, with no male help available, could no longer manage the running of the enormous place. They were bought a bungalow property in settlement, which was very close to the church. The joy of their lives – and the bane of ours because they stank of mothballs – was to have two of us 'gels' join them in their pew. On this particular day, it was my turn.

The Sunday breakfast was always the same: boiled eggs, bread and butter and a cup of tea. When my egg arrived I wondered what sort it could be because it was a sort of pale blue colour. It took more breaking into than usual but when I made it, out came a puff of dust, and lying in the very base was a little black marble about the size of a pea . . . *it stank*.

'Cor, my egg's bad, Miss,' I exclaimed, temporarily forgetting my manners and wafting said egg around for all to see.

'We do *not* serve bad food, Susan Davis, get it eaten or leave the table or you won't have lunch either.' I realised she was serious, deadly serious, and the thought of no Sunday roast spurred me into what I would have otherwise considered impossible. Wrapped in a hunk of dry bread I swallowed it down in one go.

Off then to church and my turn with the three sisters; I found them not only smelly but also rather threatening. They were always in the same long, black gowns that rustled a lot when they moved; they wore boots with goodness knows how many buttons up the sides. I liked to read Dickens, and these three were exactly of that era. I made my way to them with the other girl who shared my fate that day, and I soon realised something was going wrong.

My head and body began to feel a bit warm, then a bit warmer until I was very hot; my tummy was burning. I burped – it smelt just like the egg. The tummy ache, the heat and the mothballs all contrived to make me feel very poorly indeed and I exclaimed in a loud panic, 'I feel sick.' A wasted late piece of information really, because just as I said it, I vomited all over the black dress of sister number two. The kid who was with me announced, in an equally loud voice,

'They made her eat a bad egg – that's why!'

I felt a thousand eyes upon me as clearly the entire congregation heard. Staff was very soon on the scene and whisked me out into the fresh air – where I continued being sick all over the neatly trimmed grass. I didn't give another thought to the poor old lady; I was in a fair amount of distress. Staff had said not one word at breakfast when the egg had to be eaten; it was wonderful justice that she should have to be in attendance when it came back up. I thought I was in serious trouble and would be punished, and would definitely not have my roast, but to my astonishment neither fate beset me. An example I think when Boagey's stupidity could have again gone too far, and the public place would have caused her enormous embarrassment. *She* would not have been believed for a change if she had called *me* a liar – the stock label given to anyone divulging a painful truth – the bad egg smell was there for all to experience. The girl who had been sitting with me had her lunch too; clearly a situation best brushed under the carpet and forgotten.

Sundays, like every other day, followed the same routine week in week out. There were numerous restrictions placed on 'The Lord's Day' – their preferred terminology – and one of these was that we were not allowed a bath.

On the nights of the week when we were allowed to bathe, we had to follow a strict routine. Three of us had to go separately into each bath of water, the level barely covering our knees. The cleanest went in first and so on; needless to say, because of the games and mucking around, I was always in at number three; quite an achievement at cricket, but not so for bath time. I became expert at removing mud and grass stains sitting in tepid water; it was only when I left, in my teens, that I experienced the joy of bathing in water both hot and clean. The nights it was not your turn to bathe we had a 'strip wash', which was much preferred because at least the water was hot!

One last thing about our Victorian-style Sundays: we attended Morning Service at church, Sunday school and Evensong. This did not allow time for much else, and we were closely monitored. We were allowed to read; that was the sum total of our amusement: no knitting, sewing or playing music.

Oh, we were permitted to speak!

~ 8 ~

The call to go to Boagey's office was always the precursor of fear and trepidation; every single one of us felt the same. If the call came via a kid from another playroom, whom Boagey had used as a messenger, her announcement prompted a unanimous groan from the whole room. And this was what the messenger brought me on this occasion. 'Susan Davis, Miss Boagey wants you in her office.' Always with the emphasis on the 'you'.

My knock was greeted with 'Come,' in an already cross tone. Gawd, what have I done *now*? I thought. The matron sat at her huge desk, the first line of intimidation I always felt. She was ugly usually, but levels of this affliction deepened with the varying levels of her anger. Today, she looked very ugly indeed.

'I have reached the end of my patience with you, young lady. I have had enough of your behaviour altogether. You are now going to come with me. I'll show you where I put horrible children like you.'

I was utterly bewildered! I had been feeling much happier after another wonderful visit to the Dodds'. I had been in a few scrapes, but little trouble, because since Easter, the weather had been so lovely that we spent hours outside. I would spend most of my time running alone. I didn't know what she was talking about, but you didn't argue with Boagey.

I followed her up the main stairs, up the staff stairs, and then to a part of the Home I didn't even know existed, a very steep narrow flight of stairs that opened into a small room. I was fearful (I was alone with Boagey, and confused as to why) but I was also intrigued as to where I was. The room was very light, but the windows were too high for me to see more than just the sky. The floorboards were bare, indeed so was the room, save for a single bed. The light in the ceiling did not have a shade; it looked like a prison cell.

Up to this point, she had not said a word. Now, in a quietly threatening voice, she ordered me to 'Get undressed, put on the nightdress on the bed and get in.'

As I did so she watched me and I felt a dreadful nausea wash over me. I controlled myself so as not to shake and met her eyes with a steady, unafraid stare. But that was not how I felt at all.

'You will get into that bed, and you will lie there and consider what a dreadful child you are. You will stay there, regardless of how long it takes, until I am satisfied you understand the error of your ways, and promise me you will change in the future. Under *no* circumstances are you to get out of that bed.' Then she was gone.

I lay there with thoughts crashing through my mind. I remembered the mangle incident with dread, but then I decided that no, Boagey couldn't do anything like that. She was a bully of the first order, but she was the head of the Home – the matron – she would not stoop so low. I managed to convince myself of this, and tried to put that harrowing experience to the back of my mind again. Then I tried to think of what dreadful thing had happened, of which I now stood accused – but nothing. My thoughts slowed down because I was going round in circles and getting nowhere. I looked around the prison. I traced in my mind's eye the route taken, and then it dawned on me – I was in the tower. We had just learnt about the 'Princes in the Tower' in history at school – but I thought that that was a bit extreme – even for Boagey! Gradually I realised I could just make out the sounds of the kids outside; they would be a bit impressed if they knew where I was. But even if I had stood up on the bed, I was not tall enough to be able to look out the window and down to the grounds below; I could see sky and that was it. There were bird droppings on the glass, but it would be too high up for someone to clean. I wonder if there is any way out through the top of the house, I thought to myself. I bet the three sisters would know. I would ask them next time I sat with them, if I ever did again after the rotten egg incident. From the depths of the house, I could hear the sound of cooking pans; they seemed to be miles away. I wondered many things: how long till lunch? Will I get any? What time was I brought here in the first place? I mused away in the peace and quiet of this rather strange environment. I still could not think what Boagey was getting at, and then I remembered I was supposed to be deliberating just that. But where would I begin?

I had been right with my first evaluation of the room; there was nothing but the bed, and a few dead flies in the corner on the floor. I felt okay really. I'd had worse punishments than this to cope with; I just wished I knew why I was here.

I realised that the sounds from outside, and from the kitchen, had ceased, which meant that it must be lunchtime. At least there were no foul smells reaching this far, so that was a bonus. I strained to hear if someone was approaching with a tray of food. Boagey did say I had to stay here until I was good. Blimey, that could take years, I thought. As I lay there I realised I needed the toilet. I had not been to the toilet since I first got up, at about 7.20. They had just had lunch, which made it 12.30 when they started, so when I heard again the sounds from the kitchen, it had to be gone 1pm. No wonder I wanted to go. Then, a dreadful thought occurred. 'Under *no* circumstances are you to get out of that bed,' she had said.

I realised suddenly that there was perhaps more to this punishment than I had first imagined. I should have known really.

The more I lay there, the more I wanted to go. What could I do? There was no way I could lie there and wet the bed, I had seen enough of what was dished out to Gennie, and anyway, I couldn't physically do that. I had to get up. On the way up the stairs earlier, I had seen a little door on a half-landing behind which was a toilet, so I knew there was at least somewhere close. But how to get there? I suddenly became very afraid of what was waiting for me outside the door, but I would have to make a move, I was busting. I very gingerly sat up, and put my feet over the side of the bed, but that immediately made me more desperate. I stood, very purposefully placing my feet silently on the floor, and with cautious, measured steps, slowly made it to the door. I opened it, which made just a little squeak, but so far, so good. My heart was thumping as I met the first step down, half expecting to see Boagey, but no, all was quiet. I made it to the little door and sat down with such relief. I was as quiet as possible. Then another dilemma, do I flush or not? I sat there and decided against it. There was no way I had made any sound up to now, and by not using paper she would never even know I had been here.

As quietly as I had arrived, I opened the door to leave . . . *and there she was, not one foot away from me*! I jumped at the shock, and then saw her face bearing the most dreadful glower. With one hand, she silently pointed me up the stairs. In the other, she held a brand-new, thick rubber-soled gents' slipper. I ran up those stairs in terror and jumped on to the bed, but there was no time to get the covers over me. She hauled me upright, tore the nightdress off me, and then it started.

She started to beat me – to rain blows down onto me with the slipper; the immediate pain was unbelievable as I was still on my back to begin with. She hit me between the legs and on my chest before I could curl up; she just thrashed away mindlessly. There was no escape, no part of me was safe from the attack – head, face, back, legs – even my feet – she had gone completely mad! Then suddenly it stopped but I could feel her behind me. She had her knees against my bed, and she was rubbing herself very hard. I had no idea what she was doing. Her breathing was weird, as if she had run too far. A disgusting smell came from her and it was beginning to make me feel sick. She was making the bed tremble. I was scared stiff, waiting for the beating to start again. Her breathing turned to stifled grunting sounds, then, unbelievably, it was all over. Without a word, she turned and was gone.

I lay there straining to hear her go all the way down the stairs, which she did. I stayed as still as possible, barely daring to breathe, for what seemed like ages before moving a muscle. My skin had never hurt so much, a bruised stinging sensation all over me. Upon examination, I could see just what she had done; the marks were little blood veins on the skin, great red patches the shape of the sole and others already turning to blue bruises. The stinging was the worst thing, the *slightest* touch of the sheet made me wince, but I was naked still and had to cover myself.

Then I heard it! The sound of someone coming back up the stairs. Oh God, I thought. Please, no, no more, *please*.

I lay back down with my back to the door, covered completely by the sheet and thin blanket. With my heart beating right up in my throat, I felt I could take no more – I knew I couldn't. The door opened; someone came in, I heard a tray being placed on the floor. Not a word was said, and I heard whoever it was leave. I stayed turned to the wall for an *age* before I decided they really had gone and were not coming back. I slowly turned over. Sure enough, there was a tray, upon which was a large bowl of stewed apple and thick custard which was cold, presumably the dessert from lunch. Beside this, folded on the floor, was a brand-new, thick, long-sleeved nightdress. I had examined the original; it had a great tear in it, but a brand-new one? That was a first. I put it on and ate the food. I felt sick to begin with, but that passed and I realised how hungry I was.

She kept me in the tower for some days, and each time I heard the stairs creak, I turned away from the door. The food was left, the tray removed later, still without a word; I used the small toilet to wash, only cold water, but better than nothing. I was obviously there until the marks had all gone. The whole thing – the lack of knowledge of why I was here, the solitary confinement, the senseless beating and what had come after – was an unbelievable and harrowing experience, but one I realised I had faced with far more fortitude than the mangle incident. I was a bit older I know, going on eight and a half, and the accepted normality of the bullying quite clearly had toughened me up. I was physically stronger from my running, and had satisfactorily proved to myself that I was in control of my mind throughout. Try as I might I once again could not work out what Boagey's reasons were for putting me in the tower. I had been terrified, as much of what Boagey could do to me as of the eventual outcome. I realised, too, that she would never scare me as much again, ever. It was only as I grew older that I realised I had suffered that awful attack and its aftermath for the physical gratification of a sexual pervert.

~ 9 ~

The awful fear of another call to the office dissolved completely – and turned to happiness – at the news of yet another outing with Uncle Tom and Auntie Dodd. This was particularly exciting because I was to stay over, sleep at their cottage; something I had never done before, *sleeping out*! I was so excited when I saw the car coming up the drive I was gone, out through the huge front door and on to the drive in a second. I jumped up and down with glee until the car stopped and Uncle Tom had lifted me into his strong arms; a moment of sheer elation that will never be forgotten.

He put me down when Boagey appeared, but Auntie Dodd was now at my side and had a protective arm across my shoulders. Boagey, always the fraud in these situations, had her Visitors' Persona on display. With a plea that I behave myself, Boagey shook hands with Uncle Tom. Then we got into the car and were gone. Sweeping down the drive in the now familiar big black Rover; me already standing on the hump in the middle, a hand already on each shoulder, eating up the miles between Hell and Paradise, off in a car with two angels on earth. That is *exactly* what it was for me, it was wonderful. Behind me, on the red leather seat, was my bag containing nightwear and a flannel. I had a tummy full of exciting butterflies; I still could hardly believe this was all real. When we arrived, I got out immediately – opening and closing the big gate, as I had before.

'No need to look up "initiative" any more,' said Uncle Tom,

laughing. When we parked at the top of the drive, they left the car and I turned to get my bag.

'Oh, you won't need that,' said Auntie Dodd.

I felt devastated. They said I was staying the night. I could not believe that they were going to let me down.

I stood, frozen to the spot, as they walked up to the cottage; they reached the front door and still I couldn't move, I was stunned. As Uncle Tom unlocked the door, Auntie Dodd turned and saw me waiting. She came back, knelt in front of me and said quietly and sweetly, 'What's the matter, Susan?'

I blurted out, close to tears now, 'You said I could stay.'

'But you *are*, darling,' she assured me, and then looked at my bag still in the back of the car. 'Ah, *now* I know. You come with me and I'll show you why you don't need YOUR bag.'

Still not entirely convinced and with my head down, I followed her indoors. We went straight upstairs and she opened the door to the room that was to be my bedroom.

The decor and the bedding were mainly white, and laid out on the beautiful white quilt was an array of pink things. I could hardly believe my eyes: before me lay a pink nightdress, a dressing gown, fluffy slippers, a new flannel, even a bar of pink soap. I turned around, and ran into the waiting open arms. I apologised for misunderstanding, but she assured me it was all her fault; we cuddled each other until we both felt better.

Gosh, what a start, but the rest of the stay was wonderful; I spent most of the time outside with Uncle Tom, accompanied as ever by his faithful dog. We walked all around the grounds as before; I was shown the process of feeding the hens. Cook kept all the peelings and scraps from the kitchen; these were put into a very old pot on the Aga and boiled. We together collected this hot pot and carried it into one of the sheds; there Uncle Tom added what he called 'mash', a dry meal.

Squatting down on my haunches – armed with an enormous

wooden spoon and revelling in the emanating steamy warmth – I was allowed to help with the stirring, being shown that all the dry ingredients had to be well blended in. It smelt wonderful. I followed him into the hen run; as soon as they saw us they started their loud clucking sounds and from many different directions they ran over to us in a flock, heads thrust forward, wings out and going as fast as their little skinny legs would carry them. They looked hilarious which made me squeal with delight and jump up and down with glee; that in turn made him roar with laughter. He shared the meal out into the long trough and we left them to it. 'The eggs we can collect later,' he promised.

Next, we crossed to the paddock to visit his horse; the well-remembered whinny of recognition was our greeting, but this time I had a special nuzzle too. For a great big beast he was so gentle; not swinging his head around nearly as strongly as he did with his owner. Uncle Tom had a supply of the special cake in his pocket, and once deciding all was well, he suggested we go in for a hot drink.

I held his hand as he walked and I skipped the short way back; the comfort of that was now sheer joy, no pain or tearful feelings any more. I felt he too was as happy as me; the strong grip in which he held me was that reassurance. My normal life was totally devoid of any form of contact, except punishment, thus this tender warmth was almost overwhelming. Auntie Dodd greeted us both with a kiss on our glowing cheeks, and I was offered a hot cocoa; 'Nothing will warm you quicker,' she explained.

There was still a while before lunch so we left the house again and headed for the pond, which indeed was full of fish, as Uncle Tom had said. Great golden carp, from China originally, he explained. We watched as they seemed to just glide near the surface – then suddenly dart away as if startled. They were called 'golden' but there were all colours from pink to deep red and most had white on them. I lay on my tummy my chin resting comfortably on cupped hands. I could have stayed and been fascinated for hours, but my dreamy state was punctuated with 'Come on, young lady. Time to go in and wash your hands ready for a welcome meal, I think.'

After lunch I helped Cook clear away again, while they both rested in the drawing room. The familiarity of carrying out activities I'd enjoyed on my previous visits gave me a feeling of belonging, and Cook's fulsome praise and appreciation was so encouraging.

In the afternoon, a real adventure awaited me. Uncle Tom had a .22 rifle, and he was demonstrating how to use it. He had a box containing targets: little paper circles with a red bullseye in the centre. He showed me how to hold the barrel, with the stock firmly into my shoulder. How to line up the sights, hold my breath, squeeze the trigger gently . . . and fire. After a very short space of time, I actually hit the target, and with a bit more practice, scored in the bull! We danced around in joy and jubilation, bringing Auntie Dodd out to investigate. She said she would keep the target, as a memento of the achievement; Uncle Tom said they could do with me in the army! He was so pleased with me it made me feel very proud.

That was also the moment I learnt Uncle Tom was a high-ranking officer – perhaps a colonel or even a general, my eight-year-old mind didn't quite know the difference – but surely that accounted for his bearing, and his enthusiasm when I scored a bull! He took my hand again and led me to an outside room near the kitchen. When I entered, the smell of leather was wonderful. Around the walls on great wooden pegs was an assortment of tack for the horse: a huge leather and brass saddle, other harness and the rope halters. Although this area housed only a very small window, all seemed bright and gleaming.

He lifted me gently up on to a stool, which was just like a miniature chair with arms and a back and very long legs; I could now see the top of the large bench and placed upon it was a solid wooden box. He explained this contained the leather pieces of his uniform. 'I leave it out here until it's all cleaned and ready to wear next time. The ladies don't like the polish indoors,' he joked.

His boots were knee-high, thick-soled and very heavy; he laughed when I struggled to lift them. They were gleaming and the deep rich colour of a conker immediately after it's removed from its prickly coat. He showed me then a very odd contraption. 'A Sam Browne,' he explained and added, 'and remember it ends with an "e".' He demonstrated the fitting for me; a belt arrangement around his middle and another part which went over his shoulder. 'I'll show you a photograph when we go back indoors,' he promised.

'I do lots of polishing too,' I explained. 'When I'm on shoeshine duties for the week, I do sixty pairs each night, and on Mondays there is double work with another sixty pairs from our Sunday best. It is my favourite duty and there is always one kid to "put on" and another to "take off", so we laugh a lot and make it more fun. It takes ages on a Monday and we are always late for play time. I don't like that bit so much though'.

'And what other jobs do you have on the other weeks?'

'Well, we do table clearing and washing the dishes as soon as you can reach in the big sinks – I can't yet. We do the playroom, well, all of the cleaning really. The staff do the washing and ironing but we do the rest. We make our own beds and take it in turn to do the dorms; there are three helping then but it's still not much fun. Miss Warren is always coming in and saying things aren't done properly and they have to be done again. The hardest thing is the floor; the polish is called "Ronuk", it's stinky and thick and takes *ages* to shine off. We do that with a "bumper"; that's a square piece of wood with a pad on the bottom and a hole in the centre. Then you have a heavy cannon-ball thing on a sort of thick, long broom handle and that sits in the middle of the square in the hole. It has to be swung backwards and forwards over the floor; it's ever so heavy and I can't keep doing it for long yet. The big kids have to do the windows though; we don't and they moan about that a lot!' I laughed and he chuckled too. 'The worst of all is helping to sort out the stuff to go to the laundry with all the smelly things. I hate the sluice room and I always get out too late to play as well.'

'Hmmm,' was all he said.

We put everything back tidily in its place; then he lifted me again off my stool, giving me a big hug and a kiss on my cheek. I didn't go back on the ground; instead he laid me across his shoulder with my head nuzzling deep into his neck. He just stood still and I suddenly felt a new deep sense wash over me; like a wave clearing my mind. His physical strength was supporting my frame on his arm; his other hand was ever so gently stroking my hair. I lifted my head; his eyes were twinkling and smiling as he looked at me, and I kissed his cheek. I felt a new confidence and said, 'I love you, Uncle Tom.' I put my head back on to his shoulder. 'And we love you too, little princess; and don't ever forget that,' he replied, almost in a whisper. Slowly and quietly, we left the room and went into the garden. His Harris Tweed jacket, though rough on my face, smelt of his pipe and the woods. I could hear the hens and other familiar sounds. I was too young then to name this newfound emotion, but now I realise it was trust. Confident of their love for me and mine for them, I knew these people would never hurt or harm me; they would only ever love me. Everything inside me had new warmth; I felt so safe – I wished I could explain how happy I was, but I felt he knew anyway.

Still cuddled in his arms we walked slowly, the long way round, and returned indoors to a delicious smell. Cook had made more cakes for tea, and I tucked in with gusto. I was not greedy but the fresh air had put an edge on my appetite; to have all I could eat and feel full up was such a new experience I made the most of it. I worked off some of the food by helping again in the kitchen. It was strange how exactly the same chores I did at the Home were so much fun here, carried out with enthusiasm, because they were appreciated. What a difference a genuine 'thank you' made. We ended up in the drawing room. I still found it hard to believe that I did not have to leave that night. A thrill ran through me each time I thought about it.

I did some more reading, to the same warm praise, and then the time arrived for me to get ready for bed. Although not a really cold day, Cook had lit a small fire in the drawing room, and when Auntie Dodd had said that it was time for a bath and bed, they asked me to fetch from the wall what looked like a copper banjo with a long handle.

'It's called a warming pan,' explained Uncle Tom. I watched in awe as he opened the lid. He then proceeded to scrape some of the hot ashes from the grate, tipping these gently into the pan. He closed the lid very firmly, and then Auntie Dodd returned.

'We haven't used that in years,' she remarked.

'This is only for our guest of honour,' replied Uncle Tom; I could still not really believe this was happening to me. Auntie Dodd had already run the bath while we were doing the pan. She was carrying a tiny tray, upon which was a glass of milk and two home-made biscuits. She led the way upstairs and I followed her. Uncle Tom brought up the rear, holding the pan out ahead of him. What a procession!

My bedroom door was painted white, with a black latch that had a comforting 'clunk' when opened. Once in the room, the bed covers were folded back and the warming pan was moved up and down and side to side until the area where I was going to lie had been covered.

'Feel this now, Susan,' It was amazing, really hot, with a gorgeous smell from the linen sheets. 'We must cover that up again now. When you come back from your bath, the temperature will be perfect.'

The bathwater was deep and hot, with oil added to make my skin soft; it was perfumed and Auntie Dodd laughed when I said it was better than carbolic! We laughed and chattered all the time and occasionally she would lean forward and gently kiss me. I decided I was in some sort of Heaven. She soaped me thoroughly with something derived from bees. I felt like royalty. On the wall was a framed picture by Mabel Lucie Attwell; a chubby smiling face of a little girl, peering over the side of a green bath, explaining in verse about bathroom protocol. I did not learn it all on that visit, but I would by the next one. I had used my special pink soap; was now wrapped in the biggest thickest towel I had ever come across, also pink, and cuddled up snugly I was carried into the bedroom. The rest of my new things were ready for me.

Slowly I got dressed and ready for bed – *my own, warm, bed*. Once in dressing gown and slippers, I made my way to the window. The tray was on the dearest little table imaginable beside which was an equally small chair; I was invited to sit down. I looked out across the front garden and pond as I sat and politely ate the biscuits. In all honesty, I had eaten enough for tea, but I did not want to refuse any part of this wonderful experience. Once I had finished my supper, Auntie Dodd came over and placed a mirror on the table. I watched in fascination as she brushed my hair; very black and shining more with each stroke. This was another new experience for me; we were not allowed to have mirrors, being warned that vanity is one of the seven deadly sins. There was constant chatter throughout these proceedings; we went over the details of the day – it was the best day of my life, and I told them so.

'We'll have many more like this, Susan,' they promised. Finally, biscuits and milk consumed, teeth cleaned and hair brushed, bed time had come. The mattress was high off the ground; I really did have to climb in. When I got under the bedclothes – what bliss – the smell and the warmth seemed to embrace me. They both, in turn, gave me a huge cuddle and a goodnight kiss, then off went the light. Auntie Dodd went to the door, but then returned for another kiss.

'You are a darling little girl and we love you being here.'

Then she was gone. I drifted off to sleep knowing I was the luckiest little girl ever, and that no one else on earth was as happy as I was at that moment.

*

I enjoyed many more wonderful visits to the Dodds', each one heralded with a call to Boagey's office. At one time, such a summons would have caused deep apprehension; now I looked forward to them.

The call had come from one of the kids who had to find me in the garden. I knew immediately what it was about, so, full of excitement for the imminent promised visit, I ran all the way. Boagey's usual 'Come' was the response to my bold knock on the door and I almost *ran* in. There was an instant reversal of my excitement however when I saw her unsmiling face staring at me with those hateful beady eyes.

Did she look almost smug? I couldn't make her out.

I stood at her desk as usual, but I was puzzled. She continued to look at me in a very strange way and I sensed that there was something *dreadfully* wrong – my heart was sinking fast, it was as if my mind was standing still. She leant slightly forward and then pronounced, in a voice combining triumph and malice, 'There is to be no holiday, not now, or in the future. They have gone abroad, for the sake of Tom Dodds' health. *You* will not be visiting them *or* seeing them again – *ever*!'

She was sneering at me.

I could not move a muscle, I stood stock-still in front of her, not seeing her at all, and my mind was reeling. I recalled, with clarity, all my experiences, all my visits, each more wonderful than the last. Some seemed now to flash before me.

The Mabel Lucie Attwell poem that I had learnt off by heart.

Uncle Tom leting me sit in front of him; holding me tightly and me clutching the mane, we rode quietly and gently around the paddock – bare-back on his beautiful horse.

Bathing his white English bull terrier in an enormous tin bath outside – and how Uncle Tom and I almost had convulsions laughing at the antics of the dog trying to get out. I was soaked but it didn't matter; no one told me off.

Mixing the cakes and baking them all on my own with Cook's careful guidance; learning how to make them into 'butterfly cakes', and icing them carefully.

Spending hours in the woods opposite the cottage. Once, when we heard a woodpecker, Uncle Tom had explained they were a territorial species; he asked me to stay motionless as he picked up a stone and made a 'rat-a-tat-tat' sound on a tree. He 'called' the bird like this until it was close enough to be clearly seen; the bird thinking we were invading its space. And always after these long walks, Uncle Tom would lift me again into his strong arms; I would cuddle into his neck and smell the pipe and the woods on his Harris Tweed jacket. He would carry a very tired and happy little girl all the way home.

The beautiful new dress they bought me, even nicer than the one I had at St Christopher's. This was for a visit to some very important people in Eridge; I saw Uncle Tom in his uniform for the first time and Auntie Dodd had a dress of a flowery, floating material. I thought she looked like a queen.

Auntie Dodd showing me all the things on her dressing table, trying on her jewellery and dabbing her '4711' perfume on my wrist.

This was my life with them: learning good English and social graces, a life full of adventures, and being shown an all-embracing loving affection that touched my soul.

Now it was all over – all gone for ever.

These two darling people had applied to adopt me, to take me away to live with them for good. Barnardo's had contacted my mother, a woman I had never seen since she had disposed of me to these monsters – and she had refused them. Barnardo's had gone along with this, and that was the end of it. That simple.

On that black day, with a few malicious words, my wonderful world of love ended, for ever.

Without a word, and before the tears came, I ran from Boagey's office; through the hall and side conservatory and across the lawns as fast as I could go, diving into my hidey-hole, my secret place. It was a great bamboo bush. The upright stems were thick and scratchy, especially when gone through at the rate I had just launched myself. They formed a circular perimeter, in the centre of which was a thick, soft covering of mossy grass, always wet. I threw myself down, let the tears explode from me, and wept uncontrollable gulping sobs. I had never experienced anything like it; I had tried so hard never to cry at the Home.

The tears of emotion I had shed at Pluckley were nothing by comparison. I did not know how I would manage if I never saw them again. Thinking about it was the most painful thing, but then I knew what I wanted. I imagined the little dead birds on the drive again and that is what I wanted to be. Dead. No more daddies dying, no more Michaels going away, no more aunties and uncles leaving me and no more cruel staff. Just no more of any of it. I was not yet ten years old . . . but I had had enough.

I awoke some time later. I had cried myself to sleep and had no idea of the time. I cleaned my face as best I could, sat up and listened, but there were no sounds of kids playing. I did not want to leave this safe place but I dragged myself back to the house. I must have been in a state of shock because I don't remember what time of day it was, whether I missed a meal, or anything. All I do remember is, I received no admonishment or punishment. And I really would not have cared if I had.

I felt I had gone into my shell when Michael went, but that was nothing compared with this. I walked in a daze, had nothing to do with anyone, even feeling no sympathy with Gennie the wet-bed. In fact, any feeling, physical or mental, eluded me. I was numb. I went over repeatedly in my mind all the promises that had been made regarding future visits. The toiletries purchased just for me; the Wellington boots, the clothes that hung in the closet there that would not fit anyone else. The more I dwelt on this, the stronger became my conviction: Boagey was a Liar!

In a world where love is a stranger, you recognise it when it presents itself. I knew, I *knew*, without any doubt whatsoever, that these dear people *loved me*! There was no way they would do what they had done without good, no, essential reason. I nursed this realisation and it made me stronger. I knew now that I was not the 'revolting specimen of humanity' Boagey would have me believe. I *was* capable of being loved, *had* been loved.

My enduring memories of all the displays of affection were mine to hold as a treasure, never to be shared. The legacy they had left me was both my inspiration and, in later years, my aspiration. I would do what Uncle Tom had said, when we had laughed, joyfully, in response, 'You fight the buggers.' *I will, my darling Uncle Tom and Auntie Dodd, I will, but it will be so much harder without you near me.*

The school holidays held no more charm for me. Thank God I could run. I pounded around the house for lap after lap, never feeling physical or mental tiredness. Swathes of these hours I spent recalling the Dodds. I went over repeatedly all we had said, done, and hardest of all, what we were going to do. I could think, eventually, without the accompanying lump in my throat, but it took a long time to reach that stage.

I can truthfully say that, even now as I write this, I have never got over that loss. Each new loss, throughout my life, has always brought back the dreadful pain I endured then. I was utterly bereft.

*

The holidays continued without drama, I had little enthusiasm for what was going on around me; I was just looking forward to being back at school. However, another call to Boagey's office brought an unexpected result. She explained I was to have a visit from my mother. I greeted this news with little interest, recalling a previous similar arrangement.

It was a day when I was six years old and at St Christopher's; scrubbed and made ready to go out with my mother, whoever she was. I had never heard mention of her, in fact 'mother' was a word heard at my infant school, or read about lumped into the category of trades people like 'the milkman'. I had waited with a degree of excitement and anticipation, looking forward more to going out for the day rather than with whom. I was sitting on a large, hard chair in the main hall, legs swinging and my eyes cast down staring at the huge black and white tiles on the floor. I waited and waited. Eventually Miss Mitchell had come and taken me back to her office.

Without explanation, she arranged for me to change out of my best clothes and told me to return to her office; there I was treated to ice cream for tea, to make up for the disappointment. Being so very young, the full impact of my mother failing to turn up to see me since my admission to the Homes did not really register. I had never seen her; I had never received a birthday or Christmas card, so the disappointment was not immense, and the ice cream had made up for it completely, as far as I was concerned.

This time I waited for the meeting with my mother with scant enthusiasm. I could not see Boagey giving me ice cream as a consolation if she didn't arrive. However, she did. A black London taxi came up the drive. That was her, or rather, them, as the driver was a man.

My mother came in and greeted me with a lukewarm embrace; while I waited in the hall she went into the office with Boagey, 'for a word'. On reappearing, I was informed we were going to the seaside. That's better, I thought, but accompanied with a still dubious optimism.

We went out to the car and I was introduced to the driver, Uncle Walter, who solemnly and awkwardly shook my hand. Once we were underway he apologised for the slow and noisy progress of the vehicle and explained it was his. He drove it in London; its speed was clearly an unimportant factor I decided. Maisie (I find it impossible to refer to her as my mother) then informed me I was going to meet my brothers. What brothers? I thought.

'That was why I went to the office, to make sure it was all right.' She explained they were called Frank, Colin and Trevor, adding they were all down together on a family holiday in Dymchurch in Kent, which was why they had come to see me. I felt distinctly uneasy at this news. Why were my brothers together with Maisie and Walter, and I was only going for a day?

Maisie turned around and offered me a bar of Turkish Delight in a pink wrapper; Auntie Dodd had once let me have a taste of this rather unusual treat but I couldn't bear the perfumed smell. 'Sorry, but I don't like that,' I said. Her sigh was audible, even over the sound of the engine. This was not going well. From my vantage point in the back seat, I studied her. She did not have the same gentle look or the beauty of Auntie Dodd and was rather short and plump. There was a strange air of superiority about her in the way that she held her head; it was tilted upwards as if there were a nasty smell just below her nose. Her face had a thick layer of powder and her thin lips were a bright red line across her face. That sigh had made it patently clear she had little patience; to survive the day without being told off was going to be a miracle. I would not have minded going back then, but there was no chance of that and eventually we arrived at our destination.

The boys were playing on the beach and I was introduced to them in turn. Frank, the eldest, was enormous and very loud. Colin, just one year older than me, seemed to like me, and I could see a resemblance in our appearance. Trevor the youngest was a skinny, mean-looking kid, the sort I would have avoided at school – he looked like a sneaky type.

'Wanna play?' they asked. Cricket was a love in the Home. One of the staff even knew some of the rules, enough of them to get us through.

The surface was a damp, sandy track, with the crease scored out with a strong stick. The stumps were more sticks, but the bat was real, far too big and heavy for me, but real. Walter elected to bowl, and sent down quite a fast one that didn't touch the ground. Didn't touch the bat either! A unanimous cry of OWZAT! went up, and I walked. Walter was grinning with pleasure that he had me out first ball, and was receiving due congratulations from the brothers. Blimey, I thought, even we gave the little kids a second chance!

I sat on the sea wall and watched them play; there was nothing else to do. Maisie was in the car but I didn't have the courage to join her; she had made no real effort to make me feel welcome and she had an air I found most unsettling. She did come down eventually, with some food she had prepared. I felt disappointed that she had not noticed my inactivity and asked me to help her; I would have loved that and it would have made me feel included.

'Would you like a sandwich, or will they save you a meal for when you get back?' With that comment, she had confirmed all my doubts about her; she had no idea about what life was like for me, and more than that, was completely uninterested in learning the reality of my existence. Utterly fed up now with the whole situation, I opted for the sandwiches and kept up with the boys' intake, I knew there would be nothing else on offer. I was right too.

On the return journey between the small talk, and with courage drawn from the fact that I no longer cared about her reply, I asked why I never saw her.

'We live such a long way away,' she explained, with a pseudo sound of regret in her tone of voice.

'Where's that then?' I asked, determined to find out more.

'Chelsea,' she answered.

'Why don't you ever write to me, or send birthday and Christmas cards?'

With an overt display of absolute insincerity, she replied, 'We could never be sure you would get them.' That was the best that she could come up with; I had a word in my mind, *and* I knew what it meant – *lamentable*.

There were very few occasions when I would admit to not minding going back up the drive of the Home, but this was one of them. The taxi had been slow, noisy and smelly. Not like Uncle Tom's Rover.

Walter, it appeared, lived with Maisie. This I gathered just from their conversation, and he had greeted me with a shake of the hand! She had all the mothering instincts of a Brussels sprout, and the boys were single-mindedly happy with their own company. Sister? I could have been any old kid from Barnardo's as far as they were concerned.

Once I was back at the Home another surprise awaited me. Night Staff was on duty (it had been dark for ages on the journey) and she asked me had I had anything to eat. I was amazed; could Maisie's reputation as a mother have preceded her? I explained about the sandwiches, but she was not happy. Boagey had said I was not to go to bed hungry – I could not believe my ears!

Staff took me down to the kitchen, normally well out of bounds, and fed me. As days out go, I had had more fun on a Sunday school outing. I took the opportunity to ask Staff where Chelsea was. She said it was in London, which did not mean anything to me. When I explained why I wanted to know, she said it was less than two hours away on the train. Therefore, the reason for not visiting was as lamentable as the reason I received no cards.

Nice to be cherished!

~ 10 ~

The Home was a huge mansion and the internal dimensions were vast, but there was always the sixth sense awareness that someone was watching you at all times.

There was a rule that once inside from playing in the garden you were not allowed back out. We frequently challenged this with attempts to 'escape', and there had been many a near thing, but not one of us had made it. It was my turn to try and I set off through the hall, creeping as invisibly as was possible through the passageway until I reached the lean-to conservatory. Inching along the wall that gave me the most shelter, I reached and very quietly opened the door. I was just on the outside when from behind a voice boomed out, 'And where do you think *you* are going?' With insides turned instantly to jelly I replied, 'I'm not *going* anywhere, Miss, I'm just coming *back in*.' She looked at me with a face betraying utter confusion and ordered me back to my playroom. Once my successful exploits were explained, we all had a good laugh and I had a real hero's welcome.

Each playroom accommodated twenty girls, for dining as well as relaxation. Even on a wet day, when outside play was forbidden, there was plenty of room for us all. Some would read, sitting in the window seats. That left the tables for painting, drawing, or jigsaws. We had no radio but there was a good selection of books and games. The place came into its own at night though. Ghost stories abounded, and one of the staff swore blind there was a priest hole behind the panelling in the hall. Maybe even a priest!

There were sixteen in my dorm, with plenty of space to move around, even with the melee of us all up at the same time in the morning. Strict rules governed everything we did and none more so than upstairs. I only ever went into one other dorm all the while I was there; fraternisation was a no-no.

Our challenge to all the rules was customary and constant. One thing we older 10-year-olds did was to approach the little ones, already fast asleep. This had come about from a lesson at school, which dealt with autosuggestion. We would go to the side of the bed, bend down and very, very slowly and quietly whisper, 'Do you want to go to the toilet?' Within a short space of time, the little kid would wake up and call Staff to be escorted to the toilet. If Staff had thought she was going to have a quiet night, she was wrong!

The hardest thing to get away with was talking after lights out. Night staff got the job after proving they had the hearing of bats. I am sure they used sonar! We were lucky sometimes; even if caught, the punishment would only be a short spell standing in the corner. One night, once everyone had washed and got into bed, and Staff had said, 'Goodnight everybody, go straight to sleep,' switched off the light and closed the door, I lay awake, straining to hear her footsteps leaving the room, but you never could tell for sure after they closed the door.

'Pamela, is it right you are changing dorms?' I asked, in very hushed tones.

'Not as far as I know,' she replied.

'*I told you to go to sleep*,' screamed Staff. The old bag had not left the room when she closed the door!

While my ears recovered, and my heartbeat returned to normal, she was there, very forcefully dragging me out of bed. 'You go and stand in the corner, Susan Davis, and the rest of you, *settle down*!' Not a big price to pay for entertaining the whole dorm, all of whom were awake after her screaming. She marched me off to the corner.

On the way, we met Warren.

'What have *you* been up to?' she asked me, while looking at Staff. 'I'll take over now.' She marched me to the corner and with some force pushed me in – hard. She leant her weight against me – I could barely breathe. When she moved away, I backed up to get my balance; with her open palm, she pushed my forehead into the right angle of the corner and pressed for what seemed like ages. This was frightening and extremely painful but I fought the urge to make a sound. I was no longer the same vulnerable infant she had shaken the living daylights out of; eventually fed up, she left.

Standing there I thought about Warren. I hated her. She was a spiteful bully; to stop or smother your breath was a particular favourite of hers. Undoubtedly the worst was when she approached you from behind – one hand covering nostrils and mouth completely – then lifted you bodily, clear off the ground. It was *impossible* to breathe – but to 'fight' her made it even worse. I had witnessed this treatment *and* the fighting back; some kids had gone almost blue in the face; quite clearly she was mad. I learnt the answer was to fight back for a very short while – then go suddenly limp. The first time I did it she dropped me like a hot brick, scared of what she might have done; I could tell this from the expression on her face. I always adopted the same method but it did not reduce the attacks and it was agony on my already dodgy neck from her shaking. How she didn't really damage one of the smaller, lighter kids was beyond me.

I had heard some of the kids call Staff, but still I stayed there. Then the lights went out downstairs; the other staff were saying goodnight to one another. At this stage I was too scared to turn around, it was pitch black and I had convinced myself that Warren was still behind me! By now, the whole house had fallen quiet; I was absolutely freezing, wearing no slippers or dressing gown, and I needed a wee.

The trouble was, the corner was right at the end of the landing by Boagey's quarters; calling out and disturbing her was not a good idea!

At last I heard someone approaching; it was one of the night staff doing her rounds on the landing just behind me. 'Miss . . . ' that was all I said. There was a muffled scream, then realisation dawned.

She scurried over to me and in a loud whisper asked, 'What on earth are you doing still there?' I felt like saying I would give her three guesses, but felt it not the best idea! We both had the same idea dawn simultaneously – she had not checked my dorm; if she had, she would have known I was missing. I could have been in London by now; I must have been there for two hours or more. Consequently, she was utterly charming, allowing me plenty of time for the toilet and letting me stand by the radiator to warm myself up before returning to bed. Once by the radiator she got some cream to put on my bruised forehead. I told her how it happened. She did not condemn Warren, of course, but she did say 'Ahhh.' A barely audible expression of sympathy?

We all felt this same oppressive daily routine and suffered the 'punishment', but inside restrictions were almost forgotten at the pleasure of being outside in the grounds. Staff always attended; we were strictly supervised as to where we could and could not go, but we enjoyed the opportunity to use our voices without rebuke and generally feel free. Except for the rain and having to do extra work as punishment, we played out every day after school and before bed time.

The less active would sit around on the vast slightly up-sloping lawn at the front; this was where we would all meet up and read or decide which game the sporty were going to play. In the middle of the lawn was a grand old tree, an oak I think, and this was something to lean against when reading, gave shade from the sun on hot days and was a place to flop down tired after a game. To the left was a large field where we could really let off steam, and happily did.

I would join in any activity, especially if there was a ball involved. I always maintained our success at school with Rounders was because we invariably played games of twenty per side; with those numbers, to place the ball to miss a catch required consummate skill. Because I had deemed it so crucial to increase my physical strength to cope with the assaults, I performed every task with a degree of competition that made me a formidable opponent. We were all very competitive but it was real fun and always in a good spirit; even at play we were all still in the same boat, and there was no animosity. I was always fine, just so long as I won!

My real passion was not a team game: I loved to run. The action of just running doggedly around the perimeter of the lawns filled me with a deep joy. Occasionally, one of the kids would drop in beside me and do a couple of laps, but they considered me completely barmy, soon tired, and went off to do something more interesting. I just kept going, varying my breathing, adjusting my speed, sometimes a slow jog followed by a lap at real pace. I loved the feel of my legs pumping, my stomach tightening and supporting my back, my arms pushing and balancing me as I swerved around tight corners. After a while I became fed up with running on the lawns and took to running around the building itself. There were three flights of steps, one steep short climb and a similar drop, so it was far more challenging.

I was not a particularly big kid and soon became quite lean. I had no role model, as we never read comics or newspapers. I did however have all the staff and other kids in the Home and at school with whom to compare. I knew that I was as fit and strong as any of them, and more so than most. Not a very girly achievement – but I didn't live in that sort of environment. My one aim was to get too strong to approach as a target, and thus beat them down, as they tried to do to me. It was working.

~ 11 ~

There was to be a holiday by the sea. We were awakened very early in the morning and, though tired, that in itself was a change and therefore exciting. We were informed we had to be washed and dressed, collect a kit bag from the landing, and then stand by our beds. Sounds of excited voices echoed around the cold dorms – it was a madhouse – and so we were all silenced! They really had no idea at all; the thrill of this new experience was overwhelming.

I did not say a word. I knew they would have taken considerable delight in telling me I could not go, and they would have been as good as their word. I was so much wiser now, without any doubt. Once by our beds we were directed to the clothing piles and each selected the appropriate undergarments, socks, and clothes. I smiled when I saw Pamela – aka Nicholas – right at the front of the queue, determined to get the correct size this time! We then stripped our beds, folding the dirty sheets for the laundry. A kit bag was put on top of the bed and we all trooped down, now in silence, for breakfast. We were given just bread and jam – because we were going on a long journey, they explained that they did not need anyone to be sick en route. I wondered where we were going and how we were going to get there – all sixty of us. Boagey told another kid and me that we did not have to do our usual jobs, but were to go upstairs with Staff.

'Right you two. The kit bags have been checked during breakfast; now take them downstairs, leave them in the hall, and then return to this dorm.' The other kid did her half of the rooms, we ran competing for speed, and then returned as ordered. I was astonished at the next instruction – what on earth was going on? We were told to take each mattress from every bed, along with the pillows, and these went into the hall, right up by the front door. I was intrigued.

'Back to your playrooms, you two, I will see you in a minute.'

I had kept silent, moved everything as ordered with enthusiasm, and had been, for this short time at least, a paragon of virtue. But I was just then filled with doubt. I still had a dreadful, nagging feeling that I would not end up with the others.

Boagey came in. 'I am glad this playroom is quiet too, I would have hated for someone not to go.' She looked directly at me. I met her gaze.

She looked away and continued. 'We are all going to the seaside for the week.' One of the little ones squealed in delight; Boagey just glared at her. 'The transport will be here very soon. On its arrival, you will listen to Staff and do as she tells you. You may talk again now, but keep it down.' We went from zero to decibels off the scale, in about twenty seconds!

There was a scream of delight from a kid by the window. Rushing over, I looked, my jaw dropping at the sight. Trundling up the drive were two pantechnicons – large vans operated by a local firm of removal and storage experts, so the legend on the side informed me. The place erupted with even more excitement. Staff appeared in moments; I shut up immediately. I *was* going on this trip if it bloody killed me. I was a bag of nerves, but I'd contain my excitement and give them no reason to exclude me again.

'Susan Davis, come here.' *Ugh*, I groaned, silently. 'You are always boasting about being so strong. Go and help with the loading up. The rest of you, sit down and *be quiet*.'

I was so relieved to be out of there, I ran out to help.

The loading of the vans illustrates the quality of our mattresses: at the very back of these vans was a gap for the bedding in the average house. The drivers said they would take probably four or five mattresses. They were amazed, and amused, when they stowed thirty in each lorry's space . . . plus thirty pillows and palliasses. I took great delight in replying yes when they asked if we really slept on those every night. They were fascinated, perhaps shocked. Once the bedding had been safely installed, we were next. Each kid carried his or her own kit bag, with names on by now. These were placed on the lorry floor and would act as our seats. Brilliant! Divided into age groups, off we went.

We still did not know our eventual destination, but it really didn't matter. It was away from the home for a week. Better still, we were told that Boagey wasn't coming.

'She can't be visiting friends . . . she hasn't got any,' pointed out one wag.

The lone staff member looking after us did not say a word.

'She's going up North, apparently.'

'Well, let's hope she gets stuck in the snow, dies and never comes back.'

'She couldn't come back if she was dead, idiot.'

The speed with which we had degenerated into this disrespectful banter was astonishing – but I kept my mouth shut, still wary they might send me back.

'Shall we sing?' suggested poor Staff, totally out of her depth with this new, moronic behaviour. She was on her own too. So we sang, all the way down to Seaford in Sussex.

The men came round and dropped the huge half-doors, ready for our exit. It had been a marvellous journey; Staff was in a good mood, and no one had been sick! We all stood, picked up our bags and for the first time I saw our holiday home: a huge church hall with a high roof. We filed in, not before noting that half the kids in the town had turned out to watch the spectacle. Lined up against one of the long walls, we could see the many colourful posters for the Cubs and Brownies and other groups who met here; it looked like a popular, well-used place.

The drivers brought in our bedding and I decided I was really on holiday for I was not told to help. As each mattress arrived, we slid it into a gap along both the main walls; having already been warned by staff to take care of the stacks of chairs at the end, obviously moved to make room for us. Any space was greatly reduced as the hall filled up, ultimately giving us very little room to move around, but nobody cared. On top of each bed, we laid out our palliasse; at the foot, on the floor, lay our kit bags. As ordered, we then sat cross-legged on our beds and I could see the dust we had created floating about through the shafts of sunlight coming through the high windows. With everything completed without drama, we thanked the drivers by singing, or rather shouting, a rousing chorus of 'For They Are Jolly Good Fellows'. They looked embarrassed, thanked us and left.

Asked to sit again after standing for this rendition, Staff had a word with us. We were here for a week and would have to manage with the spartan conditions – there was, for instance, no bath. 'Ahhh,' we all groaned, in mock disappointment. She laughed. Breakfast would be basic, maybe just some fruit, because we were largely at the mercy of the church organisers who had invited us. 'Three cheers,' was the response. Staff was great; away from the watchful glare of Boagey, she was really beginning to enjoy this.

'Today we will all stay here. There is ground at the back of the hall for playing on. Tomorrow, and every day thereafter, visitors will come and take you out for the whole day. They will be left to decide and will take one or maybe two of you at a time. Some will prefer younger ones as they may have small families, but nobody need worry, you will all be chosen Everybody will be expected to be on best behaviour.' (Another mock groan arose from the group.) 'You are not to let yourselves or the Home down. Right, go and explore!'

I helped a couple of the little ones find the toilets, and then a thought occurred to me: where was Gennie? She hadn't been on our lorry – was she here at all? I went back in to see Staff. She said Gennie was not allowed to be here.

'Miss, I put all the mattresses in the hall, I know hers was there,' I pleaded. They had moved it during breakfast so there would not be a fuss, poor kid. No holiday – was there no end to her misery?

'Come with me, Susan, I need a word with you,' she said quite calmly. I followed her to the room at the very end of this huge building; designated for the staff for the duration of our visit. She sat down and pulled me gently to face her. 'You are a sensible girl for your age. Can you not see that a wet bed, all the washing and other problems, would be too much to cope with here? We are camping, albeit under a proper roof, but it's still camping. You have a kind nature to care, but on this occasion, it is misdirected.' I had met her compassionate look initially with a glare of hurt and defiance, but the simple explanation and her kindness in giving me time to talk through the matter won me over.

I joined the others. I had completely lost track of time. 'Who's doing lunch?' seemed to be the general query. However, we didn't have long to wait. Staff came to the back door; told us to form a line and we marched in to the most appetising smell.

'Everyone sit on their bed,' she called with excited urgency. There was a headlong rush. Three ladies then came out from the tiny kitchen area, with what appeared to be arms full of paper.

'It's fish and chips!' screamed one of the newer kids. She reckoned they were brilliant and could not believe I had never had them before, nor could the ladies! It turned out only about a half dozen of us had. They were as brilliant and delicious as the other kids had described; I had not realised how hungry I was. We had fruit for pudding and then Staff brought round an enormous teapot. Excepting the meals at Uncle Tom and Auntie Dodd's, it was the best meal I had ever had.

'And what service,' said Staff, laughing. For the second time that day, we sang, in more muted tones, 'For They Are Jolly Good Ladies'. It went down a storm.

Those who wanted to go out to play could, while we who moved the bedding in the morning helped Staff clean up. She voiced her concern over the fish and chips papers, explaining if left in a dustbin they would stink. We followed her into the garden where she announced, to great excitement and cheering, 'We are going to have a Bonfire!' Living in the countryside meant we had often seen and smelt the many garden fires; it was something our gardener did in the autumn to burn the leaves but we were not allowed anywhere near them. We set out to see if there was anywhere in the garden where there had previously been a fire; sure enough there was. Then a brilliant idea: we went around in twos, picking up all the old leaves, fallen twigs and dry sticks and any other rubbish from the grass and bushes, all of us surprised at the size of the bundle collected in the end.

'This will help by tidying up for the church, and we can have a *proper* bonfire,' she added. With the paper at the bottom and the detritus laid on top, Staff lit it. To be fair, it was hardly likely to dazzle with brightness, or produce enough heat to roast a budgie, but it was great. We sat around in two circles, the smallest of us in front of the bigger ones, while watching the flames die down to soft grey ash. We sang songs and played 'circle' games like 'Lucy Locket' until Staff decided it was safe again to be more boisterous. After more active organised games outside, we all trooped in at teatime to a drink of milk and a whopping sandwich each, again donated by the church folk.

'Although it is early there is still quite a lot to do,' explained Staff once tea was over. 'One of you check there is nothing left out in the garden and Susan come and help me organise a system; everyone else *sit back down on your beds*.' She had to raise her voice above the excited babble of us lot; there was a thrill amongst us of being away on holiday, but she was by no means cross when she said it.

I then helped – using the sparse and spartan facilities as best as we could – but washing at a row of four basins was chaotic and hilarious. Starting with the youngest: clothes off by the bed – run in to be washed – out of the cloakroom to dry off with the towel. It was the only way to make the space required for each function and we were exhausted with laughing. I helped with the little ones again but when it got to my turn, the water was freezing! However, as I said so many times that week, 'Never mind, we're on holiday!'

I don't think getting us all into bed had ever taken so long; it was bedlam. When the smaller kids got to their beds, they did not know how the bedding worked. The word palliasse is rather a grand name for what it was, a contraption forming a top and bottom sheet. It resembled a very long pillowcase, with the front piece lower down. It was a cotton version of what I had seen in the photographs of the Sir Edmund Hillary Everest Expedition; but his was a big puffy bag that he slept in. Staff conducted a demonstration; once settled into the thing I gave a nod to Pamela and we rolled her on to the floor. There were cries of delight from all, including Staff. With her arms trapped, she could do nothing else, and the 'drop' from the mattress was only a full two inches so we knew we would not have hurt her.

Staff eventually restored order; with everyone in bed, she said we could talk after lights out, but must not be loud enough to disturb anyone else. However, the freedom to talk made it much less interesting and very soon most of us were asleep. I lay quietly and mulled over the day; what an utter joy it had been. Of course, the main reason that the mood had lifted was the absence of Boagey. We had all been good on the road and everybody helped one another, without a word from Staff. The food was genuinely appreciated, and our thanks were profuse We were not necessarily the epitome of virtue, but our behaviour and the desire to be good owed much to being free of the strict, harsh regime imposed by Boagey.

I heard a noise and opened my eyes to find Staff was by my bed. I got up on to one arm as she knelt down. In a whisper she said, 'Thank you for all your help today, I appreciated it, very much.' She patted my arm gently.

'That's all right, Miss. Thank you for bringing us.' She went off to her room. *What a nice thing to do,* I thought. I had started helping because I had been certain Boagey was planning to bar me from the holiday but as the day had gone on – and we were free of the hateful woman – it was easy to help a grateful Staff. I realised they weren't away to relax and still had us lot to look after so it was nice to make it as easy for them as we could. I realised too I had felt no fear while she was by my bed, not as I would have done in the Home. I knew this was going to be a great holiday.

*

The morning brought with it more bedlam at the basins. The previous evening's chaos was not simply a rehearsal; the consensus seemed to be that as it was going to be like that, so let it. If Boagey had arrived, she would have passed out at the noise we were making! Then we sat back on our beds for a cup of tea and an apple or orange. Pamela and I cleaned the washroom while others helped everywhere else, still with no bidding. We agreed, between us, Staff could look after the little ones and we would do the chores. We announced this to her, proud of ourselves. She was so grateful, we were glad we had suggested it.

It was soon ten o'clock and time for the town people who were taking us out to arrive. I could hardly wait.

They trooped in and began to look around, a bit like sorting from a jumble sale really. A large, jolly lady with a halo of frizzy blonde hair appeared next to me.

'Can I take you?' she asked. I was up like a shot.

She was as much fun as her first impression had suggested. Once through the door, she gave me a huge hug, like Cook at the Dodds'. I offered to carry her huge bag, not heavy but so large that it nearly touched the ground. We turned left out of the gate, and walked hand in hand chatting easily together down a gently sloping hill, where I could already see the sea. We had driven in from the other direction and had not come this way at all yesterday so I hadn't realised the beach was so close. It was wonderful to take in the surroundings and find my bearings, and reassure myself that this was going to be enjoyed for a whole week.

The beach was stony. Great big pebbles at the top but decreasing in size until it became shingle by the water's edge. I was wearing ordinary outdoor lace-up shoes and the slippery soles made it hard work to walk, even with my strong legs. 'We'll get you some sandals later,' she said kindly.

I did not like to ask why, but we seemed to be going miles along the beach. Surely one lot of pebbles was pretty much like the rest? We were puffing away and then she said, 'Here we are, darling.' With that, she turned and unlocked a beach hut!

I could not believe my eyes; it was like having your very own doll's house. 'Oh, *wow*! Can we go in?' In reply, she lifted me bodily up to the railing, and in I went. Following, she filled and put a kettle on the tiny gas stove.

'You sit in that chair for now. Do you drink tea? Do you have sugar?' While she made the tea, I looked around. It was wonderful and my first thoughts of a doll's house were exact.

The tiny stove was in one corner with an equally tiny circular sink next to it; the water for the kettle had to be 'pumped' with a foot pedal connected to a container below the flooring. Running across the back wall was a narrow work surface with cupboards underneath, and that was it! Our two small but comfortable armchairs filled the rest of the space – but the open door gave a view right down to the sea. I loved it.

Once settled down with our hot cups of tea, she said I was to call her 'Auntie'. Her name was weird, she said, everyone just called her 'Auntie'.

'They call you Susan? That's a formal name for a fun kid like you – you are fun, aren't you?'

I nodded.

'Well, I want to call you Sue. It's friendlier and we're going to be friends and have a lovely holiday.' And so my name changed then and there. I was, and still am, called Sue to this day.

While drinking my tea, I asked what *her* real name was.

'*Promise* you won't laugh and I'll tell you.' I promised, and stared, waiting in almost breathless anticipation because of the twinkle in her eyes.

'It's Hermione Geraldine.'

I know a promise is a promise, but I nearly fell off my chair! So did she.

We were wiping our eyes when someone appeared at the door. We were making so much noise we had not heard their approach.

'Hello, Davy. Meet my new friend, Sue. You'll like her, she's mad as us; anyone with you?' Roughly half the town it seemed to me. They all congregated around the door calling 'Hello, Auntie.' They appeared to be mostly my age; clad in baggy shorts and sandals and brown as berries from living by the sea. I was offered the option of going with them or not; I was longing to get on the beach and be by the water's edge so I happily joined them. We had a brilliant time playing tag but mainly throwing pebbles into the sea; 'You throw okay for a girl,' praised Davy. I had not felt a bit out of place with only boys – especially with Davy, who if not the eldest was most certainly the leader. It made a great change from the all-girl world of my own. Auntie had asked that we stay in her sight and a little later called from the door. 'Come in now, Sue, we need to go to the shops.'

Davy and the rest of his company all disappeared, promising to return tomorrow. 'You will be here, won't you?' Auntie assured them, and me, that we would, and off we went.

We chatted all the way. She explained her husband was away working and she had a son she rarely saw, so the chance to have one of us had really cheered her up. She was an earthy, honest lady. Not a lot to give, but you would always be welcome to share it. 'A diamond,' Davy called her.

She held my hand all the way, which was a lovely comforting thing to do. First stop, sandals. 'Nothing too posh . . . you want to be able to run around free, without worrying about scratching the blooming things,' she said. I loved the shops; I had very rarely been shopping. All our things 'came in' from outside.

'What shoe size are you, Sue?'

My acute embarrassment at my ignorance of this detail must have shown; her reaction was immediate. 'We'll be back in a minute,' and we were out through the door. I thought she was cross at my lack of knowledge, but no. 'I am so sorry, darlin', what a stupid thing that was to say.' She suggested I didn't play with the others later. 'We need to sit and chat and find out all about you, and then I won't be so silly again.'

We did get the sandals – dark blue with a buckle; I loved them. She also bought me some baggy shorts like Davy's and a bathing costume. Then we were off to get food.

'Anything you don't like? Probably haven't had a big enough selection to know really,' she added, with new understanding. I told her to choose, I would try anything! She bought the biggest, crustiest loaf I had ever seen, it weighed a ton. She also purchased a great hunk of cheese, and other items I was not too sure of. She let me wear my new sandals immediately; they were comfortable and made it a lot easier to walk on the beach.

We carried the bags between us. She said I was very strong which pleased me. We ate an enormous amount of bread and cheese – I was bursting. Once again it was nice to feel full up.

'We will have this today, but tomorrow we will organise some hot food. Even when the weather is warm, you still need some heat inside you.'

True to her word, after lunch, we sat and chatted; I felt a little bit uncomfortable at first as I wasn't used to talking about myself and the world in which I lived and it was hard to know what to say and what not to say. My life was 'different' I knew, mainly from comments at school and the reactions of the new kids who came to the Home. I didn't want to talk about the punishments, mainly because I was on holiday – but there was also the chance I could have spoiled everything. I was honest when she asked about the work we did and the strictness of the staff but did not go into any details that might upset things. She laughed her head off when I told her Boagey's name and that made everything light-hearted again. 'Blimey – it's worse than mine,' she said.

The whole week continued in this happy relaxing way. Invariably I was the first one out as I longed to get back to the games on the beach, or the fun in the sea in my new bathers with Davy and friends. There was loads and loads to eat, and we talked to each other all the time. I was also always the last one back. What a holiday.

The evening before the last day, we sat on the grass at the back of the hall. Staff had brought us some card, not just ordinary paper, and we could choose our colour and the crayon to match. We each did thank-you letters and drawings for our people and the church ladies; we were very careful and it took ages.

Auntie was thrilled and said she would always keep hers as a memento. She did not give me anything, as I would not have been allowed to keep it. But I've got all my memories.

I had told her how important my strong mind was and she agreed. When we parted, she had told me to go, do not look back, just kiss and go in, better for us both. I knew that was right, as that was what I did when Uncle Tom drove away. I gave her a huge hug and a kiss, and walked in. We never met again, but she was a lovely, memorable lady who had given me a wonderful holiday.

I might not have been able to bring anything back with me but I would keep one thing from that holiday: I was now known as 'Sue'. I simply refused to reply to whoever it was if they used 'Susan'. Because all the kids preferred it and used it all the time, the staff soon became used to it. Boagey balked at first, and for longer than anyone else, but I ignored her too! She came round eventually. I loved the change. I was ten, and for some reason, I felt more sophisticated with an abbreviated name. Most of the kids at school had their names shortened, just like Davy and others of his crowd. It made me feel more like one of them, an Outsider, no longer just a kid from a Home. It felt like a special present from Auntie, and one that I could keep for ever.

~ 12 ~

Returning from the holiday caused me to do a lot of thinking. I had felt completely different while I was away and once again coming back to the Home was dreadful. I felt strange and confused as if I was suddenly two people and I wanted to work out why. Right back as far as when Michael was suddenly gone – whenever anything big happened in my life – I had always tried to work out why I felt like I did. The overwhelming pain of Uncle Tom and Auntie Dodd leaving me had been just such a time; I wanted to be alone and sort it all out. I made my way to the only place I knew where I could be entirely alone to think.

My bamboo bush was my refuge. Ensconcing myself in the secret green sward, I put my mind to what, and indeed who, I was. Being away with Uncle Tom and Auntie Dodd had been the most beautiful experience ever, and would remain so in my memory. Being away this time had been very different. I needed to evaluate that.

The Dodds loved me: of that I was utterly convinced. The realisation and ability to recognise that was in itself a milestone; up to that stage my self-esteem was not even measurable. They had given me a sense of self-worth and the recent holiday had added to that feeling. With the Dodds, it was a one-to-one situation, almost a family unit. Not so this time; I had seen and been part of a very new world.

I never asked Auntie why she chose me, it had not occurred to me; the fact was she did, and made it patently obvious she had no regrets. She had a wonderful personality and said I had as well – and yet at the same time she made me feel like a little girl. Going into the Homes when still so young sometimes made me feel older than I really was, especially when new kids came in with no experience at all. Having been there for so much longer, knowing so much more and growing up far too young definitely put 'an old head on young shoulders' as Auntie had said. We were able to hold full, intelligent conversations, something I was totally unused to. She said my sense of humour was amazing for my age, especially considering my lifestyle. She doubted she would have much to laugh about if she were in my situation.

I had got on immediately with Davy and his friends. They said I was good at the games, and quite obviously enjoyed my company for its own sake. They made a point of ensuring I would be there again the next day, and their sadness that I was leaving was genuine.

I had made the holiday for the staff much easier because not only had I helped, I had organised others to do so too, and willingly. They had thanked me on more than one occasion. I could, and did, use my initiative in numerous ways; tasks were completed before staff had even thought about them.

When the church ladies called in for a visit, two of us had made orange squash for them. We were not allowed anywhere near the kitchen in the Home, so anything more demanding would have been impossible. Later, when clearing away and washing up, one of them had joined us. While we were busy she stayed, and we had a chat. Talking with adults was a very new experience and something to which I was totally unused, and yet she had admired my vocabulary. I said I loved reading and she replied that was very clear.

This appraisal made me realise that I was not the monster Boagey and her cronies would have me believe; that was why I had felt like two different people. Boagey was always ready to criticise and demean but despite her catalogue of abuse, in all its various forms, other people saw me in a very different light. I felt now I was on the winning side. There had been numerous occasions when I believed they had beaten me down but now I realised that my strength had seen me through, and would continue to do so. I had reached another clear point in my life. I decided, then and there, I would no longer be treated as I had been. If they had been unable to take the heart from me in those first years then they had no chance with natural maturity looming. I knew who I was, I liked that person, and they would never be able to change that. My mind and body were strong. Some time had passed but still the pain from my emotions was so difficult to deal with. I knew this was caused by the cruel way they had treated me and I felt they were something altogether different, a separate part of me. I decided two out of three would see me through.

This awareness of 'self' had provided me with new strength. I felt virtually untouchable, and did not have to wait long for this new feeling to manifest itself.

One day not long after our holiday, Warren told me to go upstairs – strictly against the rules under normal circumstances during the day – to check on something. It was not my dorm, and there was another rule that was etched in stone which forbade ever going to another. However, I had gone in, failed to find whatever Warren had requested, and was just coming out of the door when from right at the end of the landing appeared Giessen, a new and rather elderly member of staff.

From the end of the long landing she shouted angrily, 'What do *you* think you are doing up here?' She approached me quickly and I knew, instinctively, she was going to hit me. There was a wall immediately behind me; I knew I had absolutely no chance of escape so I slowly approached her.

I stopped walking and said in a low voice I hardly recognised as my own, 'Don't you dare touch me.' For a moment, a split second, I saw it. She was unsure, caught totally unaware. I repeated, with more confidence, 'Don't you *touch me*!' She stopped. I knew that I had worried her. She repeated her question, but with less aggression or aggravation.

I told her Warren had sent me upstairs. 'I don't believe that, you are lying. You can go to your own dorm *now* and get undressed ready for bed.'

Up here, on an empty landing, alone with you? I don't think so, I thought. I slowly walked past her towards the dorm, situated down the small landing to my right. I reached the junction with the top of the stairs; swiftly turned left instead, *charged* down the stairs and tore through the hall back out to the garden.

Once outside, I ran up the back path, as I frequently did when running around the Home. I sat down by one of the hedges, out of anyone's view. I went over the situation; it was puzzling. Firstly, I was amazed at Staff's reaction to my defiance. It was not something I had planned. I had simply reached the stage of having had enough, and reacted instinctively.

However, something about the whole scenario nagged at me. Why had Warren sent me on a wild goose chase? Why was the new staff up there at that time of day? What was her reason for sending me to bed, on an accusation that I had lied? What would she have done, with no one else around, when I was undressed? The answers came easily – obviously – as I was asking them.

I left my spot, and hidden from view, went very cautiously to the edge of the Rounders field. This was the area where we congregated at play times but I was looking for Warren. Then I saw her; she was over the far side watching catching practice. I essentially needed to get there without her seeing me, so I crept up very quietly. Once I had left the shrub-lined path there was little cover so I held my index finger over my lips, in a 'shhh' gesture; I did not want the other kids to acknowledge me. I made it and ambled up to the kids at play. I knew the instant I saw Warren's face that I was the last person she expected to see; she *had* attempted to set me up.

I did not care one jot. I was so elated about the way I had handled the situation that nothing else mattered. I felt I had turned a corner. Furthermore, I felt the staff realised it too.

~ 13 ~

Most of us at varying times had suffered measles, mumps, chickenpox and the like, but the first time I ever heard of rickets was when Esther arrived. She was the strangest little person you could ever wish to meet. She came from Newcastle, and had an accent I could have listened to all day. She had *the* most ginger of ginger hair imaginable. Her skin was the colour and substance of paper, tissue paper, almost translucent except for a heavily freckled nose. She was so thin it was frightening; she couldn't have knocked the skin off a rice pudding if you were holding the bowl! However, there was something immediately charming about her, and she attached herself to me like a limpet.

I didn't appreciate this. I still liked to do my own thing: ever since Michael I didn't like to be beholden to anybody and vice-versa. I vowed after he had gone never to have another friend; I was kind and friendly by nature but I liked the freedom to run alone or talk in the groups as I had always done. I did not want to be singled out by anyone, but meeting Esther for the first time was a new and rather frightening experience for all of us. We had never seen anyone so thin and sickly looking. After chatting about her we all decided we would try to protect her a bit and guide her in this awful new world in which she now found herself. We had seen some of the staff bullying aimed at the vulnerable; we knew she had a formidable mountain ahead of her and felt sorry for this poor little kid.

Going on 11 now, with eight and a half years' experience

behind me, I had developed a thick skin where the Home was concerned. I stopped minding the beatings by the staff, and aggravated them by not crying afterwards. I had come to realise that my previous private tears weren't because of the actions of the staff; they stemmed from my own emotions. The cue was simply the thoughts, when I was hurting, of my lost Uncle Tom and Auntie Dodd. By not allowing their presence to come to mind, *nothing else* could touch my emotions. Within a conversation, I could now occasionally mention their names without the pain. I learnt to do this with a detached mental shift away from them, and as it was at my instigation, that was fine, I could prepare myself. If I found myself in any way close to an 'emotional' crisis, I swallowed hard and forgot it, or lost my temper and lashed out verbally. I taught myself to stop wishing for the Dodds' helping presence; I had sought that comfort for quite a while until it dawned I was making the situation worse, not better.

A 'clip around the ear' is an oft-quoted punishment, frequently attached to comic-book humour. Gleefully resorted to by an awful lot of adults – not least the Homes staff – it was more annoying than painful when dished out on a regular basis. However, 'boxed ears' was something on a far more agonising level.

Miss Giessen was from Austria; she was yet another bullying clone of Boagey and Warren. Her English was not good, in fact it was dreadful; she was, more often than not, incredibly difficult to understand. This was coupled with her personal hatred of anyone enquiring 'What did you say, Miss?', which quickly became an excuse for her to hit out at any given opportunity. She was the person who introduced us to the new ear punishment. She did it to me once, and once was enough. It did not effect a change in my behaviour, I just learnt to dodge and run more quickly out of her way.

I was indoors one wet day, drawing and painting at the table with the others. Miss Giessen came over, and standing behind my chair, asked one of the kids what she was drawing. Attempting to repeat the reply, she made such a muddle of 'shepherd's crook', I laughed out loud; it was amusing but I had no intention of mockery or rudeness. In the next instant, an indescribable pain seared through my head, and she stormed out of the playroom in high dudgeon. I sat for some time while all my senses resumed their rightful place. My ears were ringing, my eyes were blurred and my outer ears were on fire – I felt as though my head had had a gale force wind tear through it. It was extremely painful. 'Blimey, what did *she* do?' I asked the other kids very quietly, so the other staff who had completely ignored the whole proceedings could not hear, and they explained.

She had made her hands into a 'wedge' shape, bending her fingers down and raising the knuckles; then she laid her thumb along the fingers' edge and that was it. With full force strengthened by her bad temper, she clapped her hands together over my ears. My ear drums were still throbbing painfully. Apparently, I had not been the first one; but this was in public so everyone witnessed the painful demonstration, and understood there was yet another old bag to avoid at all costs. She had hurt me momentarily, but I was becoming braver and much more resilient to this constant cruel treatment.

I had felt superior to many of the other children in intellectual terms for a long time. That may sound precocious, but the Dodds and school had given me confidence. I looked across at little Esther and knew if someone like me and the older ones had been around to offer advice when I first arrived I would perhaps have had an easier time. The changing force in my young life had been Uncle Tom and Auntie Dodd; I longed for all the others, but especially Esther, to find their own personal inspiration, as I had been so incredibly lucky to do.

Sitting on the edge of the lawn one day – we had been having a game of Rounders – one of the kids flopped down next to me. This movement made me turn towards her; I immediately noticed, and recognised, the marks on her arm.

Good God, I thought. Still? After more than three years? I looked at her and then gently caught hold of her arm.

'Was that the mangle?' I enquired softly, hoping she would respond with understanding, but she was up and gone like a frightened rabbit. I felt sick, for us both. Esther instantly replaced her at my side.

'Christ, what's up with her?'

It was impossible for me to enlighten her; I could never have talked about it – and besides, Esther had another lesson to take on board. I explained to this new kid that *that* sort of bad language would not be tolerated.

'I once said damn . . .'

Having been caught after a short chase I was frogmarched upstairs by Boagey and Warren to the sluice room – the room that housed the mangle – and knowledge of where I was being led immediately terrified me. On a shelf above the table was a box containing the bars of stinking, bright pink, rock hard carbolic soap used as a disinfectant and cleanser for the floors. It came in long bars and had to be cut with a knife to a usable size. Boagey removed one from the box.

Warren trapped my arms; from behind me she viciously forced open my mouth, keeping my jaws apart by cupping her strong disgusting fingers under my top front teeth and digging into the roof of my mouth with her nails. Boagey forced her thumb down against my chin to keep my lower jaw still and started to 'grate' the carbolic soap across my teeth. 'We will teach you not to swear in this house,' she shouted. She grated in loads of it – it was burning under my tongue and I was forced to swallow – that or choke. The strong acrid smell filled my nostrils; the acidic taste and the burning sensation in my mouth and throat were terrifying. I was panicking and gasping for air – it felt impossible to breathe – especially with my head forced backwards and trapped in their vice-like grip.

Once they had had enough they threw me aside and left me, leaning now by the sink still gasping for breath, a typical punishment from Warren. I was shaking uncontrollably and felt shocked at even *them* behaving like that. Fighting for breath, I gulped a draught of cold water; this immediately made me violently sick. That was particularly horrible, bringing again the extreme bitterness into my mouth and down my nose. Each time I had a drink of water I would throw up, still not managing the long deep breath I was fighting for because of the soap taste, smell and panic. Slowly I calmed and restored my breathing – but the shaking took much longer to control.

I was left with a badly bruised jaw, a mouthful of blisters and a taste in my mouth that ruined my food for days. In addition, I remembered that taste every time I washed the floors.

When I finished my story Esther's permanent smile had left her face.

'So what can I say?' she asked, quietly. I told her to stick to plain English. If she thought it *might* be swearing, don't say it.

'The soap is still in use for floors . . . and kids' mouths,' I added. She shuddered.

I told her too, for reasons I would not disclose, never to be anywhere on her own if she could avoid it, especially upstairs. No one could be completely trusted. Always wait for someone to go with when heading for the dorm, and do not trust any of the staff, even if there are two of them.

I told her about Michael, and why I didn't like to make friends. About Uncle Tom and Auntie Dodd, and how painful that had been. She roared when I told her about being sick on one of the three sisters, and laughed when I told her about Pamela's knickers falling off.

'I'll help you if you ever need it, but try and get stronger. When you begin to eat better and gain some weight, you should join me running. You are built to run and it's an easy way to get strong.' I showed her the muscles in my legs – she was very impressed. We all like hero-worship and I was no different.

She did some explaining then; and so I learnt about rickets. Apparently, her dad had deserted the family and her mum was forced to work. Esther was only eight, but her siblings were older and could look after themselves. Her mother's job was as an usherette in a cinema; she needed to take care of this little girl so had permission to take Esther with her.

'Blimey, I've only been to the pictures once,' I told her. I thought her life sounded amazing, but it was one of the reasons for her illness. She would often be there for long enough to see a film round twice, depending on her mother's shift. She ate poorly and being in the dark conditions so frequently and for so long contributed to her condition, or so she was told. She had some special stuff to take daily to build her up, but she told me that she would not be able to run with me because her bones would break. She did not appear to be a lazy kid, so I believed her. She knew the names of loads of film stars, of course, but the most amazing thing was her ability to remember words. She only had to hear a song or a few verses of poetry through a couple of times and that was it – she would know it off by heart. She also had a lovely singing voice. She said she sounded like Judy Garland. I may have agreed, if I had known who Judy Garland was.

Esther had arrived during a school holiday; we were due back soon.

A few of us went to school in Crowborough, about two miles away, called White Hill, hill being the operative word: we walked the blooming thing each school day. The Home was situated on a crossroads; there was at first an easy half-mile walk past fields and a huge apple orchard. However, there was then a long winding hill through the countryside, with just a couple of houses on our right. At the top was another crossroads; here was situated the sweet shop, which was home to my virtually unused ration book! It was level then for a little way, with White Hill being the final challenge before our arrival at the school. Although youth and fitness were on our side it was a fair trek, and horrible in the wind and rain, but fun going the other way.

It must have only been the second week of term when the walk home from school was interrupted by a shout from the path leading from the school gates up to the road where we were. 'Sue, they're beating up Esther.' I ran back up and sure enough, Shirley Newton (or just 'Newton' as we chose to call her), the school bully, had Esther in a headlock. I don't think she had actually hit her at this point and she quickly dropped Esther when she saw me charging towards her. I must have looked as mad as I felt.

Shirley was bigger than I was; Esther can only have been the weight of a four-year-old. I went right up to her but she just faced me down. She didn't see the punch coming and I hit her plum on the bony bridge of her nose, only once – but with all my strength, which was not inconsiderable. About an inch of her nose split open, it looked like the inside of a strawberry. She stood, instantly shocked, then as bullies so often do, she burst into angry tears and fled, accompanied by cheering from everyone else; even some of the Outside kids were jeering at her.

After Newton had gone and the noise had died down, we resumed the walk back. I was annoyed with Esther for allowing herself to be split up from the rest of us; but also with myself for not noticing. I thrust my hands deep into my coat pockets and stared at the road as I walked; nobody said anything. There was a distinct change in the mood; mainly from the confusion of my attack on Esther's behalf.

I was angry. *I did not ask for this*, I thought.

I didn't have the capacity to look after this child and neither did anyone else; none of us ever 'looked out' for another, we were all in the same boat. We all got on with each other, surprisingly well for so many girls together under one roof; but 'all in the same boat' was the glue that held us together. There were no favours or privilege – it was us versus the rest – simple. We had unanimously agreed that Esther was more vulnerable and we would help – but she could not just depend on us – she would have to help herself as well. Nothing challenging was being demanded – all she had to do was keep up with us and all stay together! My attack on Newton had been sheer instinct; 'how *dare* a bullying Outsider hit the weakest in the Home' was my thought. We were each treated in exactly the same way by the staff and we coped alone, even Gennie the wet-bed had to manage, and that *was* hard. I had whenever possible offered *her* my words of understanding, but it could not actually change anything. It was not a lack of compassion or care: it was the unwritten rule. We all looked out for ourselves, fought our own battles, faced up to the staff and their frequent attacks. I didn't want to have to divert my attention away from all that; blimey, it was hard enough without having some skinny little girl hanging on to my every word and creeping round me.

My thoughts were interrupted. 'Thanks, Sue . . . sorry.'

She spoke so quietly I barely heard; I rounded on her still feeling angry and glared until she dropped her gaze. She was such a bloody wimp; she was not going to last five minutes if she didn't shape up.

I shouted my response, 'Just go ahead of me and stay with the group,' then even louder and emphatically, 'Leave me alone . . . I've had enough of you . . . and if you cry . . . *I'll knock your bloody head off.*' She did not cry, she looked very hurt. I felt lousy inside, she did not know any better poor kid, but my God she was going to have to learn, *and quickly.*

I knew, but couldn't say, what was further adding to my anger: it was a dreadful fear that had caused me to lash out. Besides Esther's thoughtlessness and the disgusting behaviour of Newton, it was the unknown consequence of what I had just done to an Outsider that was now almost overwhelming me. Boagey needed no excuse whatsoever to thrash the living daylights out of me – and I had just presented her with the perfect reason to do whatever she wished. She had some pretty good ideas for punishments when not justified; God knows what she would think up for this overt 'crime'. She would do *anything* to protect her public image and I had no idea at all what the outcome of this particular incident was going to be. *I was so angry because I was so scared.* The ramifications for little Esther were one thing – but goodness knows what lay in store for me.

Later that evening, after we had eaten tea and done the late chores, someone who was sitting on the window seat said, 'Look who's coming up the drive.' I didn't have to look, I knew from the tone of her voice. In due course the messenger came. 'You're wanted . . .'

'Yes, I *know*,' I interrupted, utterly fed up.

Usual knock, usual response, usual entrance. Immediately my bad mood lifted and I very nearly laughed when I saw Newton. Two *amazing* black eyes and a white, thick sort of plaster over her nose from cheek to cheek. *That's taught you a lesson*, I thought. Mrs Newton's version of the story was related to me, so wide of the truth as to be incredible. I had been waiting my chance to respond, with my version, plus witnesses, but no. Sentence was being handed down already – no opportunity for the case from the defence.

'You are stopped from having, sweets, pocket money, and holidays away, anywhere, for *a year*!' Boagey shouted out the last word, in some sort of triumph. I did not wait to be excused;

I turned and walked out. Bet that guarantees a big fat donation in the Cottage Homes box, I thought.

When I got back to the playroom, everyone gathered round me at the table. I told them quietly, as Staff was in the room, what had happened. We all spent the rest of the time before bed, devising ways to get back at Newton; the winner by consensus being to banish her to some freezing, distant, deserted island – with only Boagey for company.

Esther had been shocked at my punishment and was so full of remorse I stopped being angry with her. I explained that I felt I had escaped lightly; it could have been very much worse for us both and she simply could not go on, or expect me to, in the way she was at present. It was wrong for her survival, and unfair to me.

I continued, with all the others at the table nodding in agreement. She would have to work things out for herself more: watch what the other kids did, listen to what they said, or left unsaid. Watch the staff like a hawk and decide who might be safer than another. With her illness and frailty, she could perhaps feel less threatened by them but she shouldn't bank on it. Be for ever on her guard . . . and one more lesson. I told her to concentrate on getting sharper; it was the only way to survive. She definitely realised now that advice drawn from my own experience was sound, and that this was different from the world she knew, this was Barnardo's. Here their intention was to 'break' you – as was done to young horses; but those animals were nurtured and re-trained, unlike us. This was why my fighting spirit prevailed. I was determined they would never break me. I had the good fortune to be admitted very young with no alternative experience for comparison; Esther had to shelve all she had ever known in the real world but I knew she would make it.

Hers was a situation when 'help' was not appropriate; it would not help at all. With the way Barnardo's worked, I could be sent to another Home the next day, and then what would she do with none of her own devices?

*

In reality, the punishment was mostly nonsense, except the holiday bit. Since I was no longer going to the Dodds', there had only been one holiday arranged, and that had been the previous year. The rest of the punishment was frankly daft. Pocket money was the only means of buying sweets and I hadn't had any for as long as I could remember! The system was simple. Everyone was entitled to 3 pence per week. However, there was a fines regime, to which we all fell victim. There was a raft of reasons for being fined 1 penny a misdemeanour. Running upstairs: doubled if by two-at-a-time. Running downstairs: ditto. Sliding down the banister was doubled automatically (but the bravest of us loved it). Whistling in the house. Breakages when washing up. Failing to clean shoes – or anything else – properly the first time, plus it had to be done again; most unfair. The list went on, but what they failed utterly to see was, once the 3 pence was used up, there was nothing else with which they could hit you! Once pocket money drill was sorted out on a Saturday morning, I would run upstairs two-at-a-time, whistling. Staff would catch me; fine me my 3 pence and then I had carte blanche to do anything I wished for the rest of the week, with impunity. The staff 'punishments' came and went whether I was right or wrong; I figured I may as well have some fun in the process.

I only ever went into the sweet shop on the crossroads on two or three occasions, and that was with another child who never did anything wrong: a rare breed. The shopkeeper had a shoebox behind the counter, full of ration books with each of our names on. Mine must have been pristine – it certainly was never used.

*

I have said White Hill was my first school; I was there for the longest time, but moved to two others in the four years I was at

Crowborough. Both were small village establishments full of charm; but my unsettled education was hard to cope with at times. Teachers and their individual methods varied enormously, but the worst thing was the difference in distance to travel. One school was in Rotherfield; it was a mile further than White Hill just to catch the necessary bus, and then another walk to classes. I was there during a winter term; my enduring memories being walking there and back in the near darkness, and when it rained, sitting all day in wet shoes and socks.

Eridge was even further away. There was another long walk for a half-hour bus ride, stopping for others en route. However, this was undoubtedly my favourite school; I much preferred being here to any of the others. Miss Rothwell was the Head and only teacher; she lived in a small cottage next door. She was a plump, cuddly lady and always wore a brown knitted dress that looked, I thought, exactly like cooked minced beef. The playground here took up more space than the school building – the classroom was like a doll's house. I didn't mind at all if my feet got wet; there was a 'chimney-pot' black boiler in the centre of the room, surrounded for safety with a circular fireguard. It almost throbbed with heat once stoked up; wet clothes were draped around it, and they not only quickly dried, they were warm to put back on as well. Miss Rothwell was a darling; every one of us did well for her. She didn't mind at all when we laughed too much to accompany her at assembly hymns. It started all right, but she had a 'trained' voice and trilled at full volume at all times; she always apologised but she just couldn't sing quietly!

There was one memorable occasion when the bus didn't arrive; the children who weren't from Barnardo's went home but we didn't dare – so we walked. It was a good four miles; hills and countryside all the way and much too far to rush! It was not bad weather and we could have made reasonable time, but there were too many fascinations to distract us. We had a fantastic time standing on every gate and talking to the cattle and sheep, counting all the birds' nests and biting – just the once – into a bitter unripe crab apple, an experience I would not recommend. We dawdled happily along and eventually arrived when it was nearly lunchtime. Miss Rothwell at first was a bit cross and said we should have gone back to the Home; when we told her we thought we would be in serious trouble she calmed down and gave us each a hot drink. She then explained she was cross because there were no buses running at all; we just looked at each other rather glumly. All the others were out in the playground but she made us sit in and rest before having some lunch. Once we had eaten our meal, and after another little rest instead of the playground, we set off to walk back! Miss Rothwell looked worried so we decided to do what she said and not dawdle and we made much better progress this time. We were not late for tea and never discovered if the staff realised what had happened – but we certainly didn't get into trouble. It had been quite a lot of miles for a ten-year-old; but it had been one of the best school days ever for me.

The next term found me back at White Hill; no reason or explanation, and there I stayed for the last year in middle school. Once again, it happened to us all and so became a natural turn of events . . . but I am sure we would have achieved very much more in a steady, settled environment.

~ 14 ~

'Boagey is leaving.'

Goodness knows where this rumour started; it was met with utter disbelief. Rumours of all sorts, spurious and otherwise, were common enough at school – but here? I plucked up the courage to approach Sylvia, the eldest girl, and the rumour became news. She was fifteen and due to leave the Home herself; we did wonder for a little while if she had made it up – and then boasted about 'knowing' something we didn't because she was about to leave. Time passed and the speculation increased but nothing 'official' was heard – and the source remained for ever a mystery. In an enclosed institution such as High Broom, any news that filtered through was considered extraordinary, but this rumour was a miracle.

The effect was immediate on everybody; when I heard I didn't know whether to laugh or cry with happiness. The relief was exhilarating.

The oppressive mantle within the Home was suddenly lifted; it was more like the atmosphere of when we went on that seaside holiday. Even though we were vowed to secrecy between ourselves, everything seemed somehow lighter. There was an air of optimism, we all smiled indoors, and laughed outdoors with a new, abandoned joy.

Words can scarcely convey how I felt. I hated the woman, and was aware that the feeling was mutual. She was a perverse bully and obviously preferred to take on staff in the same mould as herself. The shaking that Warren did to the younger children and the continuing beatings were tolerated only because she allowed them to be. To learn so recently that the rape of young bodies was still going on was a deep shock. Why I thought I was the only one, I don't know. Perhaps I hoped I was, and yet I felt an odd relief when I discovered I was not. Occasionally, especially when I had to assist with the laundry in the sluice room, and relive the incident with the carbolic soap, I would recall the trauma of that experience. To discover, albeit with sadness, that just one other kid had been through the same made me feel less of the lone target – I felt back in line, the same as all the others again. And I now no longer believed it was just the two of us either.

I had never objected to – and indeed I understood – the need for discipline; any institution housing kids with ages varying from five to 15 had to have a routine. I always felt it provided a secure feeling, an order to life that was comfortable. However, discipline was not enough for Boagey; she wanted complete control of mind and body; to demean with gratuitous bullying and punishment – *that* was what I challenged and rebelled against. Conversely there was never privilege or reward for diligence or success; no matter how hard we worked at school, no matter how many compliments she heard from Outsider adults when at Sunday school, these made no difference to her. I had won small prizes at running and schoolwork – but once back in the Home there was no praise or thanks, she was the same with us all.

Within the Home, there was just one single indicator distinguishing the difference between the age groups: the time you were put to bed. There was not otherwise a single thing that distinguished one thing from another, one day from another, one year from another – nothing. No one had personal possessions, there were no clothes that belonged just to you, no stability at school or in the Home, and no choices. All this contrived to produce an oppressive robotic existence, which was just one of the reasons for my battle to rise above it and why I enjoyed being out at school.

There had been an enormous change when Uncle Tom and Auntie Dodd had chosen to take me out; they had shown me privileges and wonderful treats, but it all reverted to the same old grey existence when I stopped seeing them.

I would never forgive Boagey for the manner in which she delivered the news that they were no longer in my life and never would be again. She had derived enormous pleasure from my pain; an almost unbearable pain I still felt when the memories came to mind. Now all this was over! 'Boagey is leaving' was music to my ears – perhaps the best news I would ever get.

However, it didn't end there, there was more good news to come. Taking over her position would be a couple, a husband and wife who would have their daughter with them. There was not, I think, ever an official announcement of all this; somehow it just seemed to trickle through to us. The accuracy of these whispers concerned me – I so hoped they were true – but slowly things unfolded and moved on and it became clear that it just might be right. Mr and Mrs Luxton, the anticipated new heads of the Home, arrived one day – albeit completely unannounced.

They had obviously had the grand tour, and then by accident or design, I met them in the hall; a warm cheerful couple with an open charm.

As I approached them, Mrs Luxton said, 'Good grief, is your surname Davis?' I assured her, rather puzzled, that it was. 'You must be Susan, Colin's sister. We looked after him once. He was athletic as well. Do you do a lot of sport?' I told her I particularly loved running, but would play any game, indoors or out, with zeal. They were both very keen on fitness and played all kinds of sports themselves. She then said, deliberately or otherwise, that they would mark out the tennis courts and get us all playing. So it is true . . . Boagey is leaving, I thought.

Mrs Luxton informed me my brother was a Wimbledon ball boy. This meant nothing to me then; I made a mental note to find out at school, and when I did, felt tremendously proud.

We spent long hours discussing the obvious and epoch-making changes this new regime was going to effect. Each of us had various snippets gleaned during the day and these were gone over in detail. The unanimous decision was that life was taking on a whole, new and optimistic aspect.

One morning shortly after the Luxtons' visit, Staff called me in from the garden. I was to wait in the hall to see Boagey. When I got there, I found about 12 of us mustered; one was Pamela. She suggested this was the day of the official announcement, and I remember thinking that they must be telling us all in small groups, it made sense.

Staff held open the office door and we duly trooped in; Boagey sat at her desk and we stood in a line to face her. My head was up, my back was straight and my heart was almost bursting with the thrill and expectancy of it all – *this was going be the very last time I would have to face this revolting woman.*

She began.

'You will have all heard by now that I am leaving High Broom. I have really enjoyed my duty here, but it is time to move on. I have been given charge of a smaller home in the north of England and am looking forward to the challenge very much. It is, however, going to be strange at first, so to help me settle in more quickly *I have chosen all of you to come with me.*'

The gasps were audible. I stood there, totally stunned. A black mist seemed to descend before my eyes, but I felt nothing – I was completely numb. *Why was she doing this?* It was incredible, *utterly unbelievable*! I looked at the others; I was clearly not alone in my shock. I could feel again the dreadful banging of my heart in my throat. We were all red-faced; as if in a state of embarrassment, but that was not what we were feeling. I looked up from the floor, where I had been concentrating my attention, and saw the expression on that vile woman's face. It was glowing with malice and triumph. She had dealt a horrific injustice and we had all felt the blow. God, I hated her!

*

Sometime later, on another visit to prepare for their imminent move, I saw Mrs Luxton again. I approached her and positively begged her not to let me go with Boagey. I explained briefly, in case I was being watched, how much I hated her and how cruel she was, but all to no avail. Boagey had the authority and the Luxtons could not intervene or alter her plans; there was nothing they could do. The only positive thing to come out of that conversation, brief though it had been, was I knew they understood and were compassionate in their sympathy; but practically speaking, what good was that?

My recollection of the arrangements, the departure from Crowborough and the arrival at St Anne's – our and Boagey's new Home – are difficult for me to remember with clarity. I travelled from Crowborough, probably by train to London, and from there made the long journey up to Lancashire with the other girls. I remained sunk in blackness, my mind not absorbing any of the things going on around me. I think I even went beyond the feeling of dread; I seemed to have lost all feeling.

As family houses go, the St Anne's Home was quite an impressive place. From the road were two sets of double gates which opened on to a flower-bordered small drive that ran along the front of the house. On each side of the house were paths, giving access to the garden at the rear. It was an attractive-looking building of red brick and had numerous large windows that looked out over the golf course. But as a Children's Home it was utterly pathetic. It was smaller than the confines of Babies'

Castle. I hated it on sight – but this was largely due to Boagey, the fact she had dragged us all there with so much malice. The fact that she was *there*.

She had wanted me with her; I wanted her to know she would regret that decision. I would always remember the look of jubilation when she first announced the news of our leaving Crowborough with her. I would look at her and remind myself of it – and it would fill me with even more determination to get the better of her.

Downstairs there was just one room for us kids. It was situated on the left of the hall and was a dining-cum-playroom: three long tables at one end filled half the room, and as at Crowborough, we ate and played on these. At the other end was a beautiful large bookcase on the left wall with a piano opposite; it was light and bright but there was little space for all twenty-four of us.

The large parquet-floored entrance hall housed Boagey's office: a ghastly, modern opaque glass affair, squeezed into the corner of an otherwise handsome area. The staffroom lay on the opposite side from the playroom; they had almost as much space as us and there were only five of them. This was the only carpeted room; the downstairs being all solid wood, the upstairs covered in new, very smelly, linoleum. The ornate stairs ran up from the centre of the hall. Through an archway beyond the staffroom was a passage leading down to the cloakroom, scullery, boiler room and kitchen. With a quarry-tiled floor this area was probably the coldest place ever deemed fit for humans; even Cook complained. I know it was in the north of England but the place in winter was so cold we had ice on the *inside* of the windows, including the dorms.

Upstairs were many rooms on two floors, but as usual we were aware only of where we slept and bathed. I started in a dorm with six others at the back of the house above the kitchen area, and in my last year was in a smaller dorm for four at the front. On this landing, there was a small bathroom squeezed into one corner. All the other rooms were 'out of bounds', even for cleaning duties.

Because everything appeared to be on top of everything else – because we were always watched – my first and enduring impression was of living in a goldfish bowl. Wherever I went, whatever I did, someone else was there. None of us had ever seen so much of Boagey and the staff.

The path from the left hand side of the drive led into the rear garden which was, well, just a garden: surrounded on three sides with a high brick wall, a small patch of lawn, a couple of trees – *and nowhere to run*. To say I was devastated would be a gross understatement. To the right of the small grassed area was a concrete yard reached from the house by a path from the boiler room; past the kitchen on the left and through a high wooden gate. On the right hand side; where the high wall joined the convent next door, were three small buildings commonly known as 'The Bike Sheds'. The fact that no bikes were allowed – and entrance was forbidden – gave these a mystery far beyond their otherwise mediocre status.

There were three support staff and a cook; Miss Plesance was the nicest one. She had a hare lip and I put her empathy and understanding down to the fact that she herself had suffered somewhat because of this affliction. She at least behaved like a fellow human being; she had a witty sense of humour and occasionally a wicked twinkle in her eyes, she could play the piano and organised 'sing-songs', especially on birthdays. The cook, Miss Smith, was an elderly decent soul but we didn't see a great deal of her; we weren't allowed in her kitchen but she was always in the playroom to serve the lunch. The others were more of the Boagey ilk. I figured Miss Plesance would not stay long but I really hoped she would.

The first day I remember in the new home was a Saturday. All congregated in the hall; Boagey sat at a table with a book in front of her. She explained the procedure to the new kids, but we from Crowborough were already familiar with the system. This was to be a weekly meeting, when we all received our pocket money. Blimey . . . that will be a first, I thought. My previous 'debt' had clearly been written off and I got my first share; it also happened to be the last, but that was by design on my part! Upon collecting 3 pence each, we disbanded. I immediately ran upstairs two-at-a-time, fined 2 pence, whistling while doing so, fined 1 penny. Therefore, no pocket money next week.

Immediately this fiasco was over for another week, our Saturday work began. During the week, for about a half hour before school, we were allotted jobs on a rota basis – exactly as it was done at Crowborough. We made our own beds, then cleaned and tidied the dorm. Every bed and chair had to be placed just so; Staff would check and if not perfect to the nth degree she would crash everything around and we would start again.

Baths, hand basins and toilets had to be cleaned; downstairs another group washed the breakfast dishes and put them all away. The attention to the minutest detail was exactly the same whatever we did. It made you learn to 'do it right the first time' without any doubt! After school we had a bread and butter tea, and once finished, we all joined in a similar schedule taking anything up to an hour, depending on the work.

Saturday was even more intense. This was literally spring-cleaning and took all of the morning. Every nook and cranny in the dorms, playrooms, stairs, hallways, cloakrooms, the porch and the scullery needed to be cleaned to perfection.

Miss Plesance was fair when she came round but we once had an 'inspection' by one of the other staff, Devlin; we had missed the top closing part of a door into the dorm.

Every bed was stripped and the bedding thrown on the floor;

scouring powder was scattered over the entire floor and the chairs. She then went outside and returned with a great lump of soil; this she threw into the sink, wet it and smeared it all over as mud. We missed our afternoon walk of freedom as all this additional mess had to be cleaned up and we simply ran out of time. If that procedure was not up to standard, it was repeated *and* with a further punishment of their choice; for me, it was 'sewing' for two hours!

There was only one other occasion when that happened with Devlin. Everything was fine, but one curtain was not hanging perfectly perpendicular. We had missed lunch to repeat the procedure the first time; we were warned we would also miss tea if we took too long on the second attempt. We made it but then after doing the tea-time chores I sewed until bed time. A hateful day.

However, there was one punishment meted out weekly. I was always the one selected to clean out the kitchen drains, yet only Cook and I knew why this was no hardship for me.

On the surface of it, it was a revolting job. All the greasy pans were washed in the enormous kitchen sinks, with just a dash of household soda to soften the water. All other dishes were cleaned in the scullery. The kitchen drain was therefore a very smelly, grimy affair. I had to scrape the fat from the sides, scoop it on to newspaper, and then clean the sides with a metal scrubber. The fatty paper was placed beside the boiler for burning, all the equipment was put away and I would then go into the kitchen. Cook would run a bowl of really hot water and I scrubbed hard, right beyond my elbows. Then came the good bit – our secret!

I would go excitedly into the dry store and sit down on a box; she would bring in a big old china pudding bowl for me to hold on my lap. Then with a kindly smile, she would hand to me a great ladle full of treacle, syrup or honey. I would devour it, savouring every sweet mouthful and catching any drips in the bowl to lick out after. Bliss! Cook said I needed it, to take the horrible smell and taste from my mouth. In addition, I deserved a treat for doing such a disgusting job every week. She couldn't see that her kindness was the very reason I made sure I got this 'disgusting job' each and every week.

15

For the first time in my life, I no longer had the countryside in which I could create a form of anonymity. At Crowborough, the older kids took us out for a walk on a Saturday afternoon without the staff; we could go for miles around the lanes and not see a house, and only very occasionally meet someone walking their dog. There was then only an exchange of polite greetings, and although we had no uniform *per se,* we all held the firm belief that any stranger we met knew we were from High Broom. Neither Babies' Castle nor St Christopher's was located as deep in the countryside, but there I played in the grounds so it was irrelevant.

Here was very different indeed; the 'goldfish bowl' feeling in the Home most certainly extended beyond its walls. One whole side of the road gave the houses, including ours, a magnificent view of openness into the far distance – but it was not the countryside. Links Gate was a 'nice' area on the edge of the town with some houses even bigger than ours, and so we had all been warned, with the threat of serious punishment as deterrent, to be on our best behaviour whenever we left the house. However, when we did happen to meet a fellow resident, although they rarely stopped for conversation, they greeted us kindly with a nod and a smile. The greatest surprise for me personally, and one about which we were all amused, was the noise of the chatter and laughter coming from the Roman Catholic Convent next door. The nuns looked so dour and serious in their black garb so the contrast was astonishing; kind and friendly, they would always stop and chat when we met. Conversation was only of the most trivial nature, but they seemed to share the understanding, I felt, of the difference in living in a closed community rather than the 'outside world'. There was an open understanding of our circumstances; one nun said that she had once worked in a Catholic Home – but she didn't elaborate. Our other neighbours seemed nice; not one was patronising, just kind and welcoming; this also became the pattern for the town in general.

Christmas in Barnardo's was, as for all youngsters, an exciting time. Dispensing largely with the bullying regimentation and allowing us the freedom of noisy activity otherwise strictly frowned upon, we woke to the loud scratchy gramophone sounds of 'Christians Awake, Salute the Happy Morn'. Excitement built up as we went through the usual routine; washing, dressing and making beds, and then we lined up in single file along the landing outside of our dorm. From downstairs, once silent order was established, someone would blow a whistle. All hell broke loose as we tore headlong down the stairs to our playrooms to run and seek the stocking hung by our own chair on Christmas Eve. These were always moved to another chair, but with individual names on, we soon found 'ours'. Each contained an apple, orange and one sweet that could be eaten immediately after breakfast; the fruit went into a special Christmas bowl in the centre of one of the tables, and was handed out during the day.

At Crowborough, we went to church only once, for the Family Service. Here at St Anne's, because of the closer proximity (about a mile away), we had to attend three services: Communion before breakfast for those who were old enough to have been confirmed, at 11 o'clock for the Carol Service and then at six for Evensong. I loved the carols and sang out lustily, sharing naughty glances with the rest also singing as loudly as possible . . . in the knowledge that Boagey could hardly tell us off for being so reverent!

We always enjoyed our Christmas lunch which consisted of proper roast potatoes like at school and an *enormous* turkey donated by the local butcher. Miss Smith served the slices of meat in much more generous portions than was usual; the cabbage was as soggy and tasteless as ever but we still all enjoyed what was, for us, a really big meal. There was a sixpence in the Christmas pudding; but this disappointingly was demanded back from the finder, presumably to use the next year.

The eldest cleared away and did the washing up; the rest helped move the tables to the very back of the room to make space for the handing out of the presents and we all sat down quietly for this event. There were only three or four who had more than one gift; Ann Short cried every year because her dad sent a present through the post; her mother was dead and he could not look after her so she was put in the Homes, but she only ever heard from him at this time of year. One of the others received a jigsaw puzzle from an Aunt but it mattered not what it was, or from whom: nothing was allowed to be kept as one's own. It went into the cupboard to share, or into the enormous sweet tin if that was the gift, then handed round occasionally throughout the year.

I waited in breathless anticipation to have my name called out and loved going up to be handed my festively wrapped present; it was the only one I received. It was from the 'Round Table Club', a charitable group of local business people who gave to each of us, a great thrill that truly made Christmas. Always a tin of Sharp's Toffees, it was the best, most exciting moment of the whole day.

They showed the same kindness with presents on every single birthday. They obviously had a list of names and dates, and not once did they let anyone go disappointed. They also organised trips; each year we went to Blackpool Tower Circus and enjoyed another evening out at the world-famous Blackpool Illuminations. The first time was a staggering experience, seeing 'The Golden Mile' along the entire sea front promenade, festooned with thousands of coloured lights; strung across the roads, wound around lamp posts, they were everywhere. No matter how many times I went, it remained a thrill; the 'Illuminations' evening always ended with a fish supper for everyone, eaten on the coach, straight out of the paper. Wonderful!

One memorable day we had arrived back from school to great excitement; erected in our absence was a strange-looking wooden frame construction out in the garden by the playroom French doors. The long cross pieces were a solid six inches square; it was about ten feet high and the same size across, looked a bit like a goal post, but with a standing bar front and back and no net! Our enquiries were left unanswered so the tension really built up as to what this might be. All we heard was: 'It is not yet finished; you are not to climb on the wooden bars, or we will see to it that it is never completed.' With this threat we all behaved; three or four weeks passed by and then we came home to the finished article. Over the wooden structure had been thrown thick rope which made a climbing frame; this was knotted into large squares like enormous mesh. Securely tied to the front and back bars, the mesh afforded hand grips to climb. It was brilliant and had hours of use from the youngest to the eldest. The Round Table friends had donated this and we all sent them what were probably the most sincere letters of thanks we had ever written.

This kindness extended to local businesses; they also 'did their bit' for us. Every two or three weeks a bakery van would arrive. They would bring into the hall many of the cakes not sold in their shop in town by closing time on the Saturday. Given a plate each, we made our choice of one and sometimes two from the tray.

These treats were then carried to the tables and we would stuff our faces as if we had never had anything like it; doughnuts and meringues were the favourite but this pleasure was clearly shared by their customers: there were rarely any of them on the trays.

One Easter, Woolworth's had an enormous chocolate egg displayed in their window; we had seen it when we had been into town with Staff. On Maundy Thursday, everyone was ordered into the hall; excitement grew. Miss Plesance had organised this, so Boagey must have been away. She told us all to sit down cross-legged on the floor; be very quiet and listen because 'the time was getting close'. We all shut up and strained to listen for anything out of the ordinary. There it was – a car engine! The car door slammed, another opened and closed, and then the doorbell rang. You could have heard a pin drop!

Miss Plesance opened the door. Two men entered and with one either side, carried a huge wooden tray upon which was The Egg. Slight murmuring now within our group as they set it down on the big hall sideboard and announced, 'This is for you!' Probably the loudest cheer I ever heard greeted the news. We sang, 'For They Are Jolly Good Fellows', and with three cheers, they were gone. Miss Plesance gave us all the opportunity for a good look. It appeared even bigger close up and smelt wonderful; the decoration of tiny flowers and baby chicks in coloured icing sugar made it look perfect. 'It will be broken and shared on Saturday,' she announced, to another rousing cheer. The only way to crack it open was with a screwdriver held point down on the egg top; this was then hit with a hammer. The chocolate was a half inch thick in places; it was delicious.

I have no idea where the American army was stationed, but it can't have been too far away. Busy doing our Saturday chores one day we heard an engine; a huge army lorry had pulled into the drive. Every window revealed a peering face and the sudden lack of activity from above made Boagey shout up from the hall,

'Get on with your work.' Fat chance! The uniformed men jumped out and dropped the gate at the rear. Covering the entire floor area were loads of boxes, which were systematically carried into the hall. We were still all upstairs; unlike the unveiling of the egg, there was obviously not going to be any ceremony offered to these chaps. Thanks to Boagey being involved, she just waved them off – and while we did too, I don't think they saw us.

Doreen, one of the other girls, and I were called downstairs. 'Get these moved into the kitchen. Miss Smith will tell you where to put them, and hurry; you will still have your work to go back to.'

It had taken those four men at least twenty minutes to get the boxes off the lorry; poor old Doreen and I were dropping. A good half hour or more of hard slog, then Miss Smith made us leave it until after lunch as we were in her way. We returned upstairs to help with the work. We had no answer when everyone asked us what was inside the boxes. '*Heavy*,' was my only – tired – contribution!

We ate lunch and resumed the lifting. Eventually completed, mounting excitement gripped us all – *what was inside these boxes?* I ventured to ask Miss Smith. 'Tinned rhubarb pudding,' she replied, I could not believe my ears! Quite what I had imagined, I don't know, but it most definitely was *not* tinned rhubarb pudding. I was immediately glad we hadn't sung to them! However, I was one of the few who actually liked the pudding; with every mouthful reminding me of the effort to get the stuff stowed away, it was just as well. It was served on a fairly regular basis for years!

Never having previously been in this type of community, the many acts of kindness shown by the local people were a constant source of comfort and I often wonder, even with our thanks and demonstrations of appreciation, whether they were fully aware of this fact; I hope so.

16

My bed was on the left hand side of the room, immediately in front of the ever-open dormitory door. I lay fast asleep but woke with a shock as a hand was pressed against my mouth. A hoarse threatening whisper, 'Don't make a sound.' She stayed, with her hand on my mouth, for a while. My mind froze. I was lying on my left side, my back to her. I presume she was satisfied I was not going to make any sound as she then lifted the bedclothes and tightly grasped my ankle.

She dragged my foot right across the bed; this hurt my hips and knee as she held on so tightly. Pushing my heel between her legs, she started a rubbing movement. I was disgusted but did not feel the same fear I had when younger – just incredulity that this should be happening now. There was a feeling of nausea more than trauma; disgust at that same horrid breathing, that same revolting smell. It stopped.

'Don't you ever breathe a word,' in the same hoarse whisper.

Good God! It wasn't Boagey – it was Devlin! I was stunned. Devlin was that night's 'duty Staff'. She may have had the same build as Boagey but she had always seemed okay. Crikey, I had been enjoying a laugh with her at bath time just a short while ago. A thought suddenly occurred to me – I had been naked. I wondered whether she was planning to do what she had just done. I shuddered and felt sick at the notion.

God knows what the time was; I felt I'd been in bed for ages. When she left, the awful sick sensation continued but I was strangely calm; I lay very still to stay that way. I remembered when I was locked into the tower by Boagey. There hadn't been a cruel beating this time, so on the face on it what had just happened seemed to be nothing like that. However, I sensed that there were similarities between the two incidents, and I realised I now understood more of what she had been doing. I felt close to tears for the first time in a long while.

I was desperate to leave my bed to try to wash away the whole disgusting experience and rid myself of the smell of her that seemed to linger in my bed, and on me. I was too scared to call her; I could not face her anyway. I felt utterly confused and alone in the filth that was her. Freezing with an inner cold I curled up in a ball; facing this time down the landing, I hugged my arms tightly around my shivering, painful body. I tried to keep my eyes wide open but managed eventually to get warm and calm enough to sleep.

Night duty was shared between the support staff and I never did know if they actually stayed awake all night, or whether they woke when someone called for the toilet. What I did know was she was at the breakfast table in the morning. As head of my table, I had to sit next to her.

I felt more revulsion then than I had during the night. It was her hands that really repulsed me. I could not bear to look at her at all, but seeing her hands was horrible. These feelings made me feel sick; I raised my hand and informed Boagey. 'Then leave the table and go to the cloakroom,' she ordered. By the time I got there, I was shaking all over. I dropped to the floor and leant against the closed door; I was not actually going to *be* sick, but the nausea was washing over me in waves.

I had thought once, very fleetingly, that nothing like that could happen here. The Home was too small and there were no sluice rooms as there were in Crowborough. I had given it no more consideration.

'Are you all right in there?' Devlin again! My mind raced; I needed to get out of the toilet.

'I'll be out in a minute, Miss,' I answered, in a strong clear voice – a voice I hoped that lied totally about how I really felt. I sat there for several minutes and tried to calm down.

When I did come out, she was gone.

I carried out my allotted chores in the normal manner, managing to summon strength from somewhere within me. I could not understand why I felt so horribly sick and weak now; at last, it was time to leave for school.

Pamela was concerned; she kindly walked with me as I couldn't keep up with the others. 'You look dreadful, all grey.' She allowed me my silence after I had quietly assured her I would be okay. I glanced across at her. Should I tell her, I wondered. I immediately decided I couldn't. How do you explain such a revolting act, and how could anyone my age begin to understand; where would I even begin? Once again, it was a perfect trap, and I could not even find the words to use. I had no wish to hurt or scare a nice kid like Pamela; it was something clearly to carry alone, but what a burden.

With my head down, I walked and thought. I had been at school for a whole term and knew all the female teachers; I wondered if there was one of them I could talk to about this. Each time I returned to the worries of explaining. I was hurting inside and felt ridiculously close to tears all the time; I felt an almost *desperate* need to tell someone. This trap *was* perfect.

By the time I reached school I was freezing cold, shaking again, and the aching pain in my hips had worsened considerably. I went straight to First Aid. I told them I had been feeling sick earlier, had come to school, but still felt unwell. They did the routine ear, nose and throat checks, then put me on the daybed to rest. I slept nearly all day, with a drink offered when I awoke.

For ages after I found it hard to relax and go to sleep. Even the nights that Devlin wasn't on duty I was restless, and always seemed to be cold. As soon as I settled on to my left side I sensed the open door behind me, and immediately felt vulnerable. I would then turn over so I could see down the landing, but as sleep came, I would turn back again, and wake myself up. I eventually decided that it was something that had happened on just that one occasion, not to dwell on it. The refreshing sleep was luxury – but just a few months had passed when exactly the same thing happened again – the hand on my mouth. I knew immediately it was Devlin again but this time I felt really frightened. She pressed down hard with her forearm against the side of my head. I could not move under her weight and could barely breathe. In no time it seemed she put her hand under the bedclothes. I had no chance to move and now I was really trapped.

I was on my side as before. She was a big strong woman; she roughly pushed my knee up, forcing my legs apart, and pushed a cold greasy finger into my bottom. A gasp escaped me with the shock and pain; she pressed down harder on my head in a threatening manner as if to warn me about making another sound; I felt I would suffocate in the pillow. She removed her finger and pushed hard into the front of me; shoving my head down even further to ensure that I could make no noise. I was in agony and the memories of what had happened to me before were making my mind spin. She took her arm from my head; I was terrified of making a sound, and then the rubbing began. Everything was so rough, that was what was most frightening. She seemed out of control, just as Boagey had been. The heat from her and the smell were just extraordinary; stifling that dreadful breathing, so as not to make a noise herself.

Then she was gone.

I lay there stock-still, straining to hear, but it seemed all the others were sound asleep. That in itself seemed so unfair. With no sounds from beyond the dorm either, I felt isolated and alone; I could *not* arrange my thoughts clearly in my head. I very gently turned myself on to my back and drew my knees up to try to relax. I was cold again and in a lot more pain; she had been unbelievably rough.

After a little while, I began to relax, but I needed to go to the toilet, and did the unthinkable. I did not call her but went on my own. I could not bear to see her and decided that, should she appear, I would scream the place down! There was blood on me again; but with no hand basin in the toilet, and too scared to go to the bathroom further down the landing, I could do nothing about it so I quietly returned to bed.

I lay there now freezing cold – shaking with shock and in pain – and with the dreadful feeling of having been beaten down again. All the old memories came flooding back, filling my head. I could barely hold back the tears.

Who did she go to last night – who will be her victim tomorrow? I wondered. There had been a considerable length of time since her first attack on me; I convinced myself I was not the only one, but that seemed to make things worse not better. I did not want to ask 'why me?' and feel alone with this; but also I couldn't bear to think that someone else was feeling so awful. In this smaller place, we were more closely knit; we knew each other so much better, it was horrible to think this was happening to any one of us.

I wanted the courage to ask if they would move my bed away from the door; away from the dreadful feeling of vulnerability. I could however have offered no explanation or reason for this request, and as soon as I thought it I knew it would be refused. I puzzled long and hard but could not begin to imagine who else might be her victims; I hated to think about that, and anyway the other dorms were a mystery. I only knew who shared with me. I had no idea as to who else slept in which room, let alone if they were by the door or not. I wondered then if that was their plan, the reason for all other rooms being 'out-of-bounds'? Once again I realised I was presenting myself with the incalculable so, by now much calmer, I allowed myself to drift into a deeply troubled sleep.

By the time we were called to get up I was in a lot of pain and had lain awake for a while fighting back tears. Waking us kids up was the final task of night Staff before she went off duty. Devlin came in and drew the curtains back; I heard this from under my bedclothes but I was determined not to look at her. I knew it would make me feel worse again, and the overwhelming feeling of wanting to cry remained; I never cried and could not understand this. I was hoping by the time she got to the breakfast table this time, I could prepare myself; I was already feeling sick at the thought of seeing her but hoped I would cope. As soon as she had gone to the next dorm, I scurried down to the toilet on our landing. I was in the most dreadful pain but worse was the recalling of the similar situations in the past. I would be in trouble if I held up the others but *had* to find an excuse to use the main bathroom – to be on my own. I had some greasy stuff and blood that had dried on me; although there seemed to be no more, I desperately wanted to wash her away from me. Thank God, there was only the merest mark on my nightdress, it was barely noticeable; the thought of talking to *anyone* at that moment was nauseating; to try to invent a reason to explain the state of my nightdress would have been beyond me.

We had a 'strip wash' or bath at night, but the morning routine was just a hands and face wash; I desperately wanted a proper wash but knew I couldn't, and once again the tears welled up. I washed and dressed in the normal way and managed to put on my underclothes and skirt while still hidden by the nightdress. I knew then that nobody had seen the dried blood on me; it was between my thighs so safely covered from view. *I* could still 'see' it though. If I could have washed the blood away, it would have made me feel clean again inside my head too.

Staff was always supervising and watching but her gaze worried me with my present anxiety so uppermost in my mind. 'What's the matter with you today, slow coach?' she asked.

'Nothing, Miss. I feel tired, that's all, I don't feel well.'

'Well get a move on or you'll go without breakfast.'

I realised I didn't care, I wasn't hungry, but I said nothing. I virtually forgot the pains inside me; concentrating on what I could do to get myself clean was uppermost in my mind. There was no possibility with Staff there. I pretended in my mind that I was asking them at school, but I just could not get the words to go right. I was feeling desperate and breathless battling with the tears, until I sat down at the table; I suddenly knew *exactly* what I could do and how, with a bit of luck, to get away with it.

Breakfast was a bowl of porridge and a cup of tea. I ate my porridge slowly, allowing the tea, which was never very hot, to cool down a bit. I picked up my cup and immediately allowed it to drop all down the front of my school blouse and form a puddle on my skirt in my lap. I was soaked and Boagey went mad! She called me all the names under the sun, and then shouted, 'Get yourself upstairs and get cleaned up, and you can stay there, on your own and in the cold, until I find you something else to wear, you stupid idiot. Don't you *dare* move from that bathroom or you will be in serious trouble.'

It had worked! I was never as relieved to suffer her harsh tongue; and because I kept my head down, Devlin had not been of concern to me. I felt my face go red with the unbelievable relief I felt; battling the desire to scream, shout, and leap in the air with joy, I slowly left them all and went upstairs.

The strip wash was perfect; I even had warmer water than usual because no one else was running it at the same time. The tearful feelings left me, replaced by a surge of relief at discovering what I needed to do. I washed myself with my dark blue knickers so nothing would show on a flannel. They were wet from the tea so I would just say I had 'helped' by putting them in to soak. Nobody came up for ages and I was freezing by the time my clothes arrived, but I didn't care, I was clean again. However, with my concentration less intense, and the moving around, I felt all the pains again. I knew, though, that once I made it to school, I would be all right; as before Pam would walk with me and First Aid would care for me, and they did.

For a long time afterwards, my sleeplessness returned whenever Devlin was on night duty. I could not bear to think of her with one of the others, and knew she had successfully silenced me, so there would be no sounds or signs. I tried to imagine, should she return, how I would scream out to alert other staff, but I knew I would never be that brave.

17

I had looked forward to my new secondary school with a mixture of excitement and trepidation; much the same as all the other first-years, I imagine. Except that in a short space of time I had to get used to a new town, a new Home, staff and kids. We who had arrived with Boagey were only half the full complement – the others were more from the immediate locality, or at least the North of England. I found, in the first instance, this dialect to be very difficult to understand. One girl called Dorothy was so broad as to be almost impossible to comprehend. To my relief she apparently hailed from Yorkshire! The Cook, Miss Smith, and Devlin spoke in a similar way, but they were much less 'broad' than Dorothy; that was good news inasmuch as I felt I had at least a fighting chance to understand the teaching staff.

On the first day of the new term, Pamela and I with about six others set off excitedly together; the sheer joy of being away from the Home dissolving any real worries we may have harboured. We talked in the loud voices this new freedom allowed, and laughed ourselves silly over absolutely nothing.

The building was old and beautiful, a red-brick edifice of the Victorian era. We entered, guided by a prefect, and were ushered around various classrooms. Happily, Pamela and I were to be together – I felt familiar company was a reassurance. I need not have worried.

Our form-master was Mr Ward; a tall, slim, elegant gentleman with the most amazing diction and not a hint of the indiscernible accent I had been dreading. He was quietly spoken and appeared mild and gentle, yet I knew instinctively not to cross him. To be with him at my first secondary school was a privilege; he inspired me to a lifetime of learning for which I shall always be grateful.

The morning proceeded smoothly after the tour of the whole school. We were guided after an introductory assembly to our own classroom; large with a high ceiling, tall narrow windows that let in plenty of light – but also a draught to freeze your toes off! It was an ancient building but had the accompanying atmosphere of Victorian high learning. We had our own desks into which went our books, paper and writing implements; each book neatly inscribed with our own name – I had never owned so much in my life! Mr Ward oversaw the filling of the desks. 'Always to be ready for inspection – they must be kept immaculate' was his ruling. Once completed to his satisfaction, he asked each of us to stand and introduce ourselves to one another; then came his first, and probably only, mistake.

It came to my turn and he said, 'This is Sue, one of the Barnardo girls, please stand.' I did, but my face was burning with anger; I *hated* that.

With determination not to waver, I replied quietly, but in a strong voice, 'Sir, I am *not* a Barnardo girl . . . I just happen to live there.'

His immediate response quelled any other reaction from the class.

'I beg your pardon, Sue, please carry on with your introduction.' I did, but my insides were dancing loops at this extraordinary rude behaviour on my part. At the end of the lesson, he asked me to stay behind.

'Why did you change the terminology I used, Sue?' His tone was soft and inquisitive, rather than accusatory.

I stretched to my full height, looked at him very determinedly, carefully chose my words and replied, 'Because I do not see myself as one, or part of them. I am *me*, Sir. I've made myself as far as I'm concerned because I can't bear what they stand for; I want to be the same as the outside kids, not them.' Then the most amazing thing happened: he shook my hand! 'I understand all of that as an explanation and I apologise again.' He smiled a big boyish grin and said, 'We are going to get along very well.'

I left the class to join the others in the playground utterly elated. I felt then I was going to love the school, and would do my utmost not to let these people down.

Pamela was standing at the side of the play area, positively bursting to know what I'd said. When I told her, she was both amazed and happy for me. We then made a pact: at school we would get on, learn, and enjoy it.

As we ambled around getting to know our new surroundings, one of the teachers approached. 'Are you Susan Davis?' My heart sank. I assured him, with pseudo-confidence, that I was. 'Well I am the sports master. One of your friends has said you are a good runner.'

My heart was buoyed back to its rightful place. 'I absolutely *love* running,' I responded with great enthusiasm.

'Right, lunchtime tomorrow, prompt, you meet me here with the others; I will have a look and see what we can make of you.'

I hesitated, 'But Sir, I don't have plimsolls yet, they haven't given me any.'

He looked at me kindly. 'See me after you've eaten your lunch, I'm sure we can fix that little problem.' And he did!

Lunch was a wonderful meal, cooked in the school kitchen, fresh and tasty. A pudding followed, then a cup of tea. Pam and I were both full to the brim and left the dining hall together. The afternoon held no more surprises, but passed in a haze of complete joy. Nobody could have had a better first day at a new school. I could hardly wait for the rest to unfold.

One kid had not enjoyed her first day at all. Lucy was a quiet, shy 13-year-old from the North and appeared one day long after we had arrived; she was the classic example of a 'fish out of water'. Clearly middle class and extremely bright, she had previously been to a grammar school; Boagey denied her this, on the grounds of unfair privilege.

Her greater disappointment however was the church; she was a devout Catholic but forced to attend the Church of England along with the rest of us. I had not understood the significance of this but she explained when I found her sobbing in the garden one day. She added that she had managed to slope off to the convent next door when she should have been out with us playing. They had been extremely sad for her and kindly offered to take her with them; Boagey refused. Lucy spent hours with them after that, and we would all 'cover' for her should any of the staff ever enquire. She never told us the reason for being in care and left before the end of the school term. She may have returned to her family, but we unanimously agreed that the nuns got her out.

Mr Dewberry, our Physical Training Instructor, had been in the army and was a superb teacher. He explained he would teach us the techniques of sprint and distance running. He would guide us in the right choice and we were to train to build strength, endurance and good personal times. 'If you don't want to work hard, push off now,' were the words that closed his introduction. Nobody left. He called us 'my runners'. There was a long way to go before that would be an accurate description, but we worked hard at it.

He enquired as to my diet in the Home; totally unimpressed, I was allowed extra milk, delivered daily to the school in one-third pint bottles. Each child should have one bottle per day, but there were a few who refused, hence my additional allowance. My daily consumption was at least three bottles: I loved it. We all trained during first-sitting lunch and were permanently allowed the second sitting; the non-participants greeted this jealously and I soon found out why: there was more food! Miss Booth, head chef, explained there always had to be enough to go round. Sometimes the calculations would be awry, then we would benefit. Frequently offered second helpings, we accepted most graciously! The fact that we didn't put on an ounce of weight was surely due to all the extra physical exercise.

One of the effects of being in the group was an immediate circle of like-minded friends. We were poles apart in all sorts of ways, but bound by the sport. When I had pounded the grounds at Crowborough, I had competed with myself. Without the benefit of a watch or a clock that I could see, I would try, not very successfully, to count as I was going round to see if I was making more speed. The better method I ultimately arrived at was to wait for the staff to shout at the top of their voices for 'six o'clock beds' – heralding the exodus of the youngest – for another call a half hour later for the next lot, and to count the laps I managed during that period. This was a bit more accurate and gave me an indication I was improving my time. It was a pleasant change therefore to compete against the others; I had a permanent feeling that I was one of a group, and they were all *Outsiders* – that was the best bit.

The grounds in which we practised were rather mediocre, but news was circulating: we were on the move. I had not realised, but there was a new school building nearing completion. After the holiday, we would not return to this grand, old – if slightly dilapidated – building, but we were only moving about a mile away. I sought out Mr Ward, having worried for days about the change. I need not have done; he assured me all the present teachers would be moving, and there would even be some new teachers as the intake would increase.

The new school was an impressive place, all concrete and

glass. The modern structure seemed garish at first, compared with the beauty of the old Victorian building. However, the facilities were brilliant: a science lab, metal and woodwork rooms, domestic science kitchen and a fabulous gymnasium.

The grounds were more extensive, affording a far superior area for athletics and games. I was making good progress with my running and slowly bringing down my sprint times. Because at least eight of us were fast, Mr Dewberry even got the contractors to make a sandpit before they moved off site. I had never previously considered long jump, but it was quickly to become not only my best discipline, but also my favourite.

The first event I recall in the new gym was of Mr Dewberry's doing. We were out in the playground when the shout went up, 'Barney!' I did not understand the meaning of this; just ran with the crowd to be nosy. I soon discovered it meant a fight had broken out. Two boys were locked in quite a brawl; we all spurred them on vocally, until a new shout interrupted the fight: 'Disperse *now*, and pack it in, you two.' Mr Dewberry had arrived. He steered them, plus all their form colleagues, into the gym. I was rather pleased at this stage as they were in my class. A small boxing ring was set up and the two boys had to put on proper boxing gloves; Mr Dewberry told them they could now 'do the job properly'.

It was hilarious, and pathetic. They shaped up to one another and just danced around the ring; we all jeered loudly, led by Sir himself, and after a very short space of time, he dismissed them to get a wash before classes resumed.

Besides the training with Mr Dewberry, we also had games lessons with another lovely teacher, Miss Thornton. She was full of infectious enthusiasm and ran around like a two-year-old.

Rounders was definitely my favourite sport; after playing at Crowborough with teams of twenty-a-side, a straight stick and a tennis ball, it was a piece of cake with the correct kit! I could hit the ball out of the park, and my speed made getting a rounder simple. I would call loud encouragement and orders to run and catch all the time, whipping the team into a frenzy. It was marvellous for me when Miss Thornton made me Captain.

We played netball and hockey and I could often be found playing football or cricket with the boys; I just loved sport. During one hockey match, made up of two sides from the school, I took a knock from another kid. She was a stocky girl, bigger than me in all departments; we had both gone down for the ball but her elbow was sticking out. She connected very hard with the side of my head, on the bony bit above my eyebrow. I went down; then got back on to my feet quickly, but the whole pitch was swimming. This caused great consternation, not least because an enormous egg had rapidly appeared on my head. They took me to First Aid to be bathed in cold compresses and I missed the rest of that day's lessons – and Miss Thornton gave me a lift back to the Home.

I would remember this incident and put it to advantageous use in the future.

We spent lessons in the gym when it was too wet outside. Miss Thornton was incredibly fit and she created assault courses that seriously challenged even the fittest of us: up and down the ropes, balancing on upturned benches, lifting and running with the medicine ball and hanging upside down on the parallel bars. Once her lesson was over you were puffed out and trembling; and in no doubt at all about having worked extremely hard.

I held the honour of being the only one in the whole school who could go up and down all sixteen ropes without a break. Even Miss Thornton was impressed.

~ 18 ~

My twelfth birthday was the first one celebrated at St Anne's. At Crowborough, the celebrations hadn't amounted to much; there were sixty birthday arrangements to be made there every year, but it was different here as we weren't so many.

Irrespective of the actual day on which your birthday fell, the party was always on a Saturday. I didn't really understand why, but I had built this one up quite a bit; a greater realisation of growing up? First one in a new Home? More awareness from the others because the place was so small? Best wishes from so many at school? I could not decide on just one reason but I was really looking forward to the big day. I had noticed other kids still had to do their work, and so it was for me; in fact, the whole day was normal until teatime – then the excitement began.

I gratefully received my card in the post from the ever-faithful Round Table, and another from 'All at the Home'. My parcel, wrapped in pretty paper, also from the Round Tablers, was placed beside my plate – but to build up the tension, this had to wait until tea was finished. Miss Smith had made sandwiches, a treat only served for birthdays, and there was an apple each. The birthday cake would arrive much later, after we had played the games.

As I excitedly opened my package, everyone sang 'Happy Birthday'. I was thrilled that they managed to extend the 'Sue' over the two syllables, and not revert to Susan.

Many factors made up the excitement of the day, cleverly stretched out to make it last. Probably best of all was that everybody could join in; unlike Crowborough when the function was exclusive to just the kids who shared the same playroom. Even Miss Smith came when she had finished in the kitchen. We had all left the table, finished the clearing up, and Miss Plesance sat at the piano, warming up for the games and songs. She had a real sense of fun; she revelled in these occasions, and would show off her obvious skill and prowess on this out-of-tune instrument.

I undid my present: a large tray of boiled sweets, individually wrapped, brightly coloured and called 'Silmos Lollies'. I handed them round, starting with Miss Plesance as she was the only Staff there. I proceeded to everyone else, then from behind me came Boagey's unbelievably rude voice, loudly shouting, 'You are a *pig*, Susan Davis . . . you have just had tea and you are already stuffing yourself with sweets.' I tried to say I hadn't even had one for myself. Miss Plesance tried to say the same . . . but it was no use. At full volume Boagey screamed, pointing to the door, 'Get yourself upstairs to bed.'

Almost total silence fell on the group – *my* birthday party, but except for some very quietly murmured dissent, there was no arguing. I knew instinctively not to cross her so I swept past, staring angrily. I stomped noisily up the stairs in a fearsome temper, washed myself and got into bed. Although close to rage at the disappointing ruin of my much anticipated day, I was also close to tears and lay there alone in the dark, waves of self-pity and anger flooding over me. Deep inside was the resentment that I had received nothing from my so-called mother again. Auntie Dodd and Uncle Tom had always sent something, but that was long ago now. Thinking of them had pushed me to the edge. I had a lump in my throat, and the pain inside was there again: *God . . . why me? Why do I have to have this for a life? What had I done at two years old to be locked up in here? Why did Boagey make me come here with her?*

Then I thought more clearly and said to myself, *I hate you, Boagey, you old cow*. That made me feel better! I could hear the party games and fun still going on downstairs; amazing to think they were having my birthday celebrations without me!

Suddenly I heard a noise along the landing. I froze with fear and begged silently, *Please . . . not on my birthday*. Someone dashed in, shoved something into my bed, and dashed away with the same haste. I quickly looked up at the fleeing figure – Miss Plesance! I gingerly removed whatever she had left – it was a piece of my cake! I could not believe it. She had taken the risk, right under Boagey's nose, to do that for me. *Goodbye, blues, I'll be fine*, I decided. I managed to eat the cake without dropping a single crumb in my bed, then sped along the landing myself to go 'to the toilet', in reality flushing the thin paper napkin evidence away.

The following day I managed to stop Miss Plesance for a moment. She had found her 'cake-run' quite exciting – and the other kids were brilliant with their sympathy and kind words. I never did see the remainder of my only present.

Boagey managed to find a reason to send me to bed on my birthday every year thereafter. It was simply one of the many methods she would apply to try and break me. However, knowing it was going to be the inevitable conclusion to my day, it was never as shocking to me after that.

Trying to 'get back' at Boagey was, without doubt, one of the most enjoyable pursuits we undertook, for most of the time this was achieved without any awareness by her. I had wondered frequently about the actual intellectual capability of this woman, and had at one time concluded that she was naive – but later decided she was simply thick!

She seemed not to have the capacity to see what was going on right under her nose – and seemed to have no apparent ability to work things out for herself. The classic example of this was her much-vaunted 'fines' system versus pocket money. She failed utterly to see that I was taking the Mickey out of her; showing her up as a fool (to me anyway) when I 'lost' my pocket money each week. She just could not get beyond her propensity for punishment and bullying and a great deal of our mocking and leg-pulling went clean over her head. The most satisfactory way to get at her though was to make her *see* what was going on, to have her fully realise, be in no doubt at all of what we were doing – that was the name of the game.

The mail was popped through the letterbox and fell into the porch. If you were passing, it was expected you would bring it in and put it on the table in the hall. One Saturday one of the kids came up to where we were cleaning. 'Don't all go at once, but go and look at the top letter on the mail pile.' I was first off the mark and came back doubled up. I explained the joke to the rest so we would not draw attention to it by all trooping

downstairs. Boagey's initials were I T, and whoever had brought
in the mail had prefixed this with S H. We never did find out
who it was – but then there was a houseful of possible suspects,
including the staff.

My own experience with the mail had a less immediate effect;
I needed to bide my time. One day I had picked up the letters
and one had come with her name typed out in full. I placed this
under the rest so nobody else would see it.

One day during the school summer holidays we were having
lunch, when for no reason whatsoever Boagey called out my
name to get my attention, then shouted, 'Why don't you sit up
straight and stop eating like a pig?' I was proud of my manners
and was livid at this criticism. My temper erupted. I slammed
down my cutlery and stood up, noisily pushing my chair rattling
into the kid behind me. With equal noise I slammed it back
under the table and stormed off.

She screamed after me, 'Come back here, *Pauline Susan
Davis.*'

Oh, yes . . . at last! I thought, with such a deep sense of anticipated satisfaction.

'Sod off, *Irene Troebe Boagey,*' I responded, nearly as loudly as
she had addressed me.

The only thing I missed was the expression on her face upon
hearing this now very public divulgence.

To have sworn as well was beyond the pale. I didn't know
who was after me, but someone was, and I had no desire to find
out. I tore through the hall and out of the boiler room door. I
ducked down as I passed the kitchen window and ran out into
the yard; past the sheds, up a drainpipe and to safety on the shed
roof. I had seen this little spot ages ago and had tried it out
before. Once up there I knew I could not be seen, but I was
taking no chances. I was next to the convent; a high wall divided
the gardens, but now on the shed roof I was level with it. I

crawled on top and then jumped to the ground; a soft landing on to leaves that had fallen from the overhanging trees. I was safe now but decided to make the most of the aggravation anyway; hidden from view under all the shrubbery, I edged towards the gate.

The coast was clear; I climbed over and hurried down the road, crouching behind garden walls. Once past the houses, I ran on a bit further, and threw myself into the bushes bordering the golf course. I lay there absolutely puffed out.

The long-awaited opportunity to *really* get at Boagey had been satisfying beyond words. I knew there would be repercussions but I was totally unperturbed. To be perfectly honest, I was enjoying myself now; it was a new experience being out when I was not supposed to be. A thought occurred to me: I was just over 14 years old and this was the first time in my life I had ever been anywhere alone and without consent; a long time to wait for such an event.

I knew no one could see me, but I rolled over on to my tummy and watched the road, just in case. I rested my chin on my hands and luxuriated in the total freedom of it all.

I have no real idea how long I stayed there, but I decided to make a move and prove to myself that I could get back in without them ever knowing where I had been. Everything was fine until I got to the dividing wall; it was impossible to climb back up! I retraced my steps and ran, crouched down, under our own front garden wall. I then sped in to where the others were playing in the garden, and joined in as if I had been there all the time.

They were great. They explained in detail about the shocked look on Boagey's face; she was puce and looked as if she would explode. It was Devlin who was chasing me apparently, a double satisfaction for me because I had out-run her and escaped. I was giving them little snippets of what I had been up to; we were killing ourselves laughing at these exchanges, then Staff came out and saw me.

'Where have you been?' she enquired, with complete incredulity.

'Nowhere, Miss, I've been playing.'

'Well think yourself lucky Miss Boagey has had to go out; you are in serious trouble, you know.' I just gave her a dirty look and carried on. Boagey was still not back at bedtime; with such a long period of time elapsing before she actually called me to her office, I knew I was safe. Like all the staff, a great deal of what she did was in temper; I had one of her long lectures on manners and obedience, and yet another 'pink slip'. This was the most ridiculous of threats, stemming back to Crowborough and her early regime there. If she considered a punishment was insufficient to deal with the crime, she would add, with some gravity, '*You* are on a pink slip.' This was supposed to be a report sent directly from her to Barnardo's headquarters, to scare us into behaving! We had frequently talked about it amongst ourselves and realised its utter futility; the question 'what would headquarters do?' had a very simple answer: *nothing*. I challenged Boagey on one occasion and asked, 'Are you going to expel me then?' She just looked blankly back at me. I got the impression she was breaking, not me.

I had been in a shop on one occasion and seen on the counter a 'spike' used for safely securing bills and correspondence. I had a mental image thereafter of a similar arrangement at headquarters – but with my name on, where they just stuck the never-ending supply of my slips.

~ 20 ~

I dealt with Devlin in the same way I handled all the people I felt I could not face – I blanked her. They did not register in my vision, even when standing beside me. They could talk, laugh, cry or anything, it made no impression on me whatsoever. I found this easy enough, no skill needed at all, just a bit of mental strength. That was how I managed Devlin. Her attacks on me were horrifying; and I did not think I could take any more of this disgusting behaviour. I had suffered a repeat of the cold sleepless nights; as young as I was, I knew they were having a detrimental effect on my general well-being. I realised I was trapped, and she knew it too. I had no great choice: quite simply, suffer it or deal with it. I decided on the latter.

The inevitable night duly arrived; it was the same as on the previous occasions but this time I was prepared and ready for her. I was only dozing when she knelt at the side of my bed and placed her hand over my mouth. I felt physically sick with the effort I needed to muster my courage and strength to execute my plan.

When I knew that she was kneeling and close enough to touch me, I cautiously brought my right arm up from my side; carefully bending my elbow so that my tightly clenched fist was touching my right shoulder. I mentally checked where she was, and with all my might, threw myself backwards so that the bony part of my elbow hit her.

I was terrified; the shocked, noisy gasp told me I had indeed connected somewhere and she was hurt. Instinctively in response, her clenched fist landed a mighty blow on me.

Then she was gone without another sound. After a short while I sat up to see if anyone had heard or woken up: clearly not. Her punch had landed high on my upper arm and was hurting like hell. Thank God that wasn't the side of my head, I thought. It would have been much more painful for me; the kind of pain she was suffering? Amazingly, after using such force, there was barely any discomfort from my elbow, but it took a while to stop the 'shakes'. This resulted from a mixture of horror and pure adrenalin, and the eventual realisation that she would never ever again visit my bed during her night duty hours. And maybe no one else's either.

The idea to deal in this way with Devlin had come from the bang to my head on the hockey field; that girl had intended no malice whatsoever, it was an accident. However, the excruciating pain and the immediate, swollen bump, made me realise what a weapon the elbow was. Considering the prone position in which I was, the force with which I hit her was amazing, like a strong spring uncoiling its natural tension. I had planned the attack for weeks; sometimes full of confidence, at other times full of terror. I knew I would have just one go at this . . . *if I missed* . . . that was the thought that brought on the terror. I had lain in bed night after night trying to sleep and dreading the next time she would be there; I decided *that* was the greater terror. There was no way I would miss with the additional anger I would feel at her presence.

The following morning she was not at breakfast; I felt elated at the news, though it was dampened because I couldn't tell anyone the reason for her absence, and was completely ignorant of how badly I had hurt her. Wherever I had landed my elbow, it was enough to keep her out of sight for a few days. I wondered what excuse she would give for the injury.

When she did eventually recover and was seen again about the Home, I spoke to her just the once. She had come to the table where we were playing; the others informed her we were doing word games – anagrams.

'And the middle letters in your surname, Miss, spell EVIL.'

I said it in a loud voice with an extremely menacing tone; all eyes were upon me as the whole room fell silent. She made no response and turned away from the table and left the room to prepare supper. I didn't utter another word to her, directly, in the following two years I was there. That was not just a battle won, that was a whole war!

The catering budgets in the Homes weren't up to much; by no means was I kept hungry but there was a feeling when leaving the table of being not *quite* satisfied. We were a boisterous lot and energy was run off at quite a rate; to eat as much as possible at every opportunity was the desired plan.

The most basic of food, bread and butter, presented its own problems, simply due to the lack of it. They cut half a pound of margarine into thirds, then divided that into eight tiny pieces and that was the 'portion' – a very meagre amount. In addition, at breakfast, we would have a spoonful of thin, watered-down red stuff, amusingly referred to as jam. There was, however, plenty of bread and I worked out my own system for maximum pleasure and consumption. On my first slice, I scraped the margarine in the middle and the jam on the outside edge. On the following slice, I reversed the process – jam middle, margarine outside. The maximum I ever achieved was four slices with something on them. (On that particular day, perhaps it was hot and the margarine was more runny than usual.)

Many school pupils called sago pudding 'frogspawn'. We had names for several more desserts. Rice pudding with jam was 'bloody nose', tapioca was 'large lumps', but the best (or worst) was the suet roly-poly. It came from the kitchen on a long narrow plate – a light greyish colour, with a faintly glossy sheen; it just lay there limply. It was known as 'dead man's leg'. Even the custard objected to being in the same dish, and would not stay on top. Our custard was yellow, which was the only clue to its identity; other than that, it rather resembled the water in which one has washed out a brush after watercolouring.

Grace was always said at the beginning and end of each meal. I had decided a long time ago that it would take more than divine intervention to improve things. I had helped a kid back from school one day; she had fallen hard and had a seriously grazed knee. This had made me late but, because I had been helping, I was still allowed my tea. They had already said the opening grace; I sat and ate my meal. Boagey then told me to say the close. Without a waver I said, amusingly I thought, 'For what I have just *about* received may the Lord make me truly thankful.'(As indeed I was.) She went berserk! I had to do loads of extra work and go early to bed.

One situation, however, held little amusement for me. I was cleaning upstairs one Saturday morning, after having done the drains. Wafting up from the kitchen was the most revolting smell. One of the kids said it was spinach, Miss Smith had told her. I had never heard of the stuff, but if it smelt that awful, how bad would it taste? Once at the table when a couple of other kids already had theirs, I decided drastic action was called for; the virtually black, stinking slop was impossible for me to cope with. I could not remember ever refusing anything put in front of me, but this was the limit.

In accordance with protocol, I rose to my feet. I very politely requested, 'Excuse me, Miss Smith, may I please have a small portion of the spinach? Thank you.' Then I sat down.

Boagey was furious. 'You ungrateful little madam; for that you can have a large helping,' she shouted.

'For *what*?' I asked loudly; she did not reply.

The server brought my plate; I could not believe it. In addition to the huge pile of spinach was boiled breast of lamb and two miserable pieces of boiled potato. This was all swimming in the water in which the meat had been boiled. It looked and smelt absolutely disgusting and I was becoming really angry at Boagey's reaction to my politeness to Cook.

I felt the whole situation to be grossly unfair so I pushed the plate a few inches from me, sat back, folded my arms and loudly announced, 'Well, I'm not eating *that*!'

Boagey looked up. 'You will sit there till you do,' she said, gloating with her authority and enjoying the situation enormously.

I stared at her. 'I don't mind if I do,' I replied, calmly and quietly. She seemed rather surprised. She knew I could be very stubborn – but she also knew we were always ready for our food.

My breakfast had consisted of a rasher of streaky bacon, bread and butter and a cup of tea. Thus, after all the routine work in the morning I was starving. In truth, we were always starving at meal times. Today was no exception, but I honestly couldn't face the plateful in front of me; I knew I had been polite, and wanted to stand up to Boagey's unjust punishment. So I sat there defiantly. Pudding and the cup of tea were served to the others; still I sat there with no offer of anything else.

'If you have not eaten that by the time the others are ready to go for a walk, you can stay in.' I shrugged my shoulders in a sulking, silent response.

And that's what happened. They all went out and I sat at the table.

I watched the mess on my plate go through some sort of metamorphosis. The boiled water must have been almost entirely fat. It had covered the plate and was now slowly congealing around the edges. It then began to turn into a grey glue over everything else, moving, it seemed, towards the centre of the plate. One of the staff was sitting with me and I asked her if I could go to the toilet. She went with me, obviously keen I didn't run away again. Then it was back to the table.

Tea was served at the usual time; it was served 'around' me – I still sat with the mess. As they sat down I could feel their eyes staring at me; I defiantly re-folded my arms, made eye contact with no one, kept my head down and stared at the plate. By now the glue had gone a bit wrinkled. A glass of water was brought for me, and when everyone else had finished tea I took my plate to the kitchen, accompanied again of course. I was sorely tempted to make a bolt for it to begin with; but decided instead to bluff her out. I was sent to bed early.

This whole thing was quite ridiculous and grossly unfair; I had been polite. Someone with my appetite would not have asked for less without good reason. Nothing would normally keep me from going out with the others. And if I could not bear the look of it initially, I sure as hell could not eat it after that length of time.

Sunday morning was boiled eggs as usual; but not for me – the plate was there again in front of me. I could see now exactly what Boagey was doing; I decided, 'If you think I'll break first you've got another thought coming.' I discovered I had developed an amazing new sense of smell as far as food was concerned: the eggs, bread and tea smelt wonderful. I was brought another glass of water. My stomach was beginning to ache. This was madness but I had to stick it out now.

After church we always returned to a roast dinner, and when we got back to the Home this time I nearly passed out at the wonderful aroma. I was praying that Boagey would now relent; I really was not feeling well. But, quite clearly, to prove her authority was greater than my stubborn defiance, it was not to be. I sat amidst all those roasts and stared at the horrible – living – plate of food, which had clearly been left out of the fridge and in the warmest place possible and was now covered in a blue hairy coating. I had another glass of water and was not allowed to go to Sunday school – she must have worried that I'd run away; she was right. I sat again and studied my plate while the others went out. I had hardly spoken a word in 24 hours except to ask for the toilet. I had not moaned or complained at all. I was determined not to show any weakness, it had gone on for too long for me to give up now.

To have the same at tea was no surprise, nor was being sent to bed early again.

To come down to Monday morning breakfast – and it was there *again* – beggared belief. The plate now not only looked odious, it was high. The only concession, before leaving for school, was a cup of tea which I thought for a moment was going to come back up.

Now my stomach really hurt, it felt bruised. I had a headache and my eyes were swimming. The others were marvellous as we walked to school. Pam said even the staff were upset, especially Miss Plesance. Pam had hoped to pinch something from the table or kitchen – but hadn't had an opportunity.

Once in school I had to pass the lab to reach my classroom. I think it was the smell of the Bunsen burners, particularly after being closed up all weekend. Whatever it was I nearly passed out; I leant against the corridor wall. People gathered round and poor Pam began crying. When Miss Percy the science teacher arrived, a mass of voices met her, each trying to explain what was going on. By now the audience was huge. Miss Percy asked for quiet and for Pam to tell her what had happened. She said, in almost a shout, 'Boagey has stopped Sue having anything to eat since Saturday breakfast.' There was an audible gasp from the crowd – which would have pleased me more if I hadn't felt so bad.

It was arranged that I should go straight to Mr Hall, the Head. He did not say he was disgusted; he didn't have to. He immediately asked Miss Booth to bring in toast and tea for me. I had it in his office with a warning not to rush, or I would bring it back. The second lot was better than the first and I quickly felt a lot better.

He said I was to stay there for the morning, and have lunch with him. I occupied my time by learning how to properly file papers, etc. and did so with great enthusiasm. Lunch was Miss Booth's own steak pie, potatoes and vegetables, followed by pudding and a cup of tea. I don't think any other meal has ever tasted quite like it.

The maddest thing about this bizarre scenario was when I returned after school; the plate had gone, tea was served as usual and not a word was said. I guessed, but never found out, that the Head must have contacted Boagey from school. She would have been fully aware I would eat there, *and* would, at the first opportunity, inform everyone we could about what had transpired. Whatever the reason, I had shown to her, and proved to myself, a rapidly developing toughness to her horrible treatment. 'I beat you that time, Boagey – only just – but that's another victory to me.'

According to Boagey, my behaviour inside the Home, my constant battling against her, made me 'borstal material'. I could be defiant, aggressive, belligerent and had a terrible temper. However, in my defence, I felt I was treated like human garbage; *treat me like an animal . . . I shall respond accordingly*, was how I evaluated the situation. Boagey had once referred to me as a 'guttersnipe'. I angrily retorted that, if I was, Barnardo's was responsible; they had raised me. That seemed to shut her up and she did not say it again.

The contrast at school was amazing. I was obedient, attentive and polite – but the teachers were always polite – and my own manners were something of which I was proud. I was highly regarded on the sports field, and was a diligent, responsive student in class. I wasn't entirely a paragon of virtue, but not far off. The Head was empathetic and probably far more aware of the situation in the Home than I had first thought; my form teacher, Mr Ward, well, he was simply wonderful. I was constantly presented with the conundrum of feeling like two completely different people; my evaluation after the Seaford holiday had partly resolved that for me. It was Boagey and the Home, I concluded, who had brought this other side out in me.

As I had been moved around so frequently I had been to many different schools. This had made some subjects quite difficult to grasp. For instance, at one school they would be covering Roman Britain, at the next it would be the Tudors, or I could be studying the Aboriginals in Australia, then suddenly shift to life on the Nile Delta.

When I was about nine years old, and in yet another new school, I was forced, along with the other kids, to completely revise the times tables; learnt initially by rote, these were deeply ingrained in our memory. We had been taught to place the common denominator first – not in the centre – the reverse of the new teacher, Mr Adamson's method. I remember well the feeling of humiliation having to stand in front of the whole class and recite these tables, and his sarcasm should I ever slip up – which I did frequently. I did not actually feel victimised because of being in the Home, but the experience did not assist in the integration I so longed for in the world outside.

Because of these unsettling changes – although I enjoyed school and learning – I constantly struggled. There was one thing I quickly realised with enormous relief: English had a constancy that never changed. Spelling, grammar and so on were the same wherever I went; even Mr Adamson couldn't take the 'H' out of adhesive or turn a comma into a full stop. I was extremely lucky, therefore, that Mr Ward taught me English as well as being my form teacher. We already had a brilliant rapport, but my love of his subject enhanced this.

One day, we had all gone, as a class, to an Elizabethan

pageant, and then had to return and write an essay on the experience. To be perfectly honest I had been bored stupid by the whole thing – but I set about the essay, describing the magnificent country house gardens in which the play was set; the actors in their beautiful costumes depicting the period; the rich tones of the speeches. I then closed by saying, 'I know the audience enjoyed it, because they both clapped.' Well, I was only 13 and I thought it was amusing. Once these papers had been marked some days later, Sir asked me to come to the front of the class. I had to read out my essay. I did so with confidence, and when I reached the end I hesitated slightly, and then delivered the punchline for maximum effect. I was delighted when everyone burst out laughing! Except Sir; he explained how and when to apply humour. He did not consider such sophisticated subject matter should be belittled in this way: he was right of course; I was suitably contrite.

Mr Ward asked me to stay behind when the class disbanded. He informed me he had read out the piece to the other staff; they had also found it amusing. 'Your sense of humour and fun will see you through in this world, Sue; just keep it to the appropriate places!'

I often tried to apply humour to otherwise miserable situations. Frequently interest was shown about the Home and why we had to live there. I briefly explained my own situation, which caused a dreadful outburst of sympathy from one of the girls; that was a sentiment I, and the others, hated. To cheer her, and change the subdued atmosphere, I cheerfully informed her that when I was born, my mother wasn't even there! We all laughed our heads off and she quickly realised her compassion, though sweet, was misplaced.

School was quite definitely my salvation. As I passed my fourteenth birthday, I was extremely aware of the difference it had made. With the other runners, a good collection of school friends and the caring school staff around me, I had grown in confidence. I learnt more control and honed my calculating skills to advantage against the Home staff. I now had an adult mind with growing confidence to match. I was beginning to feel I had won my war.

~ 22 ~

Being called to Boagey's office now was both infrequent and far
less intimidating. Infrequent simply because of the geography of
the place – she was always in our midst. Less intimidating because,
quite simply, she did not worry me anymore. All the bullying was
in the past because I was now so much stronger and I had shown
her on numerous occasions I would take whatever she threw at
me. One day, when she was about to set upon me yet again for
no apparent reason, I said to her, quietly, but with menace, 'The
Tower.' She still proceeded with one, rather pathetic, slap across
my head but I knew instinctively it would be the very last. She
knew I had beaten her; the tables had turned and I was now the
one with the control. A sense of enormous pride and relief came
over me. After years of waiting, at last I had triumphed.

For this reason, it came as something of a surprise when I was
called to her office one morning. She sat with all the authority
of a lump of lard, corsets creaking, and digging the arm of her
glasses in her ear, as was her wont. She repulsed me: I hated
having to be in the same confined space with her.

'You will be fifteen in July,' she announced. 'You will be
leaving school – and here – because your mother wants you to
go home to her.'

I could not have felt more pulled apart. My first response was
to the words '*and here*'. I would – at last – be leaving the Home.
However, this was quickly tempered by the realisation that I was
to leave school.

From the time we first start infants' to the last day of our final term, we attend school in the knowledge that we are working to leave. I suddenly realised how safe school had made me feel; the thought of leaving – being without it – worried me greatly. This ran parallel with the absolute joy that surged through me upon hearing I was leaving Barnardo's. My feelings were swinging like a pendulum.

I went to the dividing wall by the sheds. I did not run away this time, I sat alone with my thoughts. I leant back against the wall, hugging my knees.

Ultimately, Boagey had failed to beat me. *I have won, have I not?* I thought, with a wide grin on my face. Even her physical punishments had never brought overt tears. There had been hundreds of occasions when she had administered a beating causing real pain, but she rarely had the satisfaction of seeing me cry; the terrifying attack in the Tower was the only exception. I had cried my first night at Babies' Castle and I recalled a member of staff telling a weeping infant that 'Now I'll give you something to cry for' just before a hard walloping. The answer – however difficult, and at times it was – was to never give them the excuse. I had perfected this in three Homes by the time I got to Boagey; she had never seen me cry. I had achieved this by keeping tears to the secrecy of my bamboo bush, when my emotions could take no more. Now even her physical beatings had stopped.

From a mental point of view, she had no chance. There had indeed been times, when I was much younger, when something had occurred that had left me dreadfully confused. I had no idea, for instance, why I had been shaken and despised by Warren; why I had been attacked in that sluice room; why Boagey had given me the dreadful beating. These situations were beyond my comprehension. Thus I taught myself not to try to calculate the incalculable; these actions simply became wrong or ridiculous, but not for my mind to try and fathom why. I often thought about this propensity to attack and demean; I had tried to put some sort of perspective on to it, always to no avail.

Then I thought about Uncle Tom and Auntie Dodd and was *instantly* aware of the terrible damage Boagey had caused – immediately I felt the familiar searing pain run through me. To have no more opportunity to see these dear people was tragic, but the vicious venom in the *manner* she had delivered that news, *there* was the damage. As I thought these things, the pain increased and frightened me. The lump came back to my throat, my heart was beating far too fast and my face was burning; that was it – *that* was the damage over which I had no control. I drew my knees up to my chest, moved my arms forward and lowered my head to rest upon them, and tried to relax until the emotional surge had passed. I now knew that at the mere recollection of the two most beautiful people in the entire world, I would crumple. I hoped that my strength would somehow, one day, lessen the painful feelings and I would get better. If I kept to myself the deep feelings I held for Uncle Tom and Auntie Dodd; if I could manage to not make reference to them to anyone (which I had done up to now), no one would know about my pain. I felt extremely fortunate, as unlike physical and mental damage, the emotional does not show.

*

As I sat there with all these thoughts careering around my head, something else occurred to me. 'Your mother wants you to go home to her,' Boagey had said. Blimey, I wonder what that will mean, I thought. I decided there was little point in continuing to think along those lines. In 12 years, I had seen her once and had never even had a letter. My only positive thought was that this was my ticket out of Barnardo's. That was sufficient reason to be optimistic and try to look forward.

But leaving school would be a completely new experience. The obvious, accepted result was that I *would* ultimately finish my education – but that was not the key change for me. What was important, and refreshingly new, was the fact that for the first time in my life, a change was occurring in the *future*. Before now, changing Homes, schools, friends, and especially losing the Dodds, all these things had been thrust upon me, in the moment. None of these had been a *future event*; they happened as you were told, no time to think about what they meant. This was an entirely new experience for me.

My ambivalence to being 'wanted' by my mother was startling. When I looked ahead, there was a 'nothing' feeling – a vacuum. I had made very cautious approaches to the ordinary kids at school, those who lived with their parents. I had asked a few tentative questions; what they did after school, on Sundays and so on. Did they have chores to do around the house? Did they have their own bedrooms? Make their own beds? However, I seemed to get a different answer from each one. I had passed remarks to the teachers in whom I felt a trusting closeness, but I was getting no clear picture in my mind as to what a future living with my mother might actually be like.

Dear Mr Ward came up with the help I was seeking, though completely by accident. We had had a debating forum during the school year. This had proved to be not only informative but also extremely popular. All manner of subjects were covered and the debating had been lively, with Mr Ward in the chair.

Six weekly meetings held during the English lesson was the established format. Once we knew when these were starting, we had the opportunity to put 'topic' suggestions into the box on Sir's desk. He then decided on the subject, ensuring that it would be within the range of our debating skills. He gave notice to whomever was being chosen on a particular day, but no one else knew who was the proposer *or* what the topic was until the lesson opened.

Mr Ward had told me, with the accepted pledge of secrecy, that my turn was due next, so I should prepare. When the day eventually arrived, nerves nearly got the better of me, but I couldn't have let everyone down, especially Sir. The meeting was conducted in a strictly correct and formal manner that was insisted upon by Mr Ward, to create the gravitas required for a serious debate. 'What is Family?' was my proposal. Mr Ward opened the debate, and by way of introduction, loosely covered the animals-in-the-wild bit, but said we had to move on to more specifics. I was then able to ask direct questions.

Standing up in front of the class held no fears for me at all; I had thought a great deal about what I wanted to ask and learn. The feeling of 'nerves' came about because I had no idea how to begin. I realised I was more worried than I first imagined about exposing my *complete* ignorance of what I was trying find out. That suddenly made me feel vulnerable and exposed, like walking naked down a busy street.

I made a rather stuttering start and after a very short space of time, Sir halted proceedings. 'We are making no progress for Sue, I can tell from her expression,' he announced. He then explained that we were not moving forward because I had no idea of what questions to ask. I was beginning to feel extremely foolish and wishing I had never proposed a topic in the first place.

He was exactly right about the questions. I *wanted* to ask about mothers, what they did to make a happy home and would mine make me happy when I left Barnardo's, but I started to quail inside. This was becoming quite ridiculous; I was 14 and my ignorance was staggering. My hesitation did not pass unnoticed.

Mr Ward then addressed the room. 'Can anyone in class, who

does not live at the Barnardo's Home, stand up now and tell us the names of all the staff who work there?'

Silence . . . *a beautiful golden silence*. I turned my head and gave him the broadest smile ever, in my utter relief and understanding at what he had just illustrated: they were as ignorant of my existence as I was of theirs. What a very clever, kind man he was.

Settled now and encouraged by the illustration of their ignorance of *my* environment, I continued with confidence. I knew she was my mother. She was a widow. Her name was Mrs Davis. That was it. After the initial surprise at this dearth of knowledge, a full discussion took place.

It became established that one of the first things that made a family was its *history*, the hereditary factors, achievements and ideals that bind the kin together; I simply did not have that. I told the forum I had met this so-called family only once, and that meeting was with my mother, her partner and my three brothers. I had seen a distinct likeness between us children; we all had the same thick, jet-black hair and we all loved sport. I said I had an elder sister, and that I thought her name was Mary but was not sure; a few other names had been mentioned but I did not really know who they were talking about. Whether there was an extended family of grandparents and other relatives I didn't know. Other than the meeting at the seaside, I had no other contact, not even letters. I could not tell them my mother's age; but did remember two of the boys were older than me and the other younger.

I added detail to their direct questions about how I lived in the Home, compared with their 'family life'. I had drawn some comparisons when I had asked questions in the playground; they were astonished with my explanations of some of the differences between the Home and their family life. Things like us not owning anything, not even our clothes, brought audible gasps of surprise from the girls. Mr Ward stopped their questions on punishment; nearly all recalled the spinach affair and he said that perfectly illustrated some of what we coped with.

As a topic it was well received, and I was fascinated with the direction the debate was taking; the girls had one strong set of opinions and the boys had another. After heated debate, it was unanimously agreed that none of my classmates would want to be sent back to someone who had abandoned them, and they would want to question the motive for why their parent would want them back. One had said she would hate a mother who had abandoned her as much as she would have hated the abandonment itself. I told them I had at times felt that, especially at Christmas and birthdays when there was, once again, no acknowledgement from her. This had caused those days to pass without significance for me, and each time I had felt pushed further and further away until my abandonment also became isolation.

The boys decided that my mother wanted me back because I was old enough to work. They laughed when I said, 'I suppose there is some relief at not being a boy and being expected to go up chimneys.'

One of the boys had spoken passionately about his dad being almost unable to wait for him to leave school and get a job. Conscription was ending, and his family needed his financial contribution. He already had his apprenticeship arranged; he was going to be a butcher. I was surprised at how many knew the direction in which they were heading. I got a degree of genuine understanding when I explained I didn't even know where my home would be; let alone what work I might do.

At the end of the debate, I thanked them sincerely; my topic had been so thoroughly discussed that I felt much more relaxed and informed about my future. I had a feeling of immense satisfaction that the subject had been so well received.

When I returned to my desk, Mr Ward thanked me for the

proposal and the class for a full and lively lesson. 'Don't end it there, though, any of you. Keep the theme going because you will meet many more people with the same difficulties Sue has experienced.' I no longer felt afraid or embarrassed at discussing these issues – or my ignorance of 'normal' family life – and conversations went on quite naturally after that.

The rest of the term – my last – passed pretty much in the usual way but I found myself faced with a three-way dilemma. I was dreading leaving the comfortable safe environment the school had provided, I was *longing* to get out of the Home, but the future was something that I found quite frightening. I decided on a course of action. I would make the most of every moment I spent at school. I would continue to treat the Home with the utter contempt it deserved. I would not give any more thought or attention to the future; it was an unknown quantity so to deliberate on it would do no good at all.

Amid all this, my fifteenth birthday had come and gone. There was yet again no card or letter from my mother. That surprised me particularly this year, as it was to be my last one in care. She had ignored many milestones; but I had anticipated this one would perhaps have been recognised and celebrated. I tried to let the situation go without too much disappointment, but I was pretty fed up. I undid the parcel of sweets from the dear Round Table club; I gave these to the other kids without even opening them, turned and walked upstairs. Once in the dorm, I lay on top of my bed (strictly against the rules) stretched out with hands behind my head, outwardly very relaxed. Boagey arrived in no time at all, demanding to know what I thought I was up to. I moved myself up on to one elbow and stared her full in the face.

'For every birthday that I can recall, you've had the pleasure of sending me to bed. This year I have chosen to come by myself.'

She went puce, her chins shook, and then she left without a word, utterly exasperated. I lay back down. My feeling of total control over her was bliss.

Miss Plesance did not try to smuggle any cake up this time – but her 'you were *naughty*' the following day was definitely said with guarded admiration.

*

My last day at school arrived; I felt I had been on countdown for the whole term but now it was here. Even though my future held so much hope, I shed a few tears as I went around saying my goodbyes. After eating my last lunch, I went in to see Miss Booth. She was always a happy cheery lady, and she laughed at the reference to my appetite; and accepted graciously my thanks for all her cooking. 'Especially the steak pie when you hadn't eaten all weekend, aye?' she reminded me, with a knowing wink

'Oh, that was the best ever,' I assured her.

At the end of the day's lessons, I went to my beloved gymnasium to say my farewells to Mr Dewberry and Miss Thornton. They took me into their office and handed me, metaphorically at least, a gold medal. They explained that they had, after discussing my attributes and achievements, both agreed that I could get into Loughborough University and become a teacher of games and RE – Religious Education. They added it was the finest teaching establishments of its kind; I had never felt as proud. I thanked them for all they had done for me.

Mr Ward was at his desk in the form room. I told him there was no other room anywhere at present that gave me the same feeling of belonging and security. 'Because you love the subject and have done well,' he suggested. He shook my hand and wished me well with so much warmth and sincerity. I told him, from my first day with him, how much his instruction and guidance had meant to me, adding, 'I will never forget you Sir,' and in reply he beamed that grin I would also never forget.

I passed the Maths master en route in one of the corridors. 'Bye, Sir,' I said cheerily, not the slightest bit sorry I had received my last lesson. Poor chap just addressed me with a wan smile; clearly with no more regrets than I had about my imminent departure from his class. He was a nice chap and probably a good teacher; I just hated his subject.

Mr Hall, the Head, was the last one to see. I sat opposite him as I had done on numerous occasions; he had always been such a kind, sensitive man. He assured me he had a considerable understanding, more than I would ever know, of what I had survived; and had complete confidence in what I would go on to achieve with the same fortitude. I thanked him sincerely for his understanding patience with me, especially when I had found myself floundering with confusion and hurt. He offered his hand; I shook it, then left his office, and his school, for the very last time.

Dorothy and I were leaving; the walk back was unusually quiet and subdued, each thinking our own thoughts. We had never relied upon one another in this sort of situation – and today would be no different. I felt a deep sense of regret at it being my last day; but the manner in which I had left, the wonderful comments I had heard, gave me a new confidence. They made me feel – for the first time – like a mature and worthwhile person: a budding adult. I left with an enormous sense of loss but with a growing sense of optimism.

The summer holidays were upon us, but there were no breaks away arranged here, like there had been at Crowborough. We were now, with Boagey in total autonomous control, never allowed outings, not even to a friend from school. St Anne's was too small to afford us any sort of freedom or privacy. We still had our walk on Saturday afternoons to look forward to and we went in a group to the town or the beach, but a member of staff always attended. I could never see the point of going into town; Miss might pop into a shop, but looking in windows without having any intention of buying, well, to me that seemed plain daft.

Rules changed when we turned fifteen: there were four of us and we were allowed to go out on our own. The town was out of bounds but that was fine; we always went down to the beach, about a mile away.

Boagey had 'learnt' from some unknown source that I had been seen running up and down the sand dunes. She immediately banned me from doing this; no reason was given, just a ban. In my mind I was 'training'; building up the strength in my legs, and there was nowhere else to run freely. This ban was hugely disappointing; we were also banned from 'paddling on the water's edge'. When she announced this, she had not included 'swimming in the deep'; oh, I was *so* tempted. We were aware though, as at Crowborough, that everyone knew who we were or at least where we lived; and chances were they would report even the slightest misdemeanour.

One of Boagey's many rules was no cycling, but, returning from school one day, she had met us with a blasting shout, clearly enraged. 'And what have you lot been doing riding *bikes*?' We looked at one another in absolute amazement; we had been seen – and reported in less than an hour! Whoever it was must have been out in a car and seen us as they drove by. We had been on the road outside of the school and still in school hours; I looked at the others again and decided to be the one to explain. 'Cycling Proficiency training, Miss, you had a letter last week.' She stormed into her office in an embarrassed rage and we ran down to the cloakroom choking with stifled laughter.

Her bans and petty rules, this spiteful reporting invariably without substance, all made the 'goldfish bowl' syndrome feel worse. I realised I was growing up fast: my surroundings were stifling me. I had left school, I knew I was leaving the Home; I just wanted to get on with it and the rest of my life. And then, at long last, my final day at the Home arrived.

I was summoned to the office; my heart was thumping with anticipation. I knew that it would be to explain my travel arrangements and the exact time of my now much-needed departure. 'London and home' . . . I had often repeated that to myself, and begun to feel quite excited at the prospect over the last few weeks. Now school was behind me and my departure was imminent I was more prepared. With the hanging around and waiting, the days had dragged by; it seemed an eternity since I left but I felt I belonged not at all to the Home; it would be good to end the feeling of being in limbo.

Boagey told me to sit down on the chair facing her desk. It was a tiny room and I found it stifling. *I just want to go!* I thought in frustration. I watched in silence as she shuffled the papers in front of her and arranged them into a tidy pile. There was a pause; she removed her glasses and sat forward a little. Without preamble, she then said deliberately and clearly, 'Your mother does not want you yet; you are to stay for another year.'

Some seconds passed before my senses returned; I'm sure my mouth must have dropped open. I stared at the wall beyond her; and yet could see her gloating triumphal expression and hear it in her voice. Once again, life had turned around on me completely, and delivered yet another crushing, knock-out blow.

I was not going to be able to think straight sitting there. Without a word or a glance at her gloating, revolting face, I stood and rattled my chair into the wall behind me – and left. My temper was building alarmingly.

I stood confused in the hall, like a cornered animal; playroom to the left, staffroom to the right, upstairs out of bounds, all the kids out in the garden, nowhere to go. I was feeling desperate. I had to find somewhere to be on my own. My thoughts seemed to be tumbling into chaos; I looked behind me and against the office wall was the enormous wardrobe that housed our Sunday church coats. There was a small space between it and the corner. I slid in and slumped down; managing completely to hide away to allow my rage to go and my senses to return.

I recalled being addressed in that exact manner once before. Boagey had had the same gloating expression on her face as when she had told me I would never see Uncle Tom and Auntie Dodd again. Nothing could have been more devastating than that, but this was a close second.

All I could think was: *I'm unwanted again*.

After my joyous last day I would have to return to school, and worst of all, I had another year to survive that objectionable apology for humanity who had sat before me and delivered yet another shattering disappointment. Under the circumstances, I demonstrated the most incredible control. I do not think the full impact penetrated through the initial shock; I had got up and walked out in a temper but without any questions or protestations. I like to think that sickened her.

~ 23 ~

The other kids were fantastic, they soon lifted my spirits and I didn't stay downhearted for long. I was getting used to the continuing disappointments that seemed to punctuate my life; there was nothing I could do about it, so why stay down? The shock of this new revelation was devastating but also universal: the other kids felt for me, but, of course, they were fully aware it could happen to them.

Since term ended a couple of the others had already left, unceremoniously and without emotion. It seemed awful afterwards that although we lived together in such close surroundings, we knew next to nothing about each other. Kids came and went with amazing regularity all year long; turned fifteen, left school and then leaving the Home was by no means the norm. Some simply went to other Homes as Barnardo's loved to do; a shame they hadn't moved me out of this dump. My main concern was what would happen to those who had no family waiting. Where did they go? I must admit to this not taking up an enormous amount of my time, but I did consider it as a worse option than mine, perhaps. I always said we were being groomed as 'downstairs maids' like in the Dickens era; perhaps that's what they were doing now. At one time the number of ex-Homes kids employed in grand houses was staggering.

The onset of another new term at school took on a surrealism all its own. Despite the many let downs in the past, I couldn't have expected this in a million years. The feeling of incredulity had lasted through the remainder of the holidays and now here I was, walking back down the familiar road to school, as I had first done when I was 12.

As I entered the familiar playground, Jeanette, the Head Girl from last term, approached me. 'Will you go straight to Mr Hall's office?' she asked, quietly and kindly. I made my way, relieved to be away from the hundreds of pairs of eyes I felt were upon me. Everyone had known I was leaving – or rather had left – so I was glad to be whisked off while they had the chance to digest the news that I had come back to school.

Making my way through the building brought a lump to my throat. I had said goodbye to all of this and the reality of being back was deeply unsettling. When I entered his office, Mr Hall stood up and came around from behind the desk. I could not look him in the face and stood in front of him with my head bowed, staring at the floor. He lifted his hand and put a finger under my chin, gently raising my head so that I had to look him in the face. He had tears in his eyes. I was amazed and felt my own tears well up; with that he gave me a warm hug. 'Oh Sue, you must have been dreading today.' Sobbing quietly now, I nodded silently.

He escorted me gently to a chair and returned to his side of the desk. He explained that Boagey had told him, about four weeks before, and he could dispense now with all the questions I must have been asking myself: 'What will the school do with me, where will I be put for an additional year?' There was no problem; the school had been granted a new top form facility, and I was to be part of it!

That was why Jeanette was there, and David the Head Boy, plus a couple of other students from my old year. This was – at last – a lucky break. From crawling back not half an hour ago, I now found myself in an enviable position of privileged learning.

Mr Hall explained that I was to study a one-year business course. I would learn to type, do Pitman's shorthand and learn ledger work and bookkeeping. 'If you never go into an office to work, that will not matter at all. All our learning is eventually valuable and useful; just enjoy it.' He promised there would be many privileges that we, as a form, would enjoy and which would differentiate us from the rest of the school. I thanked him profusely.

'One other thing still to do,' he announced, and then pinned on my chest my old prefect's badge; I looked down at the familiar gold lettering on the shining green background. I looked back up at him and positively beamed with relief and pride.

'I remember the first time you did that, Sir, and in the same term being made up to captain of the Rounders team.'

'And being made librarian young lady . . . and playing solo violin on the school stage. You always worked hard, Sue; you deserved all you achieved. I am very proud and pleased to have you back at school . . . and so must you be as well.'

I left Mr Hall thinking that this was going to be a great year and I would not waste a minute of it. Jeanette was in the corridor. I had hardly noticed her in previous terms. She was always 'doing something' with music or in the library then; but now she seemed to be more of a colleague as she was also doing the business course; we were not mere school kids anymore. She had her Head Girl badge back on; as we met, we held forward our badges in a flaunting gesture and showed them off to each other, grinning widely. She rushed towards me, hooked her arm in mine and we laughed together in mutual celebration.

She was very much more informed about the new system than I had been; I had no idea what this year was going to bring. It turned out there had been a parents' meeting during the holidays; Boagey had apparently sent in apologies for my absence. Jeanette informed me of Mr Hall's obvious anger at this; he had immediately allotted her to be my mentor until I had settled in again. I told her I found it a complete irony that the school knew I was staying another year before I did; that was what had angered Mr Hall, she said. We made our way to the cloakrooms, chattering fifteen to the dozen, and then attended assembly.

The hymns and prayers were over and Sir asked the new top form to take the stage. He re-introduced the Head Boy and Girl, and then told the new pupils the responsibilities borne by us with prefects' badges.

He continued, 'This group has, in their collective wisdom, decided to stay on at school for another year. This will give them a further education opportunity and enhance their scope for future employment.' *Bless that man.* Quite suddenly I had been elevated from an unwanted orphan with the most dreadful fears, to a bright young thing who was only there because she had chosen to be. What a superb Headmaster he was; no wonder he was held in such high esteem.

The first, most obvious difference in the new class was how relaxed it was. Those of us from the Home had never had school uniform but now no one in the top form had either. From my very first infants' school, St James's in Tunbridge Wells, I had never worn a uniform. I still didn't . . . but at last I was the same as everybody else . . . or they were the same as me!

Jeanette and a couple of the others had a head start; they used typewriters at home. She was a natural, definitely heading for the world of commerce. I eventually got the hang of it, but found the shorthand a bit difficult. I was too pedantic to get my mind round the phonetics, but mastered it slowly. Jeanette and I giggled when I said I thought 'as soon as possible' in shorthand resembled a dead worm on the page. There was a general consensus that unless my speeds picked up I would only be fit to work in the morgue, taking dictation from the dead.

Maths was definitely not my forte, and I would really rather forget my efforts with the double-entry bookkeeping ledger system; for a start it took me a week to learn how to say it! I genuinely tried hard and put in a lot of endeavour, but never did achieve greatness, though I learnt much and enjoyed it immensely.

I had never considered that I would work in an office; I wanted the sports field. Mr Dewberry had collared me within a day or so of being back and had been so very welcoming. He had received permission from the Head for me to help him at playtime. On my first day back as one of the runners' assistants, I watched the weedy little 11-year olds line up on the track. Had I really looked like that once? I did a warm-up routine with them, and helped with technique in general. Their enthusiasm, like mine at first, far outweighed their ability, but there was huge potential. This gave me a real hankering for Loughborough and teaching.

Miss Thornton also gave me opportunities at her games sessions. I had always been a better catcher of a ball than she had. A circle would form with me in the centre. I would randomly throw the ball, which had to be returned to me as quickly as possible. The speed built up and our sharpness was greatly improved by the end of the session. We had always had good Rounders, netball and hockey teams and this term was going to carry on that tradition.

As the top form, we had the privilege of eating at a separate table, like the staff. Miss Booth did not object at all when I asked to continue my habit of eating at the second sitting. The rest of the form was delighted about this as they were able to use the library while I was in the playground. We also had more to eat of course.

I had previously had a scratch about on the violin but now had the opportunity to have proper lessons. I was not too bad really, but one-on-one instruction made a huge difference. I sat Grade

1, and I passed Grade 2 at only one mark off distinction. The town had a Youth Orchestra and I joined as second violin; I was not allowed out from the Home to do extra practice, but still managed to perform in a couple of concerts.

Another thing that struck me as very odd about the Home rules was that none of us were allowed to do any extra-curricular activities, not even standard homework. When my running was so important to me, I really missed not being able to do extra training. Without the advantage of the school grounds or space in the Home, I used to wait until we went to the beach and would lose myself in the sand dunes, until that too was banned. Barnardo's held some weird notions of their own, but Boagey beat them hands down as far as stupidity went.

The bar on homework did not necessarily preclude one from success; you just had to work a darned sight harder to achieve the same results as your peers. There were kids at school who said they would happily live in a Home for the considered luxury of having no homework to do! I found myself doing piles of it, but for others, fitting it in during breaks, and had even more to do when it was too wet to train outside. As long as it wasn't Maths I'd gladly help, and this meant I was learning more as well, so everyone was happy.

~ 24 ~

The extra year flew by; I quickly realised I had had little to fear. Mr Hall and the others expertly dispensed with the worries of the first day. I achieved so much; the staff, and the kids who had known me from previous terms, had been kind and understanding. It was not a pleasant situation in which to be placed, but it had worked out very well. Presented with so many opportunities, I like to think I tackled them all with enthusiasm. I certainly learnt the way to turn a potential negative into a positive.

I had managed to have a long chat with Miss Thornton. She had unbelievably arranged with Boagey to let me go to an international hockey match in Manchester; we went in her car. As we trundled along she asked quite pertinent questions about life in the Home; for the first time in my life, I responded openly. She was easy to talk to; I told her a great deal about the cruelty and the unnecessary punishments.

I had felt sorriest for Gennie; happily, we didn't have a wet-bed at this Home. The way Giessen boxed our ears startled Miss Thornton, who said it was extremely dangerous, as were the constantly administered 'clips,' round the ears. I said I'd shouted, 'Why do you always have to hit me in the head?' at Boagey once and she had calmly replied, 'Because the bruises won't show.' I took ages trying to fathom if she really meant it, then decided she probably did!

I admitted I was rebellious and defiant and therefore knew I'd be punished; I accepted that. It was the bullying bit I would not accept ever to be justified. She understood when I said I was determined not to show I was hurt when I could, and never to cry in front of them. 'Tears are the reward for bullies,' she said. 'So well done.'

For me, at my age and strength, a lot of this was a thing of the past, but of course, it continued for the young ones. With Boagey's desire for total control it was hard to see an end to it; it seemed just to be what they did. The thing that kept me sane was the fact that we all got the same treatment.

The exception of course to all of this was Miss Plesance; I'd seen her wince at something as innocuous as a raised voice. I told Miss Thornton about the cake episode; she thought that was wonderful.

Now that Boagey couldn't attack me physically, she bullied me in a different way, like the manner in which she made the announcement that I was to stay on for another year. That was shock, not pain, and almost impossible to hide, so she was still deriving some perverse pleasure out of hurting me.

Miss Thornton laughed heartily when I told her about the continuing pocket money fiasco, and shared my joy in the drain-cleaning procedure.

She had not been terribly surprised at what I had told her about the Home, and had already known a great deal of what went on there anyway, she told me. I was amazed. At her request I went through the whole story about the spinach. All she had understood was that I hadn't eaten for the weekend. I also told her about the bad egg at Crowborough, and this led to more laughter when I explained about sister number two.

Yet in spite of all her warmth and understanding, I could not bear to tell her about the sexual attacks; I still could not find the words, nor knew where to start. Besides which, it would have spoilt the day and I'm sure she had, at least, an inkling about that as well.

After the match, we went to a fish shop and had a delicious meal, eaten out of the paper. I explained that the first time I'd had this luxury was at Seaford and then went on to tell her about Auntie and that holiday. She then said she had been abroad the previous year to Italy. 'It cost a lot of money but it was a once-in-a-life-time thrill, so worth it.' I had never met anyone who had been abroad on a holiday; she told me all about it, and promised to bring in photographs to school.

I don't think either of us stopped talking all day but I loved it. How she ever managed to get Boagey to let me go I will never know.

Jeanette and I were good mates. We had many a laugh about the differences in our abilities. She excelled at some subjects where I was well below average – and vice versa. Her mother wanted me to go out somewhere with them as a family and stay for tea. I told her there was no chance – it did not happen. They sent a letter, hand delivered by me, then they rang and wrote again, but to no avail. None of us could understand why, and Jeanette's parents became quite cross about it. Boagey's rules were cast in stone.

The last day of school finally arrived. It was a day I was dreading and yet it turned out to be far less harrowing in reality. One year on had made such an enormous difference to my outlook; I had grown up a great deal. I would certainly never be sufficiently precocious to consider myself an equal to my teachers but I knew the gap between us had most definitely closed. The warmth in their final words of praise and encourage-ment remained an inspiration for many a year. With an education now behind me, all I had to do was to get over the next few weeks. Freedom called in a loud voice.

The confidence and maturity I had felt on the last day at school, however, rapidly dissipated in the days that followed. They dragged by as I waited for my departure from the Home.

I asked Boagey when I would actually be leaving. She took this as a personal affront and replied she had no idea; it was up to my mother to arrange. I did not believe her. I was becoming paranoid that I would never leave.

It was getting increasingly hard even to be civil to anybody in the Home. I missed school, the teachers and especially Jeanette. The summer holidays dragged on; and my feelings of frustration increased.

As my sixteenth birthday approached, I told Boagey I did not want to celebrate it; everyone else could, but I wouldn't. I did not want the disappointment of yet another year with no mail from my mother; if I ignored the day it would not then matter. But the main reason was the history of this annual event; Boagey had managed to ruin it every year in my memory.

I didn't want to aggravate anyone, but one day I plucked up the courage to ask Miss Plesance if she knew anything about when I was to leave. She was kind about it and seemed to understand. 'I certainly wouldn't know before you do, Sue,' she replied. Thus, one day followed another in that dreadful limbo.

Finally, I was called to the office. I stood and waited. Boagey did her frustrating routine of shuffling papers about; and then she slowly leant forward, which had always been the precursor for yet another message of doom. However, not this time, and I could hardly believe my ears.

'You will be pleased to know that all the arrangements have been made. Your mother has decided to take you back.'

I could not quite make up my mind as to who was doing whom the favour. Boagey went on. I was to travel by train to London with a chaperone from the Women's Royal Voluntary Service. She would stay with me until I was met and passed over to a member of my family. That was it. It was just three days away. Strangely calm, I left the office.

I managed to get through the back of the house without

speaking to anyone. I went up to the wall by the shed, climbed it, dropped quietly into the convent grounds and took the path as I had before. I tore up the road past the houses and dived into the bushes. Breathless now, I rolled on to my back. My mind was in absolute chaos. I had waited over 14 years to get out of the Homes, and now that I was, found it was almost beyond my comprehension to absorb it. I lay very still, closed my eyes and tried to slow everything down to think more clearly.

I gradually realised what the problem was: yet again it was *the way* Boagey had said it. What did she mean by 'your mother has decided to take you back'? She had dumped me there in the first place, completely isolated from the brothers – whom I had met only once – with no cards, letters or visits, which would have helped me through it. Why couldn't she have made sure I was in the south of England instead of in Lancashire – literally the other end of the country? Were they my mother's words or Boagey's?

My thoughts wandered to Uncle Tom and Auntie Dodd. How strange it was that in such a short space of time they had given me so much while my mother had had a lifetime to do the same and yet had never even tried to do so. In only two wonderful years, they had undoubtedly given me all of the love I had received in the last 14. Uncle Tom and Auntie Dodd had made me feel that I belonged somewhere; that I had an important contribution to make to this world. And above all, they'd made me feel part of something: a family perhaps, a unit. They had given me the confidence and reassurance to believe in my own identity; to understand that I was so much more than the person I was deemed to be by Barnardo's. My mood changed when I thought of them, the dreadful pain was instant. I did not think I would ever get over the grief of losing them so cruelly. However, their love was so strong, and because of this I was able to feel that I needed no more. It had dwelt within my heart and memory and sustained me throughout my years at the Home. 'I fought the buggers, Uncle Tom . . . and I won,' I said to him quietly. I missed them so much.

I thought about the debate at school. I did wonder why I was wanted now, and I concluded my classmates were quite correct: I was to return because I was old enough to earn. I wondered then, for the first time, whether that was why I had stayed that extra year. Boagey knew there was to be a top form. Mr Ward confirmed what I had previously been told: that Barnardo's received money from the council for each child they gave a home to. Perhaps I was just a source of income – nothing more than a commodity like a bag of sweets or a tin of beans.

25

I stood at the front door with the clothes I was wearing and my case: a brown cardboard affair. It contained a new flannel, toothbrush and a tin of Gibbs Dentifrice tooth powder, one clean if not new nightdress, and a couple of other essentials. This was what constituted my 'leaving for good' belongings; but at least it was more than we would normally have to travel.

I won from Mr Ward in English a leather-bound copy of H. Rider Haggard's *King Solomon's Mines*, which I had received with pride. He had set a single-word title for what he called a short essay. This was to illustrate our comprehension of a subject; its brevity achieved with good use of vocabulary. Set one day with the subject 'luxury' some had written about special trips and birthday treats. I said in a few words (inspired by Uncle Tom) that it was doing your very favourite things, with your very favourite people, whenever you possibly could. My prize was an honour; there was only one per term for English, and it was presented on Prize Day. It meant a great deal to me. The book had my name, the subject lesson and the date inscribed inside; I had read the book with enjoyment, but to my knowledge, not one other kid had. However, I still had to leave it for 'sharing' as with everything else. At least it was only a prize; Ann Short had to surrender the one gift she had from her father each year.

I held my case and stood in the drive by the front door. I heard the engine and watched as the taxi drove towards me, stopping at the right hand gate. Feeling a massive surge of excitement I thought, *This is it.*

I had said my brief goodbyes to the kids and Miss Plesance. I acknowledged her kind treatment and thanked her profusely for making a difference; she returned my words with such a sad smile. Boagey and a couple of the other staff were in the porch; she began her good wishes and offered to shake my hand. I walked away sullenly. I was in no mood to forgive. The driver walked towards me as I reached the gate, his arm outstretched to take my case.

I turned my head and looked back. They stood there waving with rictus grins on their faces. I thought of all the cruelty and abuse and just how much I hated Boagey. I raised my right hand with the first two fingers stretched into the 'V' sign and saluted them.

'Glad to be going, are you, young lady?' enquired the driver.

The WRVS escort met me from the car with, 'Has nobody come with you, dear?' That thought had occurred to me: not much of a send-off after 14 years. She took my case and I followed her on to the train – as you might expect from the WRVS, this lady was very kind and caring.

I had looked on a map at school to see where I was in relation to London and knew there was a long journey ahead. The lady offered me a comic to read; I thanked her but said I much preferred to look out of the window.

I became aware that every mile along the track was another mile away from Barnardo's. I realised too that some of the limbo-like feelings I had experienced were because I did not know, and therefore could not trust, my mother to get me out. I battled to erase thoughts of Boagey and everything else. I wanted to be positive.

My chaperone awoke from a short nap and very kindly offered me some lunch. She opened a bag with the largest assortment of sandwiches I had ever seen. It would have pleased Auntie at Seaford! As we ate, we both relaxed. The conversation was just small talk but the further we travelled the more excited I became.

I felt more enthusiastic about it all now. I told the lady about the day I met my brothers at Dymchurch. I told her their names. I could not really add much detail to this because I did not know anything else. She did not comment much but that was all right with me.

I must have fallen asleep and I awakened to her gentle pressure on my arm and the news, 'We'll be there soon.' I felt a deep surge of excitement. She laughed as I tried to determine who would be there to meet me. She explained that we handed in our tickets at the barrier and people meeting trains invariably waited there so as not to miss each other.

I suddenly felt guilty about the thoughts I had had about only being wanted at home because I was old enough to earn. I felt it wasn't very fair to jump to conclusions when I wasn't even there yet. Perhaps my mother could have written to me, but maybe she was just too busy. After all, she was now giving me a proper home. I would be with my brothers every day, I would get to know my elder sister, and maybe I had other relatives I had never even heard about yet. My excitement was growing.

I helped the lady pack all the stuff away. 'I can't believe we ate all that food,' I said, laughing. She had been really kind and the journey had flown by. She sent me off to the toilet and then I looked after the bags while she went along. I had butterflies in my tummy. All the scenery was houses and chimneys now. The train was slowing. *I am here – I'm in London!* I thought with mounting excitement.

It was the end of the line, and we joined the throngs disembarking. I couldn't believe the din; the babble of voices and the announcements. It was a squash along the platform and it was frustrating because I couldn't see the barrier. Who will it be? I wondered. I hung on to everything while the tickets were dealt with. '*Where* did you say my family would be waiting?' I asked excitedly.

There was a pause. I looked at her; something was wrong.

Out of the corner of my eye, I was aware of someone approaching. I turned to see a woman but she was not my mother.

There was a short discussion; then I was introduced to a new WRVS lady. I was informed as kindly as possible that, once again, my mother was not ready for me. I was being sent to a Barnardo's halfway house in Earls Court.

The surge of pain was shattering.

I squeezed my eyes shut, clamped my jaws together and my fists were tightly clenched in an effort to control myself. I stared ahead but saw nothing or no one; all the sounds had gone.

'Sue, there is no rush for us to go anywhere yet; you can't leave here like that, dearie. Shall we get a tea each and then see how you feel?' Her kindness and soft tone were just too much and I crumpled. I looked at her with the tears already streaming down my face, and then, in the embrace of a complete stranger, the last 14 years of one let-down after another flowed away from me in sickening, gulping sobs.

I didn't care about the tears any more, or who saw or heard; all my restraint and control had gone in one sentence: 'She is not ready for you yet.'

My childhood had been a far from joyless experience but it had been regularly punctuated with agonising lows. When I found myself abandoned yet again, on that station platform with two complete strangers, I think I knew then what I faced. Although I had left Barnardo's behind, in reality, nothing was going to change. That first realisation of my so-called mother's attitude was one that would endure.

The second lady was very kind; the sweetness of her

demeanour contrasted strikingly with the severity of her dark green uniform. We sat on a bench once the tears were under control and she bought us both a hot drink.

I sat for a time just staring at all the people milling about: couples, friends, but especially the mothers and daughters. Do you know how lucky you are to be with someone who loves you? I thought, feeling wretched and unbelievably sad.

Then I turned to the lady. 'I'm sorry for breaking down like that but it was such a shock. Do you think your friend could have *known* what was happening?' I asked, finding it hard to imagine she would have been so sweet all the way down if she had.

'No, no, not at all. That is why she was so surprised to see me. She *should* have been told by your matron and we will have to enquire what went wrong.' She talked and talked about nothing really, but had skilfully brought me back to reality. I was worried about her time; but she assured me she didn't live too far away and was going to make sure I was feeling better before she took me further. She could offer no information about the next place; she only had the address.

'And Sue dearie, it could be Buckingham Palace, but if you don't want to be there, it's just another prison.' Now that was wisdom. After another hot drink, she and I decided I was ready to go. The lump in my throat came back, and the stinging returned to my eyes, but we could not stay there all night.

In different circumstances my first walk on a London street and my first Underground journey would have held some pleasure. I couldn't take any of it in. Eventually she dutifully delivered me to the latest dump. She left me in the hall and went into the office with her papers to sign.

I looked around me; it wasn't like a Home at all, just a very large house. The smell of a meal was lingering on the air; and there was a low hum of voices from behind a closed door to my right. I could hear the traffic beyond the open porch door, but that was because the house stood near a crossroads; lots of stopping and starting I presumed. After about ten minutes, my lady left the office; she came over and caught hold of my hands in hers. 'You'll be okay, Sue. Take care, dearie.' She smiled, turned, and departed into the busy street.

The other woman who had been in the office then called me in to see her. She said that the WRVS lady was very cross at the way I had been treated, and then asked me, 'Did you not know you were coming here?'

'No . . . why, did *you*?' I asked in shocked surprise.

'Well, yes. It was arranged last week. Are you *sure* Miss Boagey didn't explain?'

That was it: uncontrollable rage boiled up inside me and I could not help myself. I stood up and *screamed* at her, 'Do you really think I would have *forgotten*? I was led to believe right as far as London station that I was going to be met by my family. *Of course* old Boagey didn't tell me – she will be up there now on her fat backside laughing still! No wonder I hate you lot. *I hate you* and I'm not staying in this dump. I'm leaving.'

My crescendo was interrupted by a simultaneous knocking and opening of the office door by a girl a little older than me; she stood there for a moment before asking quietly, 'Is everything all right?'

'No it blooming well isn't . . . *I'm off*.'

Grabbing my case, I angrily charged past the girl and stormed into the hall; I reached for the door handle but the door was locked!

Slowly I calmed; I went into the sitting room where I had heard the low voices, had a hot sweet drink and stopped my rage. Once I settled down they asked – and I explained – just what had gone on through the day. They were really understanding and supportive; even the woman who sparked it all off came in and it was discussed for ages. Apparently the WRVS did a lot of chaperone duties and they were going to make a report. She said she would write and complain too, but that didn't raise my hopes.

One of the older ones said, 'What Boagey did was diabolical . . . but your flipping mother should have been there once the date was made.' Then they looked on the notice board for me; there wasn't even a message from Maisie. I felt utterly unimportant. There were three or four unopened letters though and I asked whose they were. I was told that they were for the girls who weren't yet back from work.' Before then I had never seen a letter not previously opened! My treasured correspondence, my cards from the Round Table Club, didn't come through the post; I couldn't remember having mail. Those who did always had them censored. When I mentioned this to the others, I discovered it had been the same in all the Homes.

Yet another black day was ending and I was feeling much better considering the circumstances. The WRVS ladies and the other girls' kindness and understanding had been appreciated, and proved extremely beneficial. We all trooped upstairs; I was shown my bedroom, and although it was shared with three others, it was not called a dormitory. I was invited to have a welcome hot bath and that presented me with another pleasure; it was the first one ever without a member of staff supervising and looking on.

On waking, my first impressions were the traffic noise from outside and the domestic bustle within. Having spent my very young days in the peace and space of the countryside, the move to St Anne's and living in a road had come as a bit of a shock at first. Even there the spread of the golf club opposite had offered a feeling of open spaces and quiet; this was something else again. Looking from the bedroom window, all I could see were houses, cars and the big red double-decker buses I had only before seen in books. Now here they were, passing the house! The bustle was from the other girls washing and dressing for work; they told me to stay where I was so as to not be in the way, and to sort myself out afterwards. 'Then go down to see Matron. She will help with anything you need.' I was relieved to hear that; personally I had no idea what I needed – so clearly how no idea about how to set about getting it.

Recollections of this period in my life are chaotic and fragmented, but Matron and the girls guided where they could; each girl had left the Homes at varying times themselves. They clearly remembered the shock of this big new world with delight or otherwise; the shock at the station was the main cause of *my* extreme anxiety. Matron talked more about this when I went down to see her. She made a pot of tea and we sat in her office for some considerable time. She did not elaborate, but said she had heard of Boagey; as she had raised the subject, and without going into too much detail, I told her exactly what my own feelings were! She offered me some toast; I declined as I was feeling a bit nauseous. It was never offered again; apparently, nobody ate anything in the morning – the general opinion was that the extra ten minutes in bed were far more beneficial!

Matron understood all the new changes that were taking place for me as she had steered thousands of ex-Barnardo's kids through their first day, and she took me out on mine. She was making things so much better and I felt my spirits lifting quickly. I found myself in awe when I actually *sat* on the famous bus, *and* I paid the fare to the conductor. The ticket machine strapped to his waist I had only ever seen in a book. I laughed a lot at being called 'duck' and 'darlin'' by everyone!

When we all sat around that evening the girls discussed what they did. They said I would have no worries getting an office job as I had done the extra year's business course. It paid more than a shop girl, so something positive had come out of that time. I do not recall attending an interview, being offered a 'post', or how I got there, but my first job ever was in Selfridges in London's West End.

As the other girls were all ex-Homes kids, we spent time in the evenings having many a laugh at Barnardo's expense. We talked and enjoyed swapping stories that would make the average Outsider pale, and the similarity in some of the treatment was painfully familiar. Here was my answer to the question about what happened to kids who left without a family to go to. They said they were comfortable at least, but they, like me, just *longed* to get out. They were not going to lull me into staying in a Home though, just because it was a 'grown-up' version of what I had already been through. I wanted to be out of there with Maisie or alone; by then it mattered not.

I endured a few weeks of this monotonous, anxious existence, until one Saturday, out of the blue, my sister Mary arrived to take me to the flat – I would never call it home. Typical of Barnardo's or Maisie, once again I had no notice of this; I had no idea she was coming. With an already jaundiced opinion of what was supposed to be my family, I have to admit that I did not like Mary on sight. She was much taller than I was and overweight, and her smile was one that could be put on at will quite obviously. She had a large, pale, hard face with cold, unsmiling eyes.

The farewells to the others were remarkable in their brevity; they had been more than nice to me, but I had simply had enough. Even if Maisie's place was absolute rubbish, even if the journey ahead was just as hard, I didn't care. I was *out of Barnardo's* . . . I had waited long enough!

Mary and I caught the bus to Willesden Green. To my eyes everywhere looked the same with the terraced houses, some small, some large, but still all the same. Mary pointed out what were supposed to be famous landmarks, but not if you were educated in Lancashire. I was familiar with reading the London of Pepys and Dr Johnson, but that was the City; I was heading for north-west London. We passed a park or two, and after some miles and less conversation, we were there.

Mary pointed out the building as we walked up the hill. 'Rutland Park Mansions' sounded quite posh, and the outside was superb: four floors or more high, built in stark red brick, and the Victorian influence manifestly clear. The inside stairwell was horrible, dirty cold concrete steps where a lurking sot with his cider wouldn't have come as a surprise; I'd never seen anything like them before coming to London. The stairs had a light switch you had to press in; Mary explained it was on a timer so you had to shift if you didn't want to go up in the dark. At last we were there and Mary opened the dark green front door that went straight into the short angle of an L-shaped hall. The sitting room was the first door on the right. In here was Maisie. The welcome was a farce; she barely embraced me, and then told Mary to show me round.

The flat was immense, with large, high-ceilinged rooms and great old sash windows that made it light and bright. I was shown the dining room that faced the front door. This housed a table you could have played table tennis on. Then Mary opened the bedroom door. 'We will share in here,' she announced. This room was nothing like the size of the other two I'd seen. It faced the back of the house and overlooked the rear of the surrounding buildings; in contrast it was dark, almost dingy. There was an empty space in front of me, but behind the door was a single bed, that was it. *I'm not going to share a bed with her!* I thought.

We went right to the end of the long passage to the kitchen, passing the boys' bedrooms on the left and the bathroom opposite. The boys were around but there was no welcome; I got a warmer reception from the vicar once a week at church.

They had not seen me in years and I meant nothing to them, any of them. It was close to midday and lunchtime; I was offered a drink and a sandwich. They were chatting amongst themselves but very little had been said to me; I was beginning to feel all my expectations of home comfort draining from me. I was told to put on my coat; we were going to the local shops.

I do not think I had said more than a half dozen words; I certainly didn't feel I could ask about the shopping trip. I felt I was in the way and that I was messing up their Saturday.

I had by now been into a chemist's and a newsagent's but to my surprise we went into a furniture store called Courts. The salesmen obviously knew Maisie and Mary but I was not introduced. Without reference to me, they chose a single bed, mattress, rug and a small chest of drawers. With the promise of delivery by 4pm, I was asked to sign a hire purchase agreement for the bed I was going to be sleeping in that night! In all honesty, I had no idea what this involved; I just did what was asked of me. The salespeople were so familiar because, as I subsequently discovered, the boys had been made to do exactly the same thing and they too had no more idea than me. The leap from *not* getting my three pence pocket money to earning a small wage each week was pretty amazing. Now I found myself buying a bed, it was beyond my comprehension.

I quite obviously had not known *what* to expect, but I bet myself we could have held a hundred meetings at school and they wouldn't have dreamt up that one! I had been abandoned and isolated for 14 years; had been attacked by perverts; and this was my much-anticipated welcome to the real world. Thinking about the debate that I had all those months ago made me question things again; but no one had ever said that I would be expected to pay for my furniture; everything was extraordinary to me, and I had no benchmark with which to compare my new 'family'. My mind was in a state of utter turmoil; I felt ignorant of this new world. If I had landed on Mars, I would have been no more, or less, at home. I was unsure of when Maisie or Mary were actually addressing me, and I didn't know when to respond or what to say. The atmosphere was dead and flat, and I felt I was not functioning normally.

At Earls Court – the halfway house – I was at least spoken to and we laughed a lot, especially when sharing our experiences of our time in the Homes. *We had History.* That was the difference – we shared common ground. From the relaxed manner of the boys, it was clear they were completely at ease. We had obviously had very different experiences. They had clearly spent a great deal of time together. As a family, they had barely been separated and had most of their holidays with Maisie and Walter. They were referred to as 'son' in such a pathetic, cloying manner; I was becoming rather glad I was me.

It was a relief at least that I was not expected to share a bed with Mary, though she displayed clear resentment at sharing *her* room. Presumably, this was a first for her. Tough. I was no happier than she was. Once my new furniture was delivered, Walter, Maisie's partner who had driven that taxi all those years ago, got everything assembled with one of the others for help.

The afternoon now over, the evening closed in. I presume I had eaten but I truly have no real memory of that. I was sitting in the small kitchen by the window. For as far as the eye could see, which was only some yards in any direction, were roofs and chimneys, much like the view I'd had from the train. I was on my own and allowed myself to remember the sheer horror of that train arriving at the station to yet another rejection by these people. Now, even in their home – in my 'home' – they were still doing it. There were various sounds going on in the house, but I had absolutely no idea what they were. People were in and out of the bathroom, one of the boys would call out and receive an answer, and Maisie seemed to be everywhere, except in the kitchen with me. I felt like a bewildered rabbit caught in the headlights and had no idea what I was allowed to do. There was a newspaper on the table but I didn't know to whom it belonged, so I didn't have the nerve to read it.

Someone was coming down the corridor; it was Maisie. 'What are you doing in here on your own?' she enquired, and then went on. 'We're going dancing, to the Victor Sylvester Ballroom in Wembley. You'll have to have lessons and join us some time. Now you know where everything is so have a cup of tea and we won't be late.'

I watched her as she went to a drawer. She was wearing incredibly high heels and a black astrakhan coat. She was overweight and reminded me of an old black-faced pedigree bull who lived in a field by the Home in Crowborough. He was fat, had hooves like high heels and black curly hair exactly like the coat.

There were calls from the hall directed vaguely at me, and then all fell quiet. Straining to hear any sound at all, I got up. I slowly and quietly walked the length of the hall and into the sitting room: no one. It was dark outside now and a small blue table lamp lit the room, but there was most definitely no one else in the flat. They had all gone out.

I sat down on the large comfortable settee and tried to relax, realising it was the first time I had done so for simply ages, since I had been on the train coming to London. I looked around at my surroundings and realised that I could stay here for a hundred years and I would never feel I belonged; I was amongst strangers who did not want to know me.

From a Home to a home? Who were they kidding?

I sat pensively for some while. My body was blissfully relaxed and the strain of the stress I had suffered was leaving me. My emotions, though, were static. Fortunately, I had allowed myself no preconceptions. On the train, I had started a process of forgiveness and understanding, but *that* rejection on the station was the last I would accept.

It had occurred to me very quickly that, like the time I had escaped from St Anne's, *I was entirely alone*! This was swiftly followed with the thought that I had never made myself a cup of tea! Even at the halfway house I was not allowed in the kitchen. The scullery, yes, to prepare vegetables; anything more 'risky', definitely not. So I declined the offer from Maisie, but I'd observed the ease and familiarity with which the boys had managed. How long had they been here? How long since they left the Homes?

My suitcase contained little more than when I first left St Anne's – but only a little. One of the girls who was leaving Earls Court had given me some talcum powder; she hadn't liked the perfume. And she had also given me two blouses because she didn't suit blue; luckily it was my favourite colour.

Taking out the flannel and toothbrush, I made my way to the bathroom. The bath and sink were filthy and wet towels were draped everywhere; I left them. I had never seen a gas boiler before; of course, I knew what it was and that it heated the water, but I was not going to take any chances. It did occur to me that in tinkering with it I might blow the place up. I washed in cold water; I was well used to it in any case.

Getting into my new bed alone felt very strange, more so because I had no one with whom I could share and discuss the experience. They had absolutely no idea as to the effect all this novelty was having on me. I lay there quietly in the dark stillness, still pensive. It was hard to believe this was my first night here and they had all gone out; my first night out of Dr Barnardo's Homes and they had left me completely alone. I repeated the sentence a few times in my head but it seemed not to sink in. I had not anticipated whistles and bells but this was a situation so bizarre as to be almost beyond comprehension.

Rejection clearly takes many forms, but here we go again, I thought. I felt an overwhelming pang of loneliness wash over me and longed for the comfort and security of my days with Uncle Tom and Auntie Dodd. They would have held me close, stroked my hair, told me they loved me and kissed me goodnight. I needed that so much.

I turned over and cried myself to sleep.

I woke early the following morning; a pall of silence hung throughout the flat. I was still terribly nervous about what I could and could not do. Deciding a visit to the bathroom was acceptable, I went quietly. The clock by Mary's bed showed just after seven so I crept back to bed, not daring to disturb the others. I lay there thinking. They had been mean enough to leave me alone on the first night *out* of the Homes but I now recalled with clarity the terrifying first night *in* there. I realised, for the first time in memory, that I did not feel threatened. These people were cold and aloof, but I was positive no one here was going to abuse me.

I knew I had to have my wits about me to manage this unfamiliar situation. Out into the 'big wide world' was the terminology frequently used by many adults, and I felt I had the capacity to deal with that eventually. Once again, I felt my weakness deep within; the inability to cope emotionally. I tried to push the painful feelings as far away as possible. I would not allow myself to be hopeful of any form of kindness or affection from these people who were supposed to be my family.

As the days went by I slowly became more confident. On the Monday morning, everybody went off to work; I had to make my way to a different Underground station but did so without problems. On Friday my three brothers, the two lodgers Pete and Derek (ex-Homes mates of Colin's), Mary and myself were all mustered into the dining room.

Walter was seated at the enormous table and he opened a

ledger in front of him. My mind returned to Boagey and the weekly pocket money charade. We lined up and from each person he took a sum as rent. Additionally, sixpence for each bath; he had carefully monitored these. He took sixpence for fuel costs and one shilling for the hire purchase payments – this did not yet include the beds for which we would all pay Courts directly; it was for curtains throughout the flat and other sundries, all of which were to be a joint responsibility.

At the end of the session, Walter requested I stay behind; he explained that I was to look for new clothing immediately; because I had so few clothes I was causing more washing to be done and adding to unnecessary cost at the launderette. If I needed help then Maisie would oblige, presumably with advice only though. How he imagined I was left with enough money to buy clothes was a mystery – there was barely enough for the fare to work!

*

The following Sunday an elderly lady visited. I was in the kitchen preparing a veritable mountain of vegetables. Maisie brought her down and she was introduced as Grandma Cherie. I liked her instantly and felt the feeling was mutual. After lunch, she and I offered to wash up and I was alone with her. We exchanged pleasantries and small talk in a very relaxed way but then she suddenly became furtive and spoke close in my ear. She whispered she wanted to see me at her home and to arrange it as soon as I could.

I seemed to spend the vast majority of my time in the kitchen. I was the only one who ironed and there was always a pile of it to do with so many people living there. I became 'washer-up' as well and was not brave enough to question this.

One Saturday evening, after most of them had already gone out, I was at the sink completing the chores when my eldest brother breezed in, dropped a plate and cup on to the table and laughed, 'Just a couple more for you, I'm off to see Sandie.'

I was immediately cross and turned on him. 'You all just treat me like the maid round here, the skivvy, and you do absolutely *nothing* to help. Just because you were always together, had lovely holidays away from the Homes and felt justified in isolating as well as abandoning me, you think I'm dirt. Well, I'm *not*!' I shouted.

I thought he was going to cry; his face had changed completely. 'Oh Sue, come and sit down . . . I am so sorry.' With the others already gone, the flat had fallen into the peaceful state I enjoyed. I sat with Frank at the kitchen table and he started a flow of words that was unusual for him. I did not see him much anyway, but when I did, he had little to say to anyone, especially me.

'I can understand what you mean but you have got it so wrong,' he told me. 'Everything with our lives was wrong but Sue, I promise I tried for us kids; I wanted so much to keep us all together. Let me tell you what I remember.

'After our Dad died, we were in south Wales with different relatives. One morning I was up, dressed, and ready to go for a special day out. I remember a big car arrived and went around collecting each of us. We then set off; I was quite excited because it was an unusual thing to be happening, especially in a car with all of us together and the petrol rationing on. We drove to Cardiff, and eventually pulled up outside this really large house. Everyone except Mary clambered out; we went through a big gate on to a driveway and then Maisie turned to me.

'She put our baby sister into my arms; told me that at nearly seven years old I was the eldest and that I was to be responsible for the whole family and to make sure we stayed together. She turned away, returned to the car with Mary still inside, and drove off.'

He paused, and I could see the recollections were painful for him to think about, then he resumed.

'I was in shock, Sue, we were all crying by now, and then this woman came out to collect us. That was our introduction to Barnardo's and it was dreadful, but we were together.

'Then one morning, a short time later, I came down for breakfast and there was only me and Colin left. You, Trevor and our baby sister had gone, and I knew nothing about it. I had no idea you were due to go anywhere and even less of where you may have gone. I felt sick and very frightened because I was told to look after us all . . . and now I'd let our mother down. I struggled at school for years and I'm sure that was due to the trauma that followed.

'Don't think either that the holidays and visits were much of a joy. Okay, we were away with her but I promise you it did not amount to much and you could never rely on her anyway. She and Walter both worked up in town and we were left very much to our own devices. We spent most of the days in Gladstone Park near her flat, but it was not exactly the bundle of fun you have imagined it to be. I know she had little to do with you and she let you down badly by not turning up at St Christopher's, but that was not unusual for her.

'On Coronation Day there was a big party and festivities arranged at "Goldings" in Hertfordshire; that's the Home where I lived. I was fifteen then and was doing my printing apprenticeship. The Homes had arranged a sports day and a celebration mug each with a party and sweets. Maisie had asked me to come down to London and watch the ceremony with them and I always wanted to please her so I said yes. The Head had given me permission, on the understanding that I would miss the sports day, and receive none of the "extras".

'It was 25 miles and I cycled all the way. I jumped off my bike and banged on the front door. There was an old woman who lived in the flat above and she came to the door and asked me what on earth I was doing there. I told her and she told me that they were at a friend's place having a Coronation party. She didn't know where, and Maisie hadn't left a message. I couldn't believe it! I got back on my bike; cycled the 25 miles back as fast as I could go, but by the time I arrived the celebrations were over.'

We just sat for a moment and looked at each other, sharing a mutual pain. This account had been such a revelation to me and had touched us both.

'Frank, I am so sorry. I really didn't mean to hurt you. Perhaps we all hurt a little too much to stay reasonable.' He smiled at me with understanding; stood up giving my shoulders a little hug, gently kissed me on the forehead and went off to meet his sweetheart.

When he had first come into the kitchen, he had been a great jolly giant of a man. When he went out, he was a lost, confused and sad little boy, with too much responsibility on his shoulders.

*

I promised Grandma I would go and see her and managed to sneak out one Sunday. I found her living in one of the many magnificent London squares, in a *very* well-to-do part of the city. Ornate wrought-iron railings protected imposing stone-built houses, with tall Georgian windows; wide steps led up from the tree-lined pavement to the magnificent front doors, each proudly displaying highly polished brass fittings.

But Grandma lived below the pavement in one of the dingiest rooms one could ever imagine. I had no way of letting her know I was coming but as I walked down her steep steps, she came out of the door. We had a big hug, just so pleased to see each other. 'How on earth did you get away?' she enquired, as she ushered me inside. 'I told them I was going to watch the Selfridges team play hockey.'

She was the caretaker for the building, and this was the accommodation that came with the job. Although extremely dark, it was lovely and warm; she cared for the boiler and this was in a corner of the vast living area; the pipes ran across her ceiling, so she felt the benefit of that.

'They upstairs call 'em apartments, it's posher than flats,' she told me, laughing.

She made some tea in a brown enamel teapot; I leant against the sink while she did this and took in the vastness of the space inside. In stark contrast, all that could be seen from the tiny window was a wall and railings; and just the legs of the folk on the pavement as they walked by. With the tea made, we sat at her little table and chatted.

Although Maisie's mother, she explained she had no love for her at all. The fact that Maisie had abandoned us to Barnardo's had caused her too much hurt and she had stopped loving her own daughter. She also had a son, John, who was away in the war when we were put into Barnardo's; she nearly lost him too as he was close to suicide when he discovered what his sister had done with us. Maisie and Barnardo's thwarted all his attempts to get us out. Our dad's family would have nothing to do with her either, so her selfish lifestyle had not given her much in the end.

She then told me about my dad. He was a six-foot-four-inch giant of a man and had passed his thick, jet-black hair on to all of us. 'You are all so much like him; except you and Colin don't have his height. Looking at your eldest brother Frank gives me the heeby-jeebies, he is identical in every way. Your dad as well passed on to you all his love of sport; he could have been goalkeeper for Sunderland Football Club, but his dad would not let him. He was a very clever engineer, again like Frank; he worked in the aircraft industry.

'If only he had lived, Sue – *what* a difference there would have been. You were *born* bright you lot and would have achieved anything. Colin would definitely now be a professional footballer or boxer. Mary has done well in medicine but only because she stayed with Maisie. It is all a tragedy really, my darling'.

We cried a little then, but to adjust the atmosphere I asked her if she would clear something up for me.

'You said we were bright, Gran – but I have thought about something for years and I don't know if it's a true memory – or maybe the imagination of a child who would like it to be.'

'Well you were so tiny when you all left – but I'll help if I can,' she warmly assured me.

I told her I recalled being in what was, quite obviously, a kitchen, standing with my arms resting at ear level between the knees of a man. He was wearing thick, dark, rough-on-my-cheek trousers that were hurting my tender skin; actually not at all comfortable, but emotionally a lovely, comforting place to be. To our right was a black range, which was hot. To the far left was a door – so covered in coats, one upon the other, they must have defied gravity. Directly in front of me was a window; in the middle of this room was a woman, standing up working at a table.

Occasionally she would open the drawer, and there lay my fascination. From where I stood, I could see directly under the table. As she opened the drawer the whole under-side changed; bits showed that were not previously visible. The drawer would go back tidy again, be pulled out – change again. It was utterly fascinating to a tiny child.

'Gran – was that my dad? Was that Maisie, do you think?'

'Is it clear enough in your mind to draw a sketch, do you think? Then I could tell you for certain, and it's lunchtime so I'll make a sandwich while you do.'

I drew my sketch for her and added every detail stored in my mind; once she had studied it she looked at me and smiled. She assured me it was *definitely* a memory; I had done an exact likeness of the kitchen where we had lived in Cheshire, sharing the huge house with our paternal grandparents. She knew the place well and added, 'It must have been in the winter, because the range was not lit in the summer. By the spring everything had changed, because your dad had died and you immediately left that house and moved to Wales. You can only have been between 18 months and two years old. That's amazing.'

She then went on to tell me I was my Dad's favourite, which was a fantastic comfort and beautiful to hear.

When I got back, I went down to the kitchen. 'And where have you been to all this time?' Maisie asked in a grumpy voice. 'And don't say you went to hockey because I happen to know they played yesterday. I bet you've been with some horrible boy from work, getting up to no good,' she accused.

I immediately turned and left the kitchen, stifling my laughter until I got to the bedroom. Regrettably, I did not dare visit Grandma again because she was scared of Maisie finding out she was telling me things. However, I had met her properly and she had provided a great deal of happiness to carry with me.

I sat with them in the sitting room more frequently now. I was not exactly shy, I just never seemed to know what to do or say when around them. Their superior knowledge about everything, and my apparent ignorance, left me an open target for ridicule on so many occasions. One Sunday Mary commented on a radio programme she had wanted to hear.

'We weren't allowed to have radio on a Sunday. We were only allowed to read or talk,' I explained.

'Oh don't be so *stupid*,' responded Mary.

'That's not stupid, it's a matter of fact,' I retorted boldly.

Maisie then stood up in front of me. 'I am not going to listen to all this rubbish about the Homes. If you can't tell the truth, then say nothing.' She continued in a very cross voice, which reminded me of Boagey. 'The best thing you can do is *forget all about it* and I demand you make no further reference to it *at all*. If all you can do is *lie* about them and *condemn*, then say nothing. *I will not have it.*'

Mary sat there with her pale, fat face, looking smug.

My baby sister was fostered because she was less than six months old when we went into the Homes; Mary had stayed in the car at Cardiff and driven away with Maisie. I, as the lone girl, had always remained separated from the brothers. This sister, now sneering at me, had never left her beloved mother's side. Why did Maisie decide to keep *just* her? It was a subject frequently discussed by the boys, without any satisfactory conclusion.

Maisie had left the room, and upon her return, she literally threw a copy of *Vogue* onto my lap. 'Read that, Pudding, and learn how to grow up.'

That was the wake-up call for me; my old fire returned in spades. How dare she address me in such a manner? They could all get stuffed as far as I was concerned. I decided that once I had made some friends and could seek good advice I would leave.

Less than four months later, thanks to help from one of the lodgers, I shut the door on that flat for the very last time. I did not tell Maisie I was leaving, I just moved into my new lodgings.

It was a massive step into the unknown but I left there with pride. Terrified, but proud.

26

I remembered the way from the station to the lodgings quite easily; it was a short walk and it was indelibly printed in my brain: *my new home*. The little brass plaque on the door read 'Mr M. Judd'. The door was opened in response to my rather timid knock by Eva, the lady with whom all the arrangements had been made. She smiled and showed me into the hall with a cheerful welcoming hello. I assumed, because of the normality of it all, that I must be hiding my situation extremely well.

She was my new landlady; actually she was the first. She was Russian, with a warm disposition and an even warmer smile. She was not much taller than me, was plump and round, and clearly very kind.

I followed her up the stairs, noting again how immaculate everywhere was, and how spotlessly clean. She showed me the bathroom and then opened the door to the right. 'There you are, Sue, your new home,' which she said with a positive note of pride in her household. She kindly placed my miniature suitcase on the chair, told me to go down later for a cup of tea, and departed quietly.

Leaving the case and the unpacking for the time being, I sat on the edge of my bed and looked around my room. I felt completely at home. I lay back on the bed, allowing my thoughts to formulate independently.

The realisation of what I had done was slowly dawning on me; I had just walked away! What I dreamt to be my family home had produced yet another item to add to the catalogue of disappointments experienced throughout my life.

Derek, one of the boys who lived at the flat, had been with my three brothers at a Home in Hertfordshire. I never asked, but I think he was an orphan and the flat had become a refuge for him, and he was happy to be there. He was, however, sickened at the way I was being treated, and did not hesitate to tell me so. I shared many a miserable exchange with him.

Derek came to my rescue after a fist fight in the kitchen without knowing anything of the build-up to this affray. My youngest brother Trevor had come in while I was ironing. He had told me that he wanted me 'to do a better job of the shirts, and iron the backs'.

I had become considerably bolder as time had passed and I was *sick to death* of his and the others' attitude toward me. They could not ever let up this continuing humiliating behaviour. I was at the end of my patience. I lost my temper and without warning or reasoning, I suddenly punched him hard under his chin. He tottered away from me but I was going to finish this. I was determined to stop his mocking stupidity once and for all. When Derek arrived, he had to pull me off Trevor, who was now bent backwards over a cupboard. He was easily a foot taller than me but my strength came from weeks of pent-up anger, and in this rage I gave him a good hiding. The noise was extraordinary; ironing board, table and chairs, all had been shunted around in the melee. There was none of the girly behaviour that one sees in a 'cat-fight', this was full-on. I was determined to get some respect from somewhere!

His face was a mess and he ran off quickly to clean himself up, and to escape the cat-calling and jeers from Derek and me that followed in his wake.

Even though I was shaking like a leaf I decided then and there that nobody would *ever* push me around again and get away with it! I had battled all my childhood, and was prepared to continue to fight, if that meant I could get out of where I was. Derek gave me a great big hug, and then we sat down and laughed till our sides ached.

After about four months, when I knew I could no longer *abide* staying at the flat with these awful people, it was to Derek I went for guidance. I had no idea at all whether there was a third option to 'Homes' or 'home'.

'Oh yes, indeed there is,' he assured me. He told me about 'lodgings'. He was a lodger in the flat. I had never really thought about the word until he explained what he meant in detail. I was already paying the same amount of rent as Derek, so clearly I was just another lodger anyway, so I may just as well be one somewhere else, and hope to be happy!

He suggested we start looking for lodgings outside of Willesden Green. 'When you get out of here, you don't want to bump into them all the time.'

He seemed to know exactly where to look and what to do. He suggested I stay on the Bakerloo Line as it would make my journey into work easier. We looked at some real dumps in which Derek had said he would not lodge his dog, if he had owned one. Then we found the place where I was to be sleeping that very night.

A couple of stops away on the underground, in Dollis Hill, was a neat semi-detached house with a just as neat and tidy front garden. We had walked up the path with a sense of genuine optimism; it was completely different from all the others we had viewed.

We got over the first hurdle of Eva's misunderstanding of the situation.

She told us, in a panic, that she only had a single room. Derek emphatically informed her that that was all I was looking for; he already had somewhere to live. The amusement of this immediately broke the ice, and the viewing was a very relaxed affair.

The room was fine: a comfortable bed and chair as well as a little cupboard and chest of drawers. It was a lovely light room with a view over the rear garden from a larger window than in the flat at Rutland Park; it was perfect. Eva would provide me with beverages as required, but not food. The cost I already knew; we arranged the date that I was to move in, and that was all there was to it.

I left there on clouds!

Over the time that remained in the flat, suppressing my excitement and indeed the occasional trepidation, took a lot of control. It was lovely to be able to share the odd surreptitious grin with Derek, which at least eased the strain, and I knew he wouldn't breathe a word to anyone.

He had advised the move should take place on a Friday morning; I received my wages on a Thursday and Walter took most of it from me on the Friday evening. Besides some left-over money to use for my new commitments, I would also have the weekend in which to familiarise myself with my new surroundings,

Thus the day had finally arrived, and I was at pains to seem that all was outwardly normal. Everybody left for their usual journey to work, but I returned rather than catch my train. I collected my few clothes, left the key on the kitchen table and, closing the door firmly behind me, embarked on the greatest adventure ever: the rest of my life!

I had one regret: I would miss the look on Maisie's face when she realised what I had done. She had believed me to be an immature naive idiot of a child. Because I knew nothing about cosmetics, fashion and all the other important things in life, I was doomed to failure. Yet I had a good job at Selfridges, paid my hire purchase with the rest of them, and had made a friend of Derek who had helped me in my quest. Now I was off, never to be seen or heard of again!

This was my life. I now had it by the scruff of the neck, and I was going to run with it. I was 16 years old and could never have imagined what a roller coaster this would prove.

*

Quietly leaving my room, I went down the stairs to take up the invitation of a cup of tea. I could see into the empty kitchen so gently knocked on the closed door to my left. 'Oh, come on in and join us,' Eva greeted me. 'Maurice, this is Sue.' The gentleman sitting by the fire gave me a warm smile and offered his hand. He had been at the hospital on the day I viewed the room so it was the first time we had met. My first thought was how ill he looked; his smile had come from a face drawn with pain. He had sandy coloured thinning hair and a bright twinkle in his eyes. I decided I was going to like them both. Eva showed me to a chair and poured my tea.

'That was good timing, we had just made the pot,' she explained. I had barely settled into my chair when she looked at me in a questioning way and asked, 'Why do you need to lodge away from home?' Maurice too was looking on interestedly.

I realised instantly that I was going to have to get used to this type of mild interrogation. I was very young to be off on my own, so I gave her the very barest of detail to suppress any other queries. It worked.

'Are you not going to work today?' I explained I had managed to get the day off for my move. It was nice to have some time to settle and get to know my immediate surroundings. I knew the station was a convenient ten-minute walk away, but knew little else about the area. Maurice then explained how to find the shops, the park and so on. Nothing was very far away.

I asked Eva if I could give her my expenses then, but thereafter to do so on a Thursday when I was paid. It left me very little in my pocket, enough to get a bit of food and maybe a paper. When I requested the directions to the newsagent's, they immediately offered me their own. They had read it and would later get the *Evening Standard* delivered, so back up to my room I went, full of tea and a free paper.

It did not take long to unpack. Some weeks previously, Mary and Maisie had gone to Penberthy's in the city and bought me some clothes that Walter had demanded. I didn't go with them, so I had no choice in the matter, but I was presented with the receipt showing the total sum due and Walter was given a copy, to deduct from my wages each week! I don't think I got much for the money but then I was ignorant of the cost of anything.

There was a rather sweet pleasure in now putting these things away into my drawer in my new home in Dollis Hill. I realised that Maisie and Walter, as my guarantors, would now have to pay the balance of my clothes bill, as well as the furniture that I had signed for – Derek had given me this little bit of information.

My new room was not enormously spacious but there was plenty of space for me. The mackintosh brought with me from the Homes was neatly hung on a hanger on my door and that was it – I was home!

My new-found independence was going to be a treasure and a joy.

Once everything was folded away, I sat in an extremely comfortable chair and opened the paper. It was the *Daily Telegraph*. Painfully aware of my lack of basic general knowledge, I had decided that at least with a newspaper I would stay informed of current affairs.

There were times, at the flat and at work, when I had found myself completely at a loss to understand a conversation, let alone join in, which was an absolute disgrace. Goodness knows why Barnardo's had considered newspapers and the radio to be taboo; surely it should have been a basic right to learn more than just that which the school would provide.

As I read in my new comfortable environment, the delicate waft of cooking reached me. I looked around the room but there was no clock; either it was gone noon, or my tummy was running fast . . . I was starving. I returned downstairs and met Eva in the hall.

I explained I was just going out to get something to eat, and she then gave me my own key. Not being the owner of anything as luxurious as a watch, I rather cheekily asked her if I could have a clock in order to be up for work on time, and this she produced from the kitchen without further ceremony.

The shops were a few moments away and I made a beeline for the bakery. I knew my money was short and I would have to manage it carefully. I was used to eating less than was completely satisfying, so that would not be a problem.

I studied the display in the window, aware that for the first time ever, I was fully responsible for my well-being. With my running training, I had always been told that a good, nutritious, balanced diet was essential and I must always remember that. I studied the prices again. I bought myself a loaf of bread.

By the time I had finished that loaf, spread over two meal times, I was as full as could be. There was a tumbler in my room; I had filled this with fresh water from the bathroom and, with Eva's cups of tea, had kept nourished. I slept more soundly than I had done in months.

~ 27 ~

I awoke on the next Monday morning to a new day, new week, new life. A thrill of excitement ran through me as I absorbed all of this. The weekend had flown by; I felt a deep satisfaction in how far I had come in just a few short days.

Eva had promised a cup of tea each morning, and as I left the bathroom, she was at the head of the stairs. With a cheerful exchange of greetings, I took my cup and returned to finish getting ready for work.

A surprise awaited me at the station; I was short of money to get to and from Oxford Street right through to Friday. I bought the ticket to the closest station I could afford, and with a brisk walk, still got to Selfridges with time to spare.

I worked in what was called then the Dissecting Office. Credit customers made purchases in various departments; these were recorded in a duplicate book and then came to us. We proceeded to bill the customer with the correct amount and work out the commission percentage for the sales staff.

An interesting occupation, but not one that would keep me interested until I could draw a pension. Unlike the Head of Department Miss Bullen, who was at least one hundred years old, and had probably been there from when she left school.

The following Monday, this dear lady called me and I went to her desk. There was another person there, who asked me to follow her to her office. The legend on the door plate said that she was the Personnel Relations Officer. She asked me to sit on the chair facing the desk.

She proceeded to read out a letter informing me that Maisie had contacted the Homes, told them I had left without a forwarding address and that she was putting me back in their care; Barnardo's were to be my legal guardians until I was *twenty-one*.

I stared at this woman in disbelief!

She allowed me my tirade in response, and once I was spent, carried on with her mission.

She explained in detail and at length all about parents, and guardians, and added that there was one situation in which I could find myself when a guardian would be a requirement by law: surgery. If I was involved in an accident and needed medical help, then my guardian would need to sign a consent form. She then went on to explain *my* responsibility to *them*. They would need to be informed of every life change; whenever I changed address, job, or got married, they were to be given full details!

Very well then, I would commit to that with no more argument or dissent. I could tell from her expression that she was pleased it had been so easy.

I gave her the address of a place I had seen while conducting my search with Derek; there was no way I was letting her have the details of my new home in Dollis Hill. Then I signed her form.

Later that week, in the carriage of the Tube, I saw an advertisement for positions with the Gas Board and took a sick day to attend the job interview. I sailed through the first interview and loved the intelligence test. They offered me the post, which I took up as soon as was possible. I did not give my notice to Selfridges.

They did not know my correct address, and they sure as hell were not going to know where my new job was – and neither were the Homes!

This turned out to be a most fortuitous move; I really enjoyed the work, the office was light and airy unlike the previous dank place, my colleagues were bright and fun, and it was a shorter distance to travel.

Another Monday, another train journey, a new job in a new office; I was living life in the fast lane. My train left from Dollis Hill and passed through Willesden Green, where Maisie and Walter lived, and I wondered what I would do if I ever saw any of them. Yet this thought brought with it no dread at all. I was filled with my new confidence that helped me brush away any negative thoughts.

I had realised, during the weekend, that the last time I had felt this good was at school. The ridiculous wait after I had left to know when I was actually going to Maisie had begun the decline in confidence. Living with her and my brothers had helped not at all, and here I was, leaving the train at Finchley Road and walking to my new office.

Mrs Lewis met me with such a warm welcome. She was an immaculately dressed, slim lady who had kindness written all over her. She was my Senior, she explained; I would sit beside her at the desk we were to share. Once settled she gave me the good news, and then the bad.

The good news was that I had come highly recommended from the interview. But the bad news was I had no cards because I had given no leaving notice to Selfridges. I knew she did not mean greetings cards but I had no idea what she meant.

I immediately asked if I could speak with her, in private. There was an empty room nearby, and we sat in there. I briefly but thoroughly explained who I was and where I had come from, and she was *brilliant*. For the first time in ages I had felt a lump in my throat, because she was being so kind. She promised me that head office would sort it all out, and the branch would not even be mentioned.

The actual work was really quite exciting. We operated the telephones in the 'Gas Escapes' department, which was virtually the 999 emergency number. On that first morning, I just had to sit and listen to the expert by my side, through an audio monitor. Hers was just the voice you would want to hear in a crisis, and I realised she put on different nuances, depending on the caller. Some were in a clear panic; some were so reluctant to give address details it was like pulling teeth! We also had the work schedule and hours sheets to do for the fitters. Later I came to know them a little. They were a lively lot and pulled my leg mercilessly but it was all in good fun. I knew I blushed at some remarks and that made it a thousand times worse.

'Right. Out with those telephone leads, Sue, time for lunch,' Mrs Lewis announced in her constantly cheerful way. 'Follow me and we will sit outside. Let's get some fresh air. Bring your sandwiches.'

I supposed this sort of moment would be with me for a while, like the time I did not know my own shoe size with Auntie on holiday. We all make assumptions based on our own knowledge and experience, and there are things that would appear to be so blooming obvious, like needing food. I just had not thought about it as there was a canteen at Selfridges. There was also the problem of money of course, but I would have to eat.

'You all right, love?' Mrs Lewis asked me kindly.

I then had to tell her everything. How I had chosen to live at Dollis Hill because it was nice, but it cost a little more than some of the dumps around. I had known from the outset that food was not inclusive in the cost, but I thought I could manage and I honestly did not realise that not everywhere had a subsidised canteen.

'Blimey, Charlie, yer lucky to 'ave a lav 'ere,' she said in the most amazing pseudo cockney accent!

She insisted I took a sandwich from her, and I must admit to my arm being not particularly high up my back.

'Don't you put yourself down, Sue. You have done miracles in just a few weeks. When we finish here, we'll go back to the desk. I'm allowed the odd free phone call and I think you can solve as many problems for me as I can for you.'

*

Mrs Lewis had two sisters, both of whom were married with children and lived in St John's Wood, not far from work or my lodgings. They were both *desperate* for help with housework and babysitting. Once she had agreed with me that I would be prepared to do *anything* to make my life better, she proceeded to make the most of the freebies!

By the time she was finished I had plenty of weekend work. On Friday, Saturday and Sunday evenings at a time to be arranged, I would babysit. Saturday morning, I'd clean one of the sister's flats. Sunday morning was when I would take the other sister's children out. Mrs Lewis worked out the sums for me, and realised it nearly doubled my wages!

This was all to start in just four days' time. I could manage on bread till then, I decided. Although I had not mentioned this quite spectacular diet to her, she had other ideas.

She reached in her bag and presented me with a 10 shilling note, which was equivalent to just over one third of my present weekly wages. My protestations fell on deaf ears and I graciously accepted; it would carry me well until pay day. What a star she was.

I was delighted when my first training day was reduced by half and I actually took calls, overheard on the audio of course. By the end of the afternoon, I was tired. We had done a mountain of paperwork between us and I had answered quite a few of the calls entirely on my own. At the end of each, she made a suggestion here and there, but she made sure to stress how pleased she was with my first day. Then she made another suggestion: groceries.

After switching off everything and ensuring a tidy desk for the next day she hooked her arm through mine and we emerged into the now dark Finchley Road.

'I love the shops when they are lit up in winter. I would never spend as much at Christmas if it was in the summer,' she told me, Completely unused to the pleasurable aspect of shopping, I offered a muted chuckle in response.

The place was crowded as everybody left their offices together, and this created a thrill of excitement through me. The noise of the traffic and the babble of the people made me feel totally part of this world.

'We are going to shop the Lewis way,' she informed me, laughing now. 'Wherever you are in the world, you head for the side and the back streets. Only the big boys can afford the cost of trading in the main thoroughfare, and only the idiots can afford to buy there.'

We had gone up a side street and turned left, and as she had said, we were somewhere completely different to where we had just left.

The narrow, dimly lit street was almost deserted, and the houses seemed to be spilling out on to the pavement. The sound of the traffic was reduced to a drone. Everywhere had such a different appearance at night, and, because of who I was with, I was seeing everything with new eyes. Mrs Lewis had shown a genuine enthusiasm for her work in the office, and this same enthusiasm carried over into shopping.

We entered a shop, causing the loud bell to break into the quiet of the grocery store. 'Hello, Mrs Lewis, and who is this?' enquired the unbelievably tiny lady from behind the counter.

'Meet Sue, my new colleague. Only started today but she's gonna be a cracker.' Colleague? *Ooooh . . . get that!* I thought to myself. I was greeted with a lovely smile, and then it was down to the task in hand.

I asked my learned companion to select what I could afford and she simply referred to me, to ensure it was to my taste.

'You can do your experimenting once you have got the extra money to cope with the risk. I have tried some wonderful-looking food when abroad on holiday, and ended up terribly disappointed,' she explained, adding, 'And remember you need toiletries.' All was done and I left the shop with a big paper carrier bag full of my selected goodies; and some change.

Mrs Lewis showed me the short cut to the station. With profuse thanks from me and a 'Cheerio . . . see you in the morning' from her, we went our separate ways. I walked down the now familiar road with my very first bag of shopping and told myself to remember this kindness.

Eva was leaving the kitchen as I entered into the hall. 'You have had a long day, Sue. You must be tired.' I leant against the doorjamb with eyes closed, feigning exhaustion, and we laughed together. 'You go on up and sort your things and I will bring you a lovely hot cup of tea.'

I put my bag down beside the small cupboard. I wanted to open and put it all away completely on my own, to savour yet another moment on this exciting journey.

I had finished washing and returned to my room as Eva arrived with the promised tea. It was clear she did not want to go back downstairs immediately so I invited her in.

She had brought a whole tray of teapot, milk and one cup. She refused my offer to get one for her from downstairs. 'No, it is for you, you must drink it all up,' she said in her beautiful soft accent. She did accept the offer of the chair, and I sat on the end of the bed.

I had been quite surprised at first that she had wanted to chat. However, after telling me how happy she was that I was such a lovely lodger, she handed me the tea she had poured and told me about herself.

'Maurice had a really bad war, as did many people. He returned to his work on the railways but had to give up on health grounds a year ago. We've tried to make ends meet on the pension they gave him, but it is very hard. He is a proud and rather stubborn man and will not seek the help that may be out there; he feels they won't believe what happened to him or how it affected him. It has made things very difficult for us both. But he did at least come home and for that I thank God.

'When we decided to take a lodger, we did so with great reluctance. I just want you to know how delighted we are that you have come to be with us. We will leave you our paper each day and Maurice had an idea. When I bring you your last cup of tea later, I will make you up his old flask he took to work. It is not used now and it will give you some extra.'

'Eva, that is so kind, and I want you to know something too. I had looked at many places and I was glad to find you. This is the first home that I have been really happy in.'

'It was meant to be,' she said, almost in tears. We stood up together and had a big hug.

I finished all my tea and made a beeline for the shopping bag. The little cupboard had plenty of space and already held a bowl and spoon, some plates, a knife and fork, and a tin opener.

To this I added a big box of cereal and a large tin of evaporated milk that would not go off, cream crackers, two different cheeses, real butter, jars of Shippam's paste and a tin of corned beef.

Right at the bottom was a small brown bag. I opened it, and that was that. I had been on the verge of tears when I had spoken to Mrs Lewis earlier that day. Then I had felt fine with all the work to occupy my mind.

When we were in the little shop, searching for what was practical and affordable, I had seen the Bath Oliver biscuits.

'Oh look, Uncle Tom had those,' I exclaimed, and *immediately* wished I hadn't. I had heard the crack in my voice, and hurriedly turned away.

I lay on my bed now and clutched this packet to me as if my life depended on it. The old pain was there again, but I could let it happen. There were no gulping sobs or anguish. Because this was my first ever completely private place, other than the bamboo bush in the Homes, I just lay quietly and let the tears come. I felt infinitely better because I had.

I realised why I had come to Dollis Hill. It was just the sort of place Uncle Tom and Auntie Dodd would have approved of; Eva and Maurice were just the sort of people who they would have held in regard and entrusted my welfare to.

I now knew in exactly the direction I was heading. If I remained aware of the Dodds' close proximity to my mind, I would be inspired. Always.

*

I had really settled in at work and I loved it. I was answering calls as they came in, no audio monitor needed now. With a problem caller, I simply placed them on hold and would discuss the difficulty with Mrs Lewis; she had been there for a good while so there were not many situations, or awkward customers, she had not previously come up against.

I had managed to swallow all my emotional lumps to thank her for the Bath Oliver biscuits. She had not said a word in response, just patted my hand. She was a darling.

The chaps in the office were a great bunch. Mr Birch was the manager. He was the only one with a car, and the number plate letters were WPB. I remember this because I always referred to it as his Waste Paper Basket!

Next to our desk was Charlie, and beyond him were Frank

and Bill; they were like a couple of old women: arguing all day and moaning about everything. On one occasion Frank had used a swear word; Mrs Lewis was up on her feet and admonished him severely, treating him as she would a child, and he barely spoke at all until lunchtime!

Charlie was the comedian. Once again, my lack of knowledge precluded me from enjoying the jokes the others found so hilarious. So much of the topical humour was based on political satire and television programmes, and I was sufficiently unfamiliar with both not to understand.

Frank was the horse man. He could tell you where every race was being run on a given day; he permanently had a racing paper on his desk. He spoke about 'odds' like Mrs Lewis did about recipes, and he reckoned he was a regular winner. Strangely enough, he was never boring. He would have made a brilliant teacher; if he could make horse-racing sound interesting, he would undoubtedly have made Maths a far more enjoyable lesson – even for me! Bill talked about his wife. He *was* boring.

The fitters were hilarious, a world apart. The dignity bestowed upon our male colleagues by Mrs Lewis and me was certainly not justified by these guys. The banter was unbelievable; half of it was a bit risqué, which I could only tell from their expressions as it went clean over my head – I didn't have a clue!

One lunchtime it was too wet to go out into the yard, so the fitters invited us to go to their area. 'Do you play snooker?' asked Joe.

'There isn't anything that I haven't tried . . . I love ball games.' This, with the innuendo attached by them, brought the house down! Mrs Lewis realised I had no idea what I had said and proceeded to give them a dressing down as well. She was a little terrier when wound up!

After all the noise had died down, I had a go. I had a 'natural bridge' as my hands were strong, and having an eye for a ball is an advantage, whatever the game. I had one problem: I could barely SEE the middle of the table, let alone reach it! At only five feet two inches in wet socks I had no chance.

After this introduction to snooker, I practised as frequently as I could. To overcome the height problem I became very good with the rest. A few months down the line, I was 'North Thames Gas Board Ladies Snooker Champion'.

Only two of us played and I beat her!

On my first evening of babysitting, I must admit to being nervous; there were more strangers to meet. Once the morning work was through, Mrs Lewis and I went back into the office quickly after eating lunch.

Concerned because I had not even spoken to her sister, she gave her a ring. Once connected, she handed the phone to me.

'Hello, Sue, Ann here, good to talk at last. Is all still okay for this evening?' she asked in a voice so like Mrs Lewis's it was unbelievable. I assured her I was really looking forward to meeting them all. 'Could you arrange, please, to come straight to us from work? We're going locally to friends for a meal. We would like to be early and then not too late home on your first visit. If you put me back to my sister I'll see what time to meet you from the Underground.'

Half of my nerves had already gone, and if she was as nice as she sounded, I had no worries. However, I would have to ring Eva and let her know, and when would I be able to have my supper?

The first concern was easily dispensed with; Eva said to take care . . . and she would leave me my paper and flask. When I told Mrs Lewis, we both said 'Aaaah' together, and then got a fit of the giggles! She assured me of no problems whatsoever with supper. 'She will have you stuffed to busting if I know my sister,' she said with feeling.

It was the end of my first week. Mrs Lewis and I chatted as we cleared away for the weekend; I said how much I had enjoyed the work. She told me how much she had appreciated the speed at which I picked things up. I had not forgotten the 10 shillings when I was paid the day before, but she said to leave it until Monday when I would have the extra.

She came all the way to St John's Wood with me, explaining she wanted to see her sister. The noise when they met and embraced, you could hear over the sound of the train! They both had the same gift for mirth and were laughing just because they were together. '*That's* family,' I thought. With a peck on my cheek, a hug and a 'See you Monday, Sue dear,' Mrs Lewis was gone.

Ann and I got on with exactly the same ease I had found with Mrs Lewis. They were like peas in a pod and I felt I had known her for ages. The walk to the flat was not long and we chatted all the way. She did say they had discussed for some time the babysitting problem; it was finding someone to trust that was the real issue, but then I had turned up. 'I would never let you down,' I assured her.

'Oh I know that, Sue,' Ann exclaimed. 'I knew from the first moment I saw you.'

She let us both in to the chandelier-lit hall with deep red-carpeted floor, and exquisite paper on the walls, and to the sound of two small voices screaming 'Mummeeeee!' Hannah and Alex ran on through and she tried to catch them both; their joy was *tangible*.

'I've only been gone for half an hour,' she chastised gently. 'And meet Sue.' They both addressed me with beaming smiles and said in unison, 'Hello, Sue.'

We all trooped through to the kitchen so that I could meet Leonard, Ann's husband. With another beam and a handshake, I had greeted all the family.

'Well, young Sue, you must be starving,' said Leonard. 'You pop down and wash your hands, and I'll serve you the best soup you will have ever tasted!'

'Mr Modesty himself!' responded Ann, and he chased her and the children along the hall with a wooden spoon!

I sat at the enormous kitchen table, and tucked in heartily to the promised soup, which was indeed delicious. 'I didn't know men could cook,' I said.

'Oh yes,' replied Leonard. 'I was raised by a good Jewish mother. I have three brothers and we all learnt to cook. Ann still leaves soup and a roast dinner to me.' We chatted as I ate and by the time I had finished, the children ran in, all bathed and ready for bed.

'Come and read us a story, Daddy,' they begged.

'Why don't I? Mummy and Daddy can get themselves ready to go out while I do,' I suggested. They replied with delighted squeals, grabbed a hand each and off we went to their bedrooms. I was presented with their favourite and they listened, joining in the pieces they knew by heart. They were lovely children.

I left the room while they were tucked in and settled. Leonard showed me into the sitting room. I said I had no interest in television; the little I had seen made no impression at all. I had the *Telegraph* thanks to Maurice; I still found all my pleasure in reading. He offered me the bookshelves to 'help yourself', and they were gone.

I sat back in the extreme comfort. This was luxury, I told myself. Everything around me displayed opulence, and yet they were so normal, so relaxed and friendly.

Going through the full bookshelves, it was clear Leonard was an architect. There were some very heavy-reading classics as well, and then I saw just the thing: *The Directory of World Art*. It was a beautiful book, leather bound with gold lettering. At school I had been taught by an art master who absolutely loved his subject. He had instilled in us all a basic interest. I particularly loved the Old Masters, so this would suit beautifully.

I very carefully opened it, and the first thing I saw was Uncle

Tom! Not really, of course, but *The Laughing Cavalier* by Frans Hals beamed out at me; overall, it was not a real likeness, but the smiling twinkling eyes were most definitely identical. I thought everyone probably knew a person like that.

Turning the pages, I had another startled surprise of recognition when I saw *The Scream* by Edvard Munch; I had not seen this picture before. I stared at the page and recognised my emotion! How could anybody paint such an emotion? I could not avert my eyes, and yet it was a most unsettling experience. I must have studied every inch of the painting, I was fascinated. Goodness knows how dark the mind of this artist was; I would go to a library and find out. I returned the volume to the shelf.

I needed to change the mood so I went quietly to the children's bedrooms; both were sound asleep. They looked utterly angelic, their black hair looking even darker on their white pillows, and with eyelashes to die for!

I made my way to the kitchen and sat again at the beautiful family table. It was good just to study the equipment at leisure. We were not allowed in the kitchens in the Homes; fair enough really, when so much could go wrong. I had prepared mountains of vegetables and stripped the fruit off the redcurrant stems (ugh!), but even at the flat, I did not get the opportunity to do more than that. I would learn, all in good time.

*

The next morning found me bright and enthusiastic about going back to St John's Wood to meet Barbara, the other sister, and cleaning her flat. I was to be met from the train, so did not want to be late. They, or rather Leonard, had escorted me back to the Tube last night; it would be so much easier for all when I knew where to go.

With the money I had been paid, I had enough to buy my weekly ticket. Maurice had given me this bit of information. I paid for one ticket and that gave me as many trips as I needed, for all seven days. Therefore, the extra journeys at the weekend were not costing me a penny, an enormous bonus.

I did not have to be a mathematical genius to work out that if I did not have the extra work I would have been in a dreadful mess. I really had not worked it all out very well at all. After giving Eva her rent, allowing a shilling per day for food, which was the barest minimum and mainly consisted of bread, and the train to work, I would have been down to literally a couple of pennies to spare. I realised, of course, the weekends were going to be tiring, but I was living in a nice house and a nice area. I was being well cared for and meeting some new and lovely people – and was keeping out of mischief!

I recognised Barbara immediately; the family likeness was uncanny. 'Hello, Sue, lovely to meet you after all the conversations with my sisters. I feel I know you already,' was her warm greeting. She hooked her arm in mine and we left the station already chattering like old friends.

We had walked in the opposite direction but, once in the flat, I was struck with the similarity and the luxury. All the decor, the furnishings, the pictures were perfectly tasteful, but I could also see the understated ease with which they enjoyed these surroundings. That was class, I decided.

Barbara explained the children were at Saturday school, and Harold had gone to his club in Town. He was a rather eminent surgeon and worked long hours; Town was his relaxation. 'Each to his own,' she said. 'Drives me mad!'

She showed me into the sitting room and explained that it hadn't been cleaned thoroughly for a long time. 'You mean cushions off chairs, all vacuumed before returning, then moved to vacuum underneath?' I confirmed.

'Oh, that is just what I mean, and more so. I'll show you where everything is kept. I'll make us a coffee while you set up, and then I'm going to leave it to the professional.'

One of the good things I learnt in the Homes was how to be thorough. Barbara left my coffee and I got on. As I cleared then cleaned the cushions, there was money everywhere! I collected this up and placed it on the mantelpiece. I had never seen so much money all in one go! There was more under the chairs too. Blimey, imagine having so much you didn't miss it!

I got on with the job, in all honesty absolutely loving it. There was no doubt that cleaning quality fabrics and furnishings made all the difference. Barbara returned.

'Good grief, look at you, what a difference – and so quick.' I felt my cheeks go red at the praise, but still enjoyed the encouragement. 'Come out now and have another coffee and sit down for five minutes. You haven't stopped for an hour and a half!'

I could not believe how quickly the time had passed. Two hours later and the room was gleaming. I went out to find Barbara. She praised me effusively, and with genuine pleasure. I felt proud that it looked so good. 'I think, young Sue, you have done enough for one day. Can you bathe at Eva's or would you like a shower before you go?' I assured her I was fine and got my bits and pieces together, but then I remembered something. 'Oh Barbara, the change up there was all down the seats and under the chairs. I put it all on the mantelpiece.'

'That's blooming men for you. As soon as they sit down the loose change runs out of their pockets.' She scooped it up and we went down the hall to the kitchen.

My wages were all ready for me in a brown envelope and this was handed to me.

She then took a large envelope from the drawer, placed all the change into it, and handed it to me! 'Oh no, please, that is yours and I am so happy with the wages, honestly.'

'That is why I am rewarding you. Honesty. I believe it is something with which we are all born, but we succumb to dishonesty through temptation. Honesty is, for me, the most admirable quality anyone can hold. You have it in abundance, along with all the other wonderful facets in your nature.'

This was said with such sincerity that I was nearly in tears.

~ 29 ~

There was less bounce in my step on the walk from the station. I was tired. I had worked very hard; for my own satisfaction, but also to impress. I could not believe the money I now carried with me. I was longing to get home and count it.

I walked through the hall and because Maurice was dozing, Eva invited me into the kitchen to join her in a fresh cup of tea. I told her all the details of the morning and I then plucked up the courage to ask if I could have a bath.

'Oh Sue, how awful of me, of course you can,' she said, with some alarm. 'And what have you arranged about your clothes washing?'

Blimey, I hadn't thought of that! I had been washing my undies in the bathroom and draping them to dry in my room, which had worked very adequately. 'Um, well, I could do them in the bath water when I've finished, and then give them a good rinse in the sink,' I suggested as a really good idea. And cheaper then the launderette.

She laughed. 'Not at all. When you have your top clothes dirty, put them in the basket on the landing and I'll do them with ours. It won't add much on me, and you are working hard enough already.'

Recalling what Davy had called Auntie I said, 'Eva, you're a diamond.' That so pleased her, and by now much refreshed, I went up for my bath.

I emptied the money from the envelope on to my bed. It was

pounds, all in silver change. This would be my nest egg. I would never ever waste a single penny of it, I promised myself.

As I lay and soaked in the welcome hot soapy water, I reflected on my short time with Eva, and realised how frequently my naivety and ignorance of everyday practicalities had been shown up. The total miscalculation of the finances I needed just to survive; being unaware of the food required at work; and the fact that I would not have *dreamt* of taking a bath without Eva's permission. I tried to think about what else lay ahead that maybe I had not considered. 'What a blooming silly idea that is,' I told myself. 'If you've not been down the road before, how the hell would you know where the turnings are?'

Nevertheless, I decided that overall I was doing not too badly. One thing I had become aware of was the difference in what I now had to think about. In the Homes, there were few distractions. Not just the normal run of childish ways in general; we had very few diversions. There was only the merest of contact with comics or newspapers, radio or television; and mixing with school friends after school was simply not allowed. The day was organised in such a way that we were either at school, carrying out the required chores or relaxing in the grounds or the playrooms. There were always masses of board games, jigsaw puzzles and books; thus I maintained an extremely introverted focus.

The outside world was part of lessons at school, in one form or another, but otherwise we had no contact with it; I was left with the reference on the page and imagination.

I went back to my room and lay down on the bed. A gentle knock came at the door. 'Come in, Eva,' I called.

She carried an armful of clothes and looked as though she had just come in from a jumble sale. 'I would hate you to think me rude, but these things I have long grown out of. I wonder if you would like to try them on and have what fits you?' She left quickly; I barely had a chance to thank her.

I had quite a 'fashion parade' for a full half hour. Blouses, jumpers, skirts and some toiletries – it was as though Christmas had come early. Having tried on everything I decided to keep it all, thus increasing my wardrobe by at least three times. I ran downstairs to thank her. We did what all women do in times of crisis or deep joy, we shared another cup of tea!

Eventually I managed to lie down and rest. I had to be out again soon to catch the train back to St John's Wood to babysit for Barbara's brood.

*

As I stepped off the train, I looked around and could not see Barbara. I stayed rooted to the spot with a feeling of panic welling up inside me. Travelling at the weekend was a vastly different experience from work days. The platform was already empty of the few people who had left the train when I did. There was a strange quiet.

Then galloping towards me was a gentleman, with his coat flying backwards, such was his speed. 'Sue, it is Sue, isn't it? I am so sorry to have left you here on your own.' He thrust forward his hand, and mine was shaken vigorously. 'Pleased to meet you, I am Harold,' he said, which was possibly the most unnecessary introduction I had ever heard!

'And I *am* Sue,' I assured him, equally unnecessarily.

He was extremely tall and used his long legs to great effect – good job I could run. As we progressed, he described the children as lively, happy individuals, who could not wait to meet me. Rebecca, or Becca for short, was nearly 11 and Joseph, known as Jo, was just turned nine.

We arrived in no time to a heart-warming reception. 'I hope you have not eaten, Sue. Jo and Becca wanted very much to wait to eat, so you could join them.' I assured them I had not.

Escorted to the kitchen, I was invited to sit at yet another farmhouse-size table. The atmosphere was of enormous warmth, and I was being treated like the proverbial honoured guest.

No silent meals here – everyone chattered away as we tucked in to one of the best roast meals I had ever tasted. 'It really is the most delicious food,' I said.

'Better than in the Children's Home?' laughed Jo.

'JOSEPH!' shouted three voices in unison.

I looked across at him, he was nearly in tears, and the silence was deafening.

'Please don't look so concerned, Jo. It is okay to talk about it. I don't do so much because I want to make a new life, a good life.' The ice was broken and we resumed from where we were.

'Right, you two scallywags, please clear away and start to wash up, we just want to show Sue where everything is.' This done, I joined in the chores, while the parents prepared for their evening out. The conversation flowed at the previous rapid pace, as did the work, and we were finished by the time they were ready to leave. They promised not to be late, reminded us of bed times, reassured me where everything was for my comfort and were gone.

We settled in the sitting room. The children were as dark-haired and strikingly good-looking as their cousins and had the same relaxed demeanour that one acquires only with confidence. They chatted with a fluent ease, obviously from the interaction with intelligent parents. I will admit to being a little envious at these seemingly perfect lives but cheered myself with the thought that they would never have experienced the chaotic fun of 20-a-side Rounders games, as I had done at Crowborough!

The games cupboard was opened and we played all sorts of games, my childhood standing me in good stead with the familiarity of most of them. Then Becca played her clarinet and Jo did a turn on the piano.

On the dot of bedtime, they both headed off to wash and get ready for bed.

'Could we have a story, please, Sue, but could we have one about you?'

I was at a loss, unprepared for this and not wanting to interrupt my bliss at this joyful evening with memories of darker times. 'You go along, I shall just pop to the cloakroom, and then I'll be with you,' I said in a voice I hoped did not have a wobble. In no time, I had collected my thoughts and joined them.

I told them about the time I had gone on holiday in a removal lorry and that the matron of the Home was called Boagey. The mood was cheery and light as I tucked them both in. 'Goodnight, Sue, I'm glad you're out of there and looking after us,' said Jo.

So am I, Jo, so am I, I thought to myself.

*

It was clear that Sunday was destined to be a very different day from the others. I had been requested to be at the station by 10.30am, which gave us all a lie-in. Leonard was there to meet me and I assured him, once we had arrived at his home, that I was now completely familiar with the route. We all sat at the family table with a hot drink, the jovial family atmosphere enveloping me like a warm blanket.

'Away you go, you two, and get changed,' requested Leonard, dismissing Hannah and Alex. Leonard and Ann then explained the planned procedure for today and every Sunday hence.

Ann and Leonard both loved sport, and they wanted very much to see the children involved. It was easier when they were younger, but difficulties now could only be overcome with help, and that was where I came in.

We were heading off to the sports hall and, while the two adults had a game of badminton, I would take the children across to the swimming pool.

They underwent instruction for the first half hour and then played until their parents joined them, and I met them again to dry and dress. I had a great view of the pool from the upstairs cafeteria, and this is where we all met up at the end of the session.

'Well, that worked like a dream,' said Ann graciously, and we all agreed.

'You look as though you could be fairly useful on a sports field,' added Leonard. I explained all I had done at school and then mentioned Loughborough. He said that he would make enquiries and we would talk about it again.

'Would you believe we have been out for three hours?'

'Yes I can, I'm starving!' said Alex with feeling. We all agreed and set off home.

'You wait and see what we are going to do when we get back,' enthused Hannah with genuine excitement.

Leonard had made some delicious soup on my first evening and now I was to learn what to do to make it! With anyone else, I would have felt clumsy and awkward, but these people were amazing. They thought it crazy that such a basic lesson was omitted from our education.

'Oh! We did have domestic science. I can wash and iron a tray cloth that would win a gold medal, but we were not allowed to take ingredients from the Home for the cookery classes until we could cook!'

I continued to enlighten them about some of the other rulings Boagey instigated with regard to our education, and whispered, 'We were not allowed to attend the sex education lessons either. During these classes, I had to go out and fill the ink wells.' Well, they collapsed with laughter and then followed a humorous discussion about *all* the stupid things Barnardo's considered to be justified.

'I am so pleased you can talk more easily now, Sue. You cannot possibly forget a whole childhood, it would destroy you,' explained Leonard.

The soup was in what looked to me like a witch's cauldron,

and was left to simmer while we adjourned to the sitting room. I had been right about Leonard's profession as an architect and said that although I enjoyed the art book, how strange I found *The Scream*.

'Alex, show Sue our favourite weird one.'

He turned the pages with care and came to Van Eyck, pointing out *Giovanni Arnolfini and His Bride*. It really was as weird as they had suggested. We took it in turns to select the oddest bits to discuss. To this day, I find it as strange as ever.

'One Sunday we will take sandwiches with us, and after the swim we will go to a Gallery. There is *so* much to see and do in Town, Sue, and now you are with us I can make plans for doing plenty on Sundays.' This pleased the children as well as myself.

During our rather late lunch, which was delicious, they explained they would not need me to stay late in the evening. 'We have decided that now we have all burned off some energy, and as you and Leonard have trains to catch in the morning, we will relax with Hannah and Alex and you can spend some time to yourself. There may be the occasional evening, but we would always give you plenty of warning.'

We all joined in the clearing away, still with the lighthearted banter, and the laughter. The day had been a huge success, and I was looking forward already to the coming weeks.

~ 30 ~

Some weeks later, on a cold Thursday morning, I had awoken feeling awful. My throat was burning, my head was thumping and I had the most raging thirst. As I sat up, I began to shake. Deciding to go to the bathroom anyway, I quietly left my room. Although it was just after six o'clock, I could hear noises from the kitchen below. It was Eva. She took one look and escorted me back to bed, with assurances that I should stay there 'and not dream of going to work'. Shortly after, she came in with some tea.

'You look a classic flu case,' she said with a knowing sympathy.

'But Eva, if I don't go to work, I won't get any money'

'Of course you will, Sue,' she responded, smiling. 'We all of us have to have days off sick, and you could not possibly be allowed to go in and give the germs to the whole office. Stay there and I'll tell you what I'll do. At nine o'clock, I will ring your Mrs Lewis, explain how you are, ask about your concern over sick pay, and come and tell you what she says.'

I felt too awful to argue or enquire further. She stayed while I drank my tea and then tucked me in before returning downstairs. I snuggled down to sleep, but worried like mad about the wages. I was already on the financial borderline anyway, even with the extra money from the weekend work.

God Almighty, I thought, that's *tomorrow* . . . What can I do? I cannot possibly expect to be well enough for then. I can't let them down; I have to make it. If I rest today and tomorrow, will I be fit then? I was deluding myself and I knew it. What a mess, all because of a cold! I tried to make mental calculations of the money situation. I knew I had some stores in my cupboard. 'Always get a bit extra when you can afford it, and you won't starve when you can't,' is what Mrs Lewis had said right from the start. Having heeded that advice, I knew I could manage a week without going to Mrs Patel in her little shop.

True to her word, I was awoken with a gentle hand on my shoulder. 'I have just been speaking with Mrs Lewis,' Eva told me. 'She said you will get paid, and you are not to go back until Monday, at least.'

'But Eva, I have got to go and see to the weekend work, I've promised.'

'Don't you worry about that, it is all arranged.'

After saying what a lovely, friendly lady Mrs Lewis was, she told me her plan. Eva would do all the work. The respective members of the families would meet her, and she would undertake to do exactly what I did. She would use my season ticket and we would come to an arrangement with my rent. I couldn't really argue with that.

I slept like a baby after Eva had plied me with the tablets Maurice took for his headaches. Noises downstairs awoke me. Then I heard footsteps on the stairs and Mrs Lewis's cheerful voice rang out. 'Oh! Good, you're awake.'

Good grief, I've slept all day, was all I could think. *What on Earth was in those tablets?*

Mrs Lewis had come all the way out to Dollis Hill to bring me my wages. What a darling. She then went on to verify that Eva was going to sort out the sisters, and I was not to worry about being sick.

'The Gas Board is brilliant in their understanding and compassion, and you will have your full pay next week,' she assured me. I thanked her, she pecked my cheek and gave me a hug, and left my bedroom.

By Sunday afternoon, I was feeling better. Dear Eva finalised her Florence Nightingale role by filling my now empty tummy with a Russian soup called borscht. It was wonderful and gave me the strength to see me back at my desk on the Monday morning.

*

One Sunday evening, I was home for my relaxation after completing the weekend work. Barbara's flat was a 'revelation', to use her own word. I had managed to spring-clean each room in turn, and now just had to keep it all up to standard. She had taken to packing me off with a wonderful assortment of food. 'Because you eat like a bird,' she admonished gently. I must admit to sharing her generosity with Eva and Maurice. There were some items I could not enjoy: olives I didn't like but they were delighted to have some luxuries.

The outings that Leonard suggested had really taken place. Hannah had chosen the Natural History Museum and Alex opted for the War Museum. We visited all the popular sites of interest, some being the first occasion for the parents as well. Sometimes we had a picnic in one of the parks, Ann and I preparing the sandwiches and treats before we left.

I also had my very first lunch out in a restaurant at a Lyon's Corner House. The uniforms made me and the children get the giggles. I had said that the waitresses looked like the Homes' staff with trays, and it was just so ridiculous, we were off! I tried hard to stop and set an example, but the more I tried the worse it became, and then the adults picked it up. Ann said that one of the old ladies looked as though she was sucking a lemon, and that set Leonard off as well. From that day on he said that the restaurant should be know as the 'Lyon's Round the Bend House'. This met with unanimous approval.

These excursions always took place after the morning had been spent playing sport, which meant that the days could often be longer than had been anticipated. It was sometimes hard work but fun, so I did not mind at all: until I had the flu.

It had taken some while to completely recover from the virus, but much longer to amend the financial problems. I was back in the routine of Gas Board and babysitting. I know it was a good life. I was unbelievably fortunate with all the things I did, but I was becoming weary with the neverending financial battle. I could feel it beating me and bringing me down.

The four days I had been sick had really set me back, and I had dipped into my nest egg to get by. I had partially satisfied my disappointment in this by persuading myself that that was what it was for, but not totally. In addition, contrary to the assurances, I had received only a percentage of my total wage as sick pay, which had been an enormous disappointment and had caused me quite a bit of concern. I had not felt fully fit on the Monday, but thank God I resumed when I did.

I had looked at the price of clothes, which were not essential after Eva's kindness, but I had no chance of affording anything new. I was desperate for underwear. After washing my bra, I would put it on when it was as dry as possible, because I only had the one. I had three pairs of knickers, but the constant drain on my finances was the stockings I needed for work. There were so many jags on the old wooden desks and chairs that it was easy to ladder them. I suppose I could have resorted to the type Miss Wallis-Myers had worn in the Homes; she could have been dragged through a hedge *forwards* and would not have snagged a single thread. It must have been like permanently wearing cloth wellies!

There was a place in Kilburn that carried out invisible repairs on this damage, and was cheaper than buying new. However, finding the time to get there and then return the following day to collect them was quite a challenge. If I could have bought five or six pairs at one time, that would have been easier, but I did not have the extra money to invest in such a luxury. When I did buy stockings it was always the same make and colour, and then when they laddered I took them all over together for repair. With what Eva had given me, and the clothes that Maisie had bought, I managed to stay clean and tidy on the outside. I just prayed I was never involved in an accident. If I ever saw some-one hesitate longer than average at zebra crossings I guessed they probably needed new underwear!

*

I had been so lost in thought that I must have fallen asleep because the next thing I knew I was awake, suddenly feeling very cold. I looked at the clock by my bed. Two o'clock? I puzzled. Slowly it dawned on me, it was morning! I was still fully dressed and had clearly just turned over and gone to sleep, with my financial deliberations still rolling around my head. I quietly got up and opened my door. 'Hello, flask,' I chuckled to myself. I crept quietly along to the bathroom, and very nearly had an accident when Eva opened her door.

'Hello, Sleeping Beauty, are you awake at last?' she enquired in a whisper.

'I am, but I must have missed out on the Handsome Prince bit,' I whispered in reply, wide-awake now.

'Well, I'm going to make a hot cup of tea, so you come down when you are ready.' I gathered up some of the food that Barbara had given me; I was starving. Eva had some as well and we had a real party all on our own, a 'just after' midnight feast as I suggested. We were not even particularly hushed. Eva said Maurice had his tablets at night, and I well recalled the effect they had on me; I think they would have knocked out a horse.

Eva poured the tea, and then fixed me with a very kind, but intent expression. 'Sue, do you think you are over-doing all this work?' she asked kindly. 'I knocked three times earlier, and then opened your door. You were sound asleep. I did not wake you because I felt you needed to rest. A fit young woman of your age only sleeps like that when they are ill or exhausted. Sue, I think it is the latter, and I am worried for you. I think you are making yourself ill. You are losing your "sparkle" and I think it's why you caught the flu and it hit you so badly.'

We chatted into the early hours. I told Eva, for the first time in detail, all about leaving the Homes, and the aftermath of that. How my wages, because of my age, were totally inadequate for my needs, and how I felt it would be impossible to stay in London.

'I was raised in the countryside; even the last Home overlooked the golf course, and was on the edge of town anyway,' I explained.

'Well, look, it's time you went back to bed, and me too. You think things over, I will as well, and we can chat later on, if you would like to.'

I assured her I would, and made my way back up to my room.

When the knock came on the door to wake me, it felt like midnight. Eva came in with my tea and said she was so pleased that we had chatted during the night. 'When you come home tonight, how would you like to have a meal with us? I have spoken a little to Maurice this morning. He feels like I do that it is time, as long as you agree, to see what can be done to help.' We had a big hug and I said I would love to have a meal.

When she went out, I sat on my bed and quietly cried. She was right on all counts, I could see that clearly. The thought of leaving London had suddenly become a decision and it was hurting me. I felt I was losing, but then decided that not all battles could be won. The extreme hours I had worked, the stress of constantly battling with finances and the new privations, these had all taken their toll.

As I washed and dressed, I cheered up. I was only seventeen and had achieved, I felt, an enormous amount in a short space of time. I set off to fight another day. By the time I arrived at work I was feeling much better, and had half decided that maybe I did not even have to move on; however, I was about to find out that fate has a strange way of working at times.

Frank had obviously finished the racing pages in whichever paper he had open. At times like these, the whole office was entertained with snippets that he found interesting. I was busily setting out my desk ready for the telephone calls to start, as there was always a rush of these very shortly after nine o'clock. Then my ears pricked up when Frank read out what he was reading.

'Imagine that. Twenty bloody years down the line and still they found him,' he announced in amazement.

'I wish you would not swear, you 'orrible little man, and who has been found?' asked Mrs Lewis. Frank went on to explain. Apparently a chap had left his wife and had disappeared completely, everyone presumed, with a woman he worked with. Through some agency or another, his wife had found him. He had married bigamously and there was all hell to pay.

I was surprised, not at any of the people involved, but at the discovery itself and the time span! Imagine thinking no one knew where you were, then discovering they did after all? I thought.

I had no other reason to stay clear of Barnardo's except the strong desire, from day one, to carry out my life as I wished. I had no time for the soft option and was prepared to do everything necessary to achieve my dream. My early life had been a hard battle with Barnardo's, and since leaving, I promised myself my only way forward was without them sticking their noses in. I had left Selfridges and changed jobs just because I wanted to keep my new address from their knowledge. I never ever wanted to have dealings of any sort with them again. They had messed up my childhood and they were not going to be given even the hint of an opportunity to be anywhere near the rest of my life. They would not, if I could help it, ever have the knowledge of where I was living or working. It had become apparent that the only way I would ever get to Loughborough, even if I were good enough, was with financial assistance. There was an after-care department at the Homes, but the idea of *me* contacting *them* for help was absolutely out of the question. I was long gone – nothing would persuade me to return.

I had started my morning wondering if in fact I could manage to stay where I was, but in that instant, my mind had been made up for me. I would leave London.

Making a decision was a relief, and the relief was immense; pressures that had been building up were rapidly leaving me. Eva had offered to help me, and the dinner table that very night was going to be the place I would sort out the next stage of this journey.

31

There were two occasions during the day when Mrs Lewis enquired, 'Are you okay, Sue?' I knew I was distracted from my work with the worries on my mind, but I had not realised it was so obvious. During our morning break, I told her of the waking and the 'midnight feast'.

'Ah, that explains everything then,' she responded with amusement, and to my relief. My preoccupation with 'opening up' was my deep concern. From the time I was very young, I had always drawn my own conclusions and made decisions after silent deliberation. None of us kids in the Homes was particularly interested in the concerns of the others. There had been times when I had actually thought, in a moment of weakness, that I could approach someone adult, but they were rare times indeed and quickly dispensed with.

That train of thought had made me focus on the problem as I saw it. My refusal to cry as a child was simple; it made the situation or punishment infinitely worse. I had toughened up and eventually become inured to the hardship I experienced. I was now viewing consultation with a third party with trepidation, which possibly wasn't fair on Eva, considering how kind she had been to me, but I decided to let the discussion take its own course.

Throughout a splendid meal, the conversation had centred mainly on the everyday. Slowly the subject of my childhood was raised, and I found an opportunity to explain my lack of ease in discussing anything, let alone seeking help and advice.

Maurice responded immediately with 'That's exactly the same as me, Sue. I had an awful war, I can accept that, and Eva understands. But tell my worries to some twerp who spent his time behind a flippin' desk? Absolutely not – and I never will! The way they responded to my physical wounds was one thing, and I was used to illustrate their level of concern and expertise; I was not going to seek out further help.' He was an angry man and my heart went out to him, but he had made my path smoother to proceed.

After a halting start, and with a great deal of input from them both, I managed to detail the problems perceived by me to be an impossible situation to maintain for much longer. I was aware I was entitled to birthday raises in pay but that was not going to ease much of the trouble. Eva asked, 'Where have you been, what friends have you made? Nowhere and none are the answers, dear.' She was right. I had the trips with the kids, which I enjoyed immensely, but I was still 'at work', and I was required to help with any request. The relaxation I managed in the whole of my week was about one half afternoon on the Sunday. That was the killer, but I could not manage without the income.

Maurice had listened intently but not said a great deal; when he did it was a speech, and he had a plan formulated in its entirety.

'Sue, dear, during the war some women who were available to do so went into agriculture. They were called Land Girls. It was a hard life, because they were doing the work of the men who had left the farms. Many of them were very unsuited, as they were from the towns and cities. However, even they adjusted and did an essential job very well. Now listen, you have the distinct advantage of being already familiar with farms and the land. You're fit and strong and would cope easily with the demands of the job, *and* you would have a roof over your head and regular meals. Your wages would be less, to pay for your room and board, but I think you would be much happier, and better off.'.

Before I could respond, Eva added, 'And don't you worry about Mrs Lewis's sisters. I thoroughly enjoyed it all, except I felt sorry that you were ill. I know they would be quite happy for me to take your place, and Sue, we would not then need to have someone else in your room. We would never find anyone to replace you. And your room will be there if anything goes wrong.'

Supper had been just what I needed. Maurice was relaxed and was an interesting, amusing and intelligent host. He was pleased I was getting so much value from their paper, and showed me some methods to assist with the solving of the crossword.

Seeking help had been far less traumatic then I had imagined; I suppose all new experiences come with certain trepidation. The solutions were brilliant. Eva could have her home to herself again and do some weekend work, bringing in a little more than I had been paying in rent, and the thought of their door open to me was kind beyond words.

The suggestion to live in on a farm was sheer inspiration. I did love the countryside; it was where I had grown up. I think my mind was made up as to that being the answer but I would talk to Mrs Lewis – seeking advice was getting to become a habit.

*

At the first opportunity the following day, I told Mrs Lewis I would like a word. 'Hmm, sounds interesting, young Sue. *And* you've got the sparkle back in your eyes. If we are going to have a heart-to-heart, I shall treat you to some lunch. Put on your coat and follow me.'

By the time our soup and rolls arrived, I had already given details of the previous evening's meeting. Mrs Lewis said that she and her family had already talked about my tiredness; so therefore my decision was of no great surprise at all to her.

'You have worked long hours, Sue, and both my sisters say

how much effort you put in to everything you take on. Only perfect will do, aye?' she said smiling. I agreed but said that was how I did things – well, or not at all.

'Right. To the practicality of all this. Where, when and how are the most important questions. Any ideas at the moment?'

'Okay. Where? I know the Kent and Sussex area – it would be a comfort to be somewhere familiar now that I'm going somewhere new. When? As soon as possible, before the money problems become more than I can cope with. How? That's where you come in – I need your advice.'

'You have just said something that has given me a brain wave.'

'Blimey! That must have been quite a statement,' I said, receiving a fake clip around the ear for my cheekiness.

'Quick . . . back to the office before Mr Birch gets back. I have a couple of urgent phone calls to make.

Talk about organisational skills! She contacted the weekly newspaper, the *Kent and Sussex Courier*, and requested that a copy be sent for a month as she was considering a move to the area. Seeing the potential of a new reader, there was no charge! I was fascinated: how could it help me?

When the first one arrived, I soon found out. Mrs Lewis directed me to the situations vacant column in the classifieds section, and what a variety of job there proved to be. We both pored over this selection, but there was nothing suitable. 'Don't you worry, Sue, there will be one for you,' she assured me, and three papers later, there was!

'Strong girl required to help on small-holding, occasional assistance with two children and housework.'

'Well, blow me,' I said in complete amazement. 'My three favourites in one go.'

'Right, to business. Tomorrow I'll go to Barbara's and tell her exactly what the plan is and then ring the number because it says after six o'clock.'

'Can we tell them Eva's suggestion because I would hate for them to think I was letting them down.'

'You are sweet to be concerned, but all will be fine. These things always have a way of working themselves out, and this will be no exception,' she assured me, and added, 'It's a Tonbridge number. Do you know that area?' I told her I knew Tunbridge Wells and Tonbridge was in the vicinity. I had not really minded whether it turned out to be Kent or Sussex, but I was pleased that it was the former. Pluckley was in Kent, which meant I would be back in Uncle Tom country. That would be a comfort in itself, and beyond that, I did not yet know.

When Mrs Lewis called the number at Barbara's later that night, I do not recall much of what was said, except it was reasonably put across that I did not wish to stay any longer with my family in London. The wage for an under-eighteen-year-old in London was too meagre, and I wished to work where accommodation was available.

I then spoke to the lady and she sounded charming. She was very warm and asked me some prudent questions about my general health, my interests outside of work, where I was currently employed and how long I had been there. She then went on to ask about notice arrangements, and when I could start with her; I requested she speak with my boss again.

During the conversation, Barbara had her arm around my shoulder and gave me a strong comforting squeeze, then her sister put down the phone.

The grin on Mrs Lewis's face was matched by all of us, and there was general whooping and hollering when she announced, 'You've got it, Sue . . . you've *got it*!'

Barbara then rang Ann and Leonard, and they came over with Hannah and Alex. Becca and Jo were so excited, and competed in their efforts to tell Harold when he came home from work. Harold went to the fridge and produced a bottle of champagne in which we all shared, including the children! There was a loud cheer as the cork flew out; all those around me seemed quite blasé as they were clearly familiar with it all, but I could not *believe* the loud bang it made. The noise we were making, the laughter and chatter, created the most sensational atmosphere and I was very aware of being at my first adult party. The champagne was the first drink I had ever had and I loved it, not only the sharp bittersweet taste, but also the gentle sensation of the cold bubbles tickling my nose. We rang Eva to tell her the good news and Barbara slipped to the kitchen and made sandwiches and other nibbles for everyone, but then Mrs Lewis ended the proceedings.

'If I don't get home and cook my man his meal I'll be coming to Kent with you, young lady,' she chastised jokingly. 'You get your coat and we'll walk to the Tube together and leave this rowdy lot to their own devices.'

More jumping around me from the children, hugs and more congratulations from the adults, then Mrs Lewis and I went off into the night with her arm hooked through mine.

The sound of my key in the door brought Eva rushing to meet me.

'Oh Sue, we are both so thrilled for you. Come in and tell us all about it.'

Maurice stood silently, came around from his chair and gave me a strong embracing cuddle. I realised he was quietly crying. 'Sue, this has all happened so very quickly. I hope it all works out for you. I will ever feel guilty for the suggestion if it doesn't.'

'I promise you, Maurice, I have spoken to the lady, I know it is going to be a success,' I replied, with fingers crossed.

'You make another promise then,' he said as he returned to his chair. 'If for any reason at all it does not, you come back to us.'

'Now I have the other work I shall tell you again, we do not need to let out your room. It will be there if you should ever need it,' added Eva, warmly.

Maurice continued, 'Sue, I can't explain to you what I saw in the war any more than you can tell me what went on in the Homes. How we deal with hardship is entirely down to us. I would no more discuss my worries and health with some so-called expert at the War Office than talk to the man in the moon. If you can get by without seeking their so-called help, you do it. You are a strong, upright, lovely girl and you will go far. Just remember two things, dear. You owe not, nor are you owed, and if you cannot have what you want . . . want what you have. Now come over here and give me a cuddle,' he said with a great smile on his kind, sensitive face.

The mood had swung back to one of laughter and joy and we sat and nattered for a long time. Maurice, I noticed, was looking tired, so I asked if they would excuse me to go upstairs. They both sweetly kissed me goodnight, and I floated on air to my room.

32

Once again, I was speeding on a train, in yet another direction. I sat back and thought about the past two weeks.

Both Ann and Barbara had told me not to do any more work. The party night was the last time I had seen them, and I preferred by far to remember that than a series of sad farewells.

My colleagues at work had been wonderful; I had a raft of good luck wishes packed in my case. I now also had a grown-up case in my possession, a gift from Eva to contain all the new clothes she had given to me. Mrs Lewis had written a personal reference to give to my new employers and had let me read it before sealing the envelope. I would have got a job anywhere with her kind words. I felt happy and proud. She had also given me another envelope to open and read when I arrived at my new home.

Eva and Maurice had come up with a huge surprise by presenting me with my train ticket; it was a relief because of the expense *and* it provided me with some spare cash for my new start. We had all cried at my departure, but I could now reflect upon the day I had first arrived at Dollis Hill with a lasting happiness. I was only seventeen but what a year it had been. I had moved from feeling like an anxious, timid waif into a grown-up woman of the world.

Maisie would have been devastated if she had seen me in a public place, still with no make-up on my face. What a shallow set of ideals she had. I loved and wore daily the perfume Eva had included when she gave me the clothes; and had treated myself to a bottle of 4711 because that was what Auntie Dodd used to wear. I dabbed it on to the hankie I took to bed, but otherwise it was not used. It was for comfort and reassurance, and was safely packed in my case with the packet of Bath Olivers.

The roofs and chimneys were now behind me; the countryside was gradually coming into view. Church spires in tiny hamlets and villages showed scattered on hillsides and in valleys; tractors and farm machinery gradually outnumbered motor cars and cattle outnumbered people. Nature's rich palette of greens and browns in the trees and landscape was having a cleansing effect on my mind, as well as my vision. I gazed almost dream-like at the scenery, realising this was where I belonged more than anywhere else. I spent my early childhood in rural Kent and Sussex – and this was Uncle Tom country.

*

Reflecting still, I felt again the shattering pain of my arrival in London, and the agonising wait in the halfway house before going at last to a family and home. The feeling of a new form of abandonment when left completely alone on the first night ever away from Barnardo's, and the misery of disappointment at the charade that was supposed to be family life. Eva and Maurice and the other good folk had shown me much kindness, but I too had behaved and worked impeccably – and nearly killed myself in the process. The burden of a constant lack of money was no reward for such endeavour.

Suddenly, the increasing distance away from Maisie and London was providing me with a refreshing, revitalising freedom; the closer I came to my rural destination, the stronger grew my feelings of love for this beautiful, familiar environment. I decided I would only ever look ahead. I would hold no hopes because whenever I had hoped in the past, life had decided differently and smashed me down yet again. 'Do it alone and wish for nothing' was going to be my new philosophy.

I knew then I would never go back to London . . . whatever the future held.

I also knew that it was time now to look to the future, rather than dwell on my past.

Acknowledgements

With many thanks to:

Janet Billington and Tyron Billington, my computer wizards.

All my friends, for their invaluable help during a very black time in my life, and for their encouragement in setting it all down on paper.

Sami, my little buddy who *insisted* I seek a publisher.

Stan, my agent, who did exactly that.

Also available from Vermilion

☐ The Step Child   9780091906993   £12.99
☐ Trouble in My Head   9780091917234   £7.99
☐ Love Child   9780091906832   £6.99

FREE POSTAGE AND PACKING
Overseas customers allow £2.00 per paperback

BY PHONE: 01624 677237

BY POST: Random House Books
C/o Bookpost, PO Box 29, Douglas
Isle of Man, IM99 1BQ

BY FAX: 01624 670923

BY EMAIL: bookshop@enterprise.net

Cheques (payable to Bookpost) and credit cards accepted

Prices and availability subject to change without notice.
Allow 28 days for delivery.
When placing your order, please mention if you do not wish to receive any
additional information.

www.randomhouse.co.uk